Icing

on the

Cake

Icing
on the
Cake

BAKING AND DECORATING

SIMPLE, STUNNING DESSERTS

AT HOME

Tessa Huff

Abrams, New York

To Brett—
my most favorite
person.
Thank you for our
wonderful life.

CONTENTS

For me, the "icing on the cake" means much more than frosting. It is taking a sweet treat and elevating it to something even more delightful. It is that little something extra that transforms our homemade baked goods into beautiful, show-stopping desserts. In a literal sense, the concept includes meticulously piped frosting on sky-high cakes and gardens of buttercream rose–topped cupcakes, but it also means ultra-chic French macarons with marbled icing, a kaleidoscope of seasonal fruit tarts, and all the sugar-filled and sprinkled-covered decorations of our dreams.

*I*f you don't know where to begin, fear not. I didn't always have the confidence to experiment with complex decorative designs. My baking journey didn't begin until I was nineteen. In a borrowed kitchen, armed with mismatched baking pans, I started down an unfamiliar path that would eventually feel like second nature to me. I taught myself how to cook and bake during my first few years away at UC Davis. My meals were quick and simple, and mainly provided the bare essentials in order to survive my communications lectures, dance team practice, and busy social schedule. However, my love for baking developed from something much more than just needing to refuel. Baking became a mental vacation from my active college life. By concentrating on a recipe or meticulously measuring ingredients, it was a way for me to escape the chaos of my rowdy roommates, the stress of exams I didn't study enough for, and any other emotional hiccup that came with early adulthood. Baking also presented an opportunity to be creative. Even if my first cakes were nothing short of a disaster, I still had fun practicing my elementary piping skills and arranging store-bought candies on top to make them extra special.

Over the years, the setting has changed, but the scene remains the same. The crowded college kitchen transformed into the one I shared with my older brother after graduation, to the local bakery where I worked nights until I could fill and frost a cake in five minutes flat, to my own cake shop, to the kitchen in the city condo my husband and I recently renovated. Whether in a professional kitchen or at home with my family, I've learned that I enjoy baking for the emotional connection and artistic outlet it provides.

I opened The Frosted Cake Shop in my mid-twenties. Making cakes for clients stunted the emotional aspect of baking, but I still enjoyed bringing their visions to life. Four years later, my husband and I moved from California to Vancouver, Canada, and closed the doors to my shop indefinitely. Missing that sense of community and working one-on-one with clients, I started my blog, *Style Sweet*. A bit lonely and lost in a new country, I began baking just for me again. Baking at home instead of in a commercial kitchen allowed me to experiment with flavor pairings, truly enjoy the baking process, and rediscover my passion for dessert design. I taught myself the art of food photography and styling in order to document my creations and share them with my online community. This turned into my first book, *Layered: Baking, Building, and Styling Spectacular Cakes*.

Having readers create and enjoy my recipes with their own families and friends and seeing copies of my book in their homes has been surreal. Writing a cookbook is an honor, and after completing my first one, I realized that I still had so much more to share! My first love will always be layer cakes, so I've included plenty of brand-new cakes in this book. However, *Icing on the Cake* contains a wider array of decorative desserts and is more of a tribute to beautiful recipes and a passion for pastry than a sequel.

When putting together ideas for this book, I sat down and asked myself, "Why do we bake?" What draws us back into the kitchen before every birthday, holiday, special occasion, or even random Thursday night to bake up something from scratch? What motivates us to stay up past midnight anxiously watching a perfect butter cake rise in the oven, to commit to making finicky macarons even after a dozen failed attempts, to research and retest pie dough over and over until it feels just right between our fingertips? Most of us don't have the time to spend countless hours hiding away in the kitchen piping buttercream roses or the like, yet if we are truly passionate about it, we find a way to do it anyway.

For me, I bake because it is both communicative and creative. I love molding, shaping, and weaving together ingredients with my bare hands into something delicious—each pastry with my own signature flair or unique flavor combination. Baking for others is how I communicate feelings of love and gratitude. Most often we don't put in all the attention and effort required for these baking projects unless they are for someone we completely adore, so when you can't find the words you need to express your love or admiration, then say it with cake and pastry!

And when I bake, I love to create beautiful food—with swirls of pastel buttercream and delicate icing flowers, as well as rustic beauty in the form of sharp sugar shards and golden rivers of dripping caramel sauce. Most of the time, my desserts would still taste great without the extra flair, but I do it because it's fun, and sometimes that's all the reason we need.

Like most bakers, I enjoy the process of creating delicious desserts from scratch; the way pastry comes together between my fingertips; and transforming a pile of ingredients into spectacular works of edible art. First and foremost, recipes should taste great, but if baking is a form of therapy, then decorating is my favorite type of creative expression. From delicate meringues to rustic pies, I strive to make each of my recipes beautiful and delicious from the inside all the way to the icing on the cake. I hope that my stories and recipes will encourage you to do the same.

HOW TO USE THIS BOOK

I hope you find this book equal parts inspirational and educational. My goal is for you to learn from my experiences, find joy in the narratives, and get so excited and inspired by the images and ideas that you are instantly drawn into the kitchen. Within these pages, I've included my favorite combinations for technique, design, and flavor. You will find a "Featured Decorating Techniques" list on each recipe, which highlights the different decorating techniques you can learn while making that particular dessert, as well as step-by-step photos for some of the more complex designs. For example, some of the designs include:

Many of the projects reflect a particular aesthetic and/or pair well with the flavors within the cake, but I encourage you to mix and match the different elements as you wish to create truly one-of-a-kind confections. There is something for everyone and every season, but do not feel limited by the images and recipe pairings I've chosen to showcase. Swap the loopy ruffles on the Cannoli Cake (page 158) for the delicate ruffle waves on the Pistachio Truffle Cake (page 84) and vice versa.

It's true. Some of the recipes in the book are slightly over the top, include various subrecipes, and take a good amount of time to build and decorate. But it's okay to be aspirational and I hope this is the book that lets you live out all your pastry dreams. Other recipes bake up quickly and have as few ingredients as plain egg whites and sugar, and most have time-saving variations. If the drippy chocolate glaze and gold splatters of the Chocolate Millionaire's Cake (page 66) excite you, then go for it! If, instead, it seems overwhelming, sub in store-bought caramel sauce and skip the bells and whistles.

Have fun, plain and simple. While learning new techniques, there are bound to be some stressful points along the way, but don't let the angst outweigh the fun. If a decoration or detail is not bringing you joy, leave it off. Save the larger, more involved cakes for special occasions and keep the quick cupcakes for casual weekdays and impromptu game nights. But if meticulously blending together the perfect shades of buttercream or hand-rolling dozens of roses out of pie dough makes you happy, then you are definitely going to love the pages that follow.

HELPFUL EQUIPMENT BEYOND THE BASICS

Cake pans: The layer cake recipes in this book call for either 6-inch (15-cm) or 8-inch (20-cm) round pans. Chose aluminum pans with sides that are at least 2 inches (5 cm) high. My Fat Daddios and Wilton pans have lasted from my bakery days and into my home kitchen. Other useful pans include a 9 by 13-inch (23 by 33-cm) jelly roll or cake pan and a 9-inch (23-cm) springform pan. A standard (12-cup) muffin pan will hold both regular and extra-large cupcake liners. In all cases, look for pans that are not too dark and that are *not* nonstick.

Candy thermometer: There are various tricks for determining the state of boiling sugar (ranging from soft ball to hard crack), but a candy thermometer makes the task much easier. A thermometer is also great for knowing when raw eggs have reached a safe temperature.

Double boiler: A double boiler is a means of using indirect heat to warm delicate ingredients like egg whites and chocolate. You can buy a set of pots specifically made for this purpose (they'll look like two saucepans stacked on top of each other), or create your own using a heatproof bowl and a saucepan. The bowl should sit securely on top of the saucepan without touching the bottom. Fill the saucepan with an inch or two (2.5 to 5 cm) of water and bring the water to a simmer over medium-low heat, then set the bowl on top. Be sure the bottom of the bowl doesn't touch the water. You want the heat of the steam to heat your ingredients, not the direct heat of the simmering water, which could scorch whatever you're cooking.

Fine-mesh sieve: A medium or large fine-mesh sieve is helpful for so many things, from sifting dry ingredients to straining custards, creating lump-free batters to refining smooth pastry cream.

Heatproof rubber spatula: A heatproof rubber (or silicone) spatula is not only great for all types of mixing, but can also be safely used when cooking components on the stovetop.

Icing smoother: For smooth sides and crisp edges, a metal icing smoother will make your homemade cakes look professional. They are fairly inexpensive and will save you a lot of sanity. Chose one with teeth on the opposite side for a two-in-one smoother and icing comb, like the one made by Ateco. Alternatively, you can use a bench scraper to smooth icing.

Kitchen scale: Using a kitchen scale is the most accurate way to measure ingredients. I highly recommend measuring flours and other dry ingredients with a scale, and using a scale is imperative for measuring chopped chocolate and delicate mixtures like when making macarons.

Offset metal spatulas: Offset metal spatulas (available in varying lengths and widths—I recommend having a small and a large one) consist of a metal strip bent at an angle at the end where it attaches to the handle. This angling gives you more control when, for example, you're applying frosting to a cake. Possibly my most used kitchen tool, offset spatulas are great for everything from frosting cakes to serving a slice of fruit tart.

Oven thermometer: An inexpensive oven thermometer is a great investment. Found at most well-stocked grocery stores (and readily available online), an oven thermometer will let you know what the actual temperature of your oven is, not just what the dial says. Once you get to know your oven, adjust the temperature accordingly.

Parchment paper: Not to be confused with waxed paper, parchment paper can be used to line baking sheets. For more delicate cakes, lining the bottoms of the cake pans with parchment, cut to fit, helps baked cakes release easily from their pans.

To cut parchment paper rounds, simply tear off a piece of parchment slightly larger than the bottom of your cake pan. Fold the parchment in half (left to right) and then fold in half again (bottom to top). You should have roughly folded a square at this point. Bring one of the folded edges to the other folded edge to create a triangle. Fold the triangle in half to create a smaller triangle. Depending on the size of the cake pan, fold the triangle in half one more time.

Flip the cake pan upside down. Place the tip of the folded parchment triangle in the center of the cake pan. Keeping the tip of triangle in the center of the cake pan, trim the edges with scissors following the curve of the edge of the cake pan. Unfold the parchment and check to make sure it fits snuggly inside of the cake pan. Trim to fit as needed.

Pie and tart pans: Metal and glass pie pans conduct heat better and more evenly than ceramic pie pans. Chose a pie pan with a lip to help secure the edges of the pie dough. For tarts, choose fluted pans, either round, square, or rectangular in shape, with removable bottoms.

Piping bags: Depending on the recipe, both disposable and canvas piping bags make their way into my kitchen. For smaller tasks like piping chocolate accents or messier tasks like using multiple colors of buttercream to create flowers, I opt for small disposable bags. For larger tasks like frosting a couple dozen cupcakes, I find that large canvas piping bags are handier.

Piping tips: Stocking a variety of piping tips—large and small, fluted and plain—will help with everything from cake decorating to filling tart shells. Smaller star and petal tips are great for finer, delicate decorations, while large round tips help with filling cakes, piping macaron batter, and much more. See page 275 for specifics.

Rotating cake stand: If you make layer cakes often (or plan to), a rotating cake stand will help you create smooth frosting finishes and various piped designs. They range in price and material. The inexpensive plastic ones will suffice, but my sturdy metal Ateco version has lasted me nearly ten years so far.

Silicone baking mats: When you're lining a pan, parchment paper will suffice in most cases, but silicone baking mats make great reusable nonstick surfaces for baking macarons and meringues.

Stand mixer: The mixing speeds and timing for the recipes in the book are based on using a stand mixer. Occasionally, I'll give you the option to use a handheld mixer, but for recipes with longer mixing times or for which you need two free hands to get things done, like French meringue buttercream or marshmallows, a stand mixer is highly recommended.

FREQUENTLY USED INGREDIENTS

Almond flour: You can make your own from blanched almonds, but packaged almond flour is perfectly acceptable. Look for almond flour over almond meal for use in macarons, and be sure to grind it in a food processor to get an even finer texture before use.

Butter: Always stock your refrigerator with and use unsalted butter, unless a recipe specifies otherwise. Even though most recipes call for added salt, it is best to control the amount by using butter that does not contain salt. Since good-quality European butter usually has a higher butterfat/lower water content, save it for pie and tart dough.

Chocolate: Chocolate is measured by weight. Look for the quantity on the packaging, or use a kitchen scale. Milk, semisweet, and bittersweet/dark chocolate contain different amounts of cacao—the higher the cacao percentage, the more intense the chocolate flavor and the lower the amount of sugar in the chocolate. When a recipe calls for dark chocolate, look for cacao percentages ranging from 65 to 70%. For semisweet chocolate, look for percentages from 50 to 60%. I recommend brands such as Valrhona, Callebaut, and Guittard chocolate. When you can, splurge on good-quality chocolate sold in blocks or fèves (bean-shaped discs).

Cocoa powder: Unless otherwise specified, choose unsweetened Dutch-processed cocoa powder. Black cocoa powder (ultra–Dutch processed cocoa powder from which all the acidity has been neutralized) may be called for to create richer flavors and deeper colors, but it is not necessary.

Eggs: The recipes in this book use large eggs. Measure the egg whites when directed to do so, as for Swiss meringue buttercream and macarons. Some free-range and organic eggs have dark yellow yolks that may impart a more golden color to your cakes and custards. They taste the same, but may affect your overall vision for the cake.

Flour: Be mindful of the type of flour that a recipe calls for because different types contain different amounts of protein, which can affect the finished baked good. Cake flour results in more tender cakes and should be used when called for in a recipe. However, different brands of cake flour may yield different results, so you may end up wanting to use a portion of cake flour and a portion of all-purpose flour to get your desired texture. For best results, use a kitchen scale to measure flour. If not, use the dip-and-sweep method (see page 21).

Gel food coloring: Gel food coloring has a higher concentration of color than liquid coloring, meaning you can use less to achieve the colors you need. This also means you are not adding too much additional liquid to a recipe, which is important when you're making something like a delicate macaron batter or meringue that might break from too much liquid. I recommend AmeriColor gel food coloring.

Instant Espresso Powder: Many of the chocolate cake recipes call for hot coffee and/or instant espresso powder. These ingredients enhance the flavor of the chocolate. You won't necessarily be able to taste the coffee, but if you prefer not to use coffee, substitute hot water in equal measures within the recipes.

Luster dust, disco dust, and edible glitter: These powders and glitters come in a variety of colors, including metallics. They can be applied like powdered food coloring with a brush to sugar paste and fondant or mixed with a clear alcohol to create a paste/paint to brush or flick on cakes and pastries.

Milk and cream: Reach for whole milk for cake batters and custards. When a recipe calls for heavy cream, look for a cream with around 35% milk fat. Keep cream chilled for better results when whipping.

Salt: Use fine-grain (kosher or sea) salt in recipes in this book. Reach for flake salt or fleur de sel when using salt as a garnish.

Sprinkles: A collection of sprinkles always comes in handy for cake and cupcake decorating. Stock different colors and shapes of sprinkles, quins, nonpareils, sugar pearls, and dragées. Do not consume silver dragées in large quantities.

Sugar: Most recipes call for granulated white sugar. Superfine or caster sugar may be used for making meringue, but it is not necessary. Confectioners' sugar is also known as powdered sugar. In this book, confectioners' sugar is measured unsifted, so measure the indicated quantity and sift after measuring, if needed.

Vanilla: Use pure vanilla extract whenever vanilla extract is called for, especially in buttercream and custard. If a recipe calls for vanilla bean paste or real vanilla beans but you can't find them, use pure vanilla extract. Vanilla bean paste and whole beans can be quite expensive, so save it for vanilla buttercream or meringue, where the flavor will really shine.

ALL ABOUT

Layer Cakes

IF MY FIRST BOOK, *LAYERED*, is any indication, my love for layer cakes knows no bounds. Cake making was my gateway into the world of baking and pastry. I thank my twenty-year-old self for picking up a few odd cake pans (6-inch springform pans, to be exact, and not something I would recommend for your first set of cake pans) on a whim one afternoon.

I grew up submerged in the performing arts. Being a dancer was such a huge part of my identity for my first twenty-five years of life that when I was forced to take a step back due to migraines and motion sickness, I felt lost. I'd tried other forms of fine arts, like watercolor, but I was never very successful with any type of painting or drawing until I started considering buttercream my medium and cakes my canvas. Cake decorating was the creative outlet I needed at such a turning point in my life and career. A blessing in disguise, it was the final push I needed to put all my energy into my budding bakery.

I ran The Frosted Cake Shop for four years prior to our big move to Vancouver. Starting in my brother's 1940s kitchen, I first turned my passion for cake making into a career. In order to be properly licensed, I quickly found space in a commercial kitchen to rent before opening my own brick-and-mortar shop.

My shop was a family affair. My mom painted the interior my trademark pale turquoise blue and my brother helped with logo design and marketing, while my dad and I spent countless hours getting plans approved by the county. Friday nights were for family takeout in my reception area, and on the weekends my husband, Brett, would help with wedding cake deliveries and washing endless dishes. During this time, novelty and gravity-defying cakes were extremely popular. In addition to classic wedding cakes covered in my signature handcrafted sugar flowers, most of the other creations leaving my shop doors were topsy-turvy style, carved characters covered in fondant, mini tiered cakes, and more.

No matter the style of cake, success came down to the foundation. In order to stack and deliver layered cakes, you must start with a great recipe and a structurally sound base. Even the most gorgeous of cakes is nothing without these two pillars of cake-making success. Here are some of my best tips and techniques for baking the best layer cakes:

WHAT MAKES A GREAT LAYER CAKE

A perfect layer cake is all about balance and texture. The cake crumb itself should be moist and tender, yet stable. Different types of cakes, like butter, sponge, and oil-based cakes, may be moister than others, but none should be dry. A carrot cake might be incredibly moist compared to a light, airy chiffon cake, but neither should be so tender that they crumble when sliced.

While I encourage you to play with the composition of different cakes and fillings, some combinations work better than others. You may find that an airy sponge cake pairs better with a thin layer of raspberry jam and sweetened whipped cream than a heavy cream cheese frosting that might weigh down its delicate layers. Genoise cakes are notoriously bland, in a good and intentional way, and rely on soaks and simple syrups to add sweetness and flavor, while a decadent chocolate cake might not need more than a dusting of confectioners' sugar to be enjoyed.

Likewise, not all fillings are created equal, and the amount used should vary based on density and sweetness. A thick layer of creamy fudge or buttercream tastes heavenly, but I recommend smaller ratios for fillings like rich ganache or sweet jam. For added texture, I like to throw in a crunchy element, like chopped nuts or even sprinkles, when possible.

Be sure to follow the storage and serving suggestions for each recipe. Most cakes are best at room temperature while others, such as a genoise cake, remain soft even after refrigeration and actually improve over time after they've had a chance to absorb some of the moisture and flavor from the filling. When in doubt, please don't eat cold, stiff Swiss meringue buttercream.

TIPS AND TECHNIQUES

Most of the butter-based cakes in this book use the creaming method. I've broken down several of the steps and the importance each plays in creating the perfect crumb. Not every cake recipe will call for all of these techniques, but they are great rules to bake by in general.

Start with room-temperature ingredients: Unless otherwise specified, all of your ingredients, including butter, eggs, and milk, should be at room temperature for a smoother, more homogeneous batter. Room-temperature (softened) butter is crucial for proper creaming (see below), and keeping the ingredients the same temperature helps them come together easier to prevent overmixing. Room-temperature butter should be soft enough to leave an imprint of your fingertip when pressed, but should never feel greasy or melted. To quickly bring eggs to room temperature, place them (in their shells) in a bowl of tepid, not hot, water while you gather the other ingredients.

Preparing your cake pans: To prevent your baked cake from sticking to the pan, properly prepare your pans before adding the batter. Most recipes will call for greasing and flouring. For best results, brush the inside of the cake pans with very soft butter, sprinkle with flour, shake it all about, then tap out any excess flour. Oil or baking spray may also work. For more delicate cakes, I also recommend lining the bottoms of the pans with parchment paper to keep their tender crumbs from tearing.

Measure and sift dry ingredients accurately: Unlike other types of cooking, baking requires you to accurately measure your ingredients. For example, as little as ½ teaspoon baking powder can make a huge difference. Weighing flour is the most accurate way to measure. If you do not have a kitchen scale, measure using the dip-and-sweep method: Aerate the flour in its container with a whisk, dip a dry measuring cup into the container, then sweep the edge of a butter knife across the top of the measuring cup to level the flour.

Sifting the dry ingredients together not only eliminates lumps, but also evenly distributes the leavening agents throughout.

Creaming butter and sugar: Want tender, velvety, melt-in-your-mouth cakes? Please take the time to properly cream butter and sugar together. I can't emphasize the importance of this step enough. Do not rush through this process, which is usually the first step in any butter cake recipe. Beat together room-temperature butter with sugar until fluffy and pale in color. This should take 3 to 5 minutes. During this process, the mixer drives air into the butter-sugar mixture as the sugar granules cut into the butter and create little air pockets. This friction helps the sugar start to dissolve and softens the butter even more. Creamed butter and sugar distribute throughout the batter more evenly for a smooth batter, and, most important, the batter is more aerated and provides better lift, resulting in a more tender crumb.

Add the eggs one at a time: With the mixer running on medium-low, add the eggs called for in the recipe to the batter one at a time, and wait for each egg (or white or yolk) to be fully incorporated into the batter before adding in the next.

Alternate adding the dry and wet ingredients: Instead of dumping all the flour or milk in at once, alternating between adding dry and wet ingredients keeps the batter smooth and helps prevent overmixing. This technique allows the batter to absorb the ingredients more efficiently. Always start and end with the dry ingredients.

Reverse mixing method: Instead of starting with the creaming technique, this method begins with the dry ingredients and ends with the eggs. I tend to favor this method when I am looking for a lighter, springy cake crumb (see Decoding Vanilla Cakes, page 265). The key to this method is to slowly stream the egg mixture into the batter, allowing it ample time to be absorbed, and scraping the sides and bottom of the bowl between additions. Be careful not to overmix or the crumb will be dry.

Checking for doneness: Because ovens bake at different temperatures, it is important to know what doneness cues to look for instead of just relying on the clock. The tops of the cakes should appear dry and slightly golden when they're done. Many sponge cakes are done when the surface springs back to the touch. The easiest way to check that a cake is done is the toothpick test: Begin checking the cake at the lower end of the baking time range. Insert a toothpick into the center of the cake and pull it out. If the toothpick comes out clean or with a few crumbs attached, the cake is done. If the toothpick is moist or coated in raw batter, continue baking and check again in a few minutes. Resist checking for doneness too often, or your oven may lose heat. A cake is typically overbaked if it pulls away from the sides of the pan (slight pulling away is probably fine, but if there is a significant gap, the cake is likely overbaked).

Cooling and leveling: Set cakes on a wire rack to quickly stop the baking process. Let them cool in their pans on the rack for 10 to 20 minutes, or until they are cool enough to handle. Do not let a cake cool completely in the pan or it may become difficult to remove. Remove the cakes from the pans by running a thin knife around the inside of the pan and then invert the cake onto the wire rack. Let the cakes cool completely, right-side up on a wire rack before removing the parchment (if used). The cake should be completely cool before leveling or cutting; this will help prevent tears and cracks. Some cakes will be slightly rounded on top after baking. To increase the stability of your layer cake, be sure to trim off the domed portion with a long serrated knife (see How to Fill and Frost a Cake, page 266).

The crumb of a cold cake holds together better, so to make things even easier, wrap the cooled cakes in plastic wrap and chill in the refrigerator before leveling or cutting the cakes into multiple layers.

Filling and frosting: Be sure that the cake layers are completely cool before filling or frosting. Heat from a warm cake may melt the butter in a frosting.

Again, a chilled cake is easier to fill and frost and creates fewer crumbs. Be sure that the frosting is not too stiff, or it may tear the tender cake when you spread it on. For more details, check out How to Fill and Frost a Cake (page 266).

Timing and storage: Unless otherwise specified, most cakes may be baked in advance. It may be difficult to bake the cake, make all the fillings and frosting, and assemble the entire cake in one day. Most cake layers can be kept in the refrigerator for up to 3 days or in the freezer for up to a couple of months before they're assembled. Wrap them very well in plastic wrap to keep them from drying out. Thaw frozen cakes in the refrigerator overnight, still wrapped, before assembling.

COMMON CAKE MISHAPS AND PROBABLE CAUSES

TUNNELING WITHIN THE BAKED CAKE CRUMB:
batter was overmixed

CAKE SANK IN THE MIDDLE:
cake is underbaked; oven door was opened too often and/or too early (before the structure for the cake was established); too much moisture in the batter; leavening agents were not fresh/active

CAKE IS DRY:
batter was overmixed; too much flour added—be sure to measure accurately; oven was too hot or cake was overbaked

CAKE IS DENSE OR TOUGH:
batter was overmixed; wrong type of flour (higher percentage of protein) was used; butter and sugar were not creamed properly

CAKE IS TOO TENDER OR CRUMBLY:
batter was undermixed; wrong type of flour was used (lower percentage of protein); too many tenderizers, such as sugar, fat, or egg yolks, were added

LARGE CRACKS ON THE TOP OF THE CAKE:
batter rose too quickly because the oven was too hot or there were too many leavening agents; cake pan was too small

CAKE IS UNDERCOOKED OR RAW IN THE CENTER:
oven was not hot enough; check for doneness—don't just rely on the clock

BATTER IS SPLIT OR APPEARS CURDLED:
cold ingredients were used instead of room-temperature ones; butter and sugar were unable to cream properly. Note that the batter may still be used, but the crumb of the baked cake will be affected

Elegant Cakes and Confections

Adorned with dainty ruffles and floral elements, this collection of cakes and sweets is dressed to the nines, all ready for any chic gathering or elegant affair. Many of the cakes are artfully decorated with piped buttercream frosting, while others are naturally stunning, like a towering pavlova or the traditional design of a green Swedish Princess Cake. Not only are their designs enchanting, but they also boast delicate flavors of lavender, almond, raspberry, and the like to match their graceful exteriors. I imagine sharing slices of Orange Salted Honey Cake at brunch or passing around gilded trays of floral cupcakes at a fancy garden party.

Orange Salted Honey Cake

FEATURED DECORATING TECHNIQUE: RUFFLE PETAL PIPING

The enticing combination of citrus and salted honey is the perfect blend of zesty flavors. It is creamy, complex (in flavor, not in preparation), and decadent while still being light and fresh. The honey in the buttercream is fairly distinct, and the touch of salt makes the flavor palette multidimensional. The cake pairs perfectly with afternoon tea, and the delicate, petal-like finish would be a gorgeous accent at any brunch or shower. MAKES ONE THREE-LAYER 6-INCH (15-CM) CAKE; SERVES 10 TO 12

FOR THE SALTED HONEY CUSTARD:

1½ tablespoons unsalted butter, diced

1 cup (240 ml) plus 1 tablespoon whole milk

4 tablespoons (50 g) granulated sugar

¼ cup (60 ml) honey

3 large egg yolks

3 tablespoons plus 1½ teaspoons cornstarch

1 teaspoon pure vanilla extract

¼ to ½ teaspoon salt, or to taste

FOR THE ORANGE BUTTER CAKE:

2¼ cups (295 g) cake flour

2½ teaspoons baking powder

½ teaspoon salt

1½ cups (300 g) granulated sugar

2 tablespoons finely grated orange zest from about 2 large oranges

⅓ cup (80 ml) fresh orange juice

⅔ cup (160 ml) buttermilk

¾ cup (1½ sticks/170 g) unsalted butter, at room temperature

1 teaspoon pure vanilla extract

3 large eggs

FOR THE HONEY BUTTERCREAM:

4 large egg whites

⅔ cup (160 ml) honey

⅔ cup (135 g) granulated sugar

2 teaspoons pure vanilla extract

2 cups (4 sticks/450 g) unsalted butter, at room temperature

Gel food coloring of your choice

MAKE THE SALTED HONEY CUSTARD

Put the butter in heatproof bowl. Set a fine-mesh sieve over the bowl.

In a medium saucepan, combine the milk and 2 tablespoons of the sugar and slowly bring to a simmer over medium heat. Remove from the heat.

Whisk together the remaining 2 tablespoons sugar, the honey, and the egg yolks in a medium bowl. Whisk the cornstarch into the honey mixture until smooth.

While whisking, stream about half of the hot milk into the egg mixture to temper the egg yolks (this slowly raises the temperature of the eggs so they do not curdle). Pour the tempered egg mixture into the saucepan with the remaining hot milk mixture and heat over medium-low heat, stirring continuously, until the pastry cream thickens and slow, large bubbles start to pop on the surface. Whisk for 1 minute more, then remove from the heat.

Pour the pastry cream through the sieve into the bowl with the butter. Add the vanilla and salt. Stir until smooth and cover with a piece of plastic wrap, pressing it directly against the surface of the pastry cream to prevent a skin from forming. Refrigerate until cool and thick, at least 2 hours or up to 3 days.

MAKE THE ORANGE BUTTER CAKE

Preheat the oven to 350°F (175°C). Grease and flour three 6-inch (15-cm) cake pans and line the bottoms with parchment paper.

Sift together the flour, baking powder, and salt into a medium bowl.

In a small bowl, rub the sugar and orange zest together between your fingertips until fragrant. In a separate bowl, stir together the orange juice and buttermilk.

In the bowl of a stand mixer fitted with the paddle attachment, beat the butter on medium speed for 2 minutes. Add the sugar-zest mixture and mix on medium-high until light and fluffy, 3 to 5 minutes. Stop the mixer and scrape down the bowl.

Turn the mixer to medium-low and add the vanilla. Add the eggs one at a time, mixing until each is incorporated before adding the next. Mix until combined. Stop the mixer and scrape down the bowl.

Turn the mixer to low and add the flour mixture in three batches, alternating with the buttermilk mixture, beginning and ending with the flour mixture. After the last streaks of the flour mixture are incorporated, mix on medium for no more than 30 seconds.

Evenly divide the batter among the prepared pans. Bake for 25 to 28 minutes, until a toothpick inserted into the center of each cake comes out clean. Let the cakes cool on a wire rack for 10 to 15 minutes before removing from the pans. Allow the cakes to cool completely, right-side up, on the wire rack before removing the parchment. Level the tops of the cakes with a long serrated knife as needed.

MAKE THE HONEY BUTTERCREAM

Put the egg whites, honey, and sugar in the bowl of a stand mixer. Gently whisk them by hand until just combined. In a medium saucepan, bring an inch or two (2.5 to 5 cm) of water to a simmer over medium-low heat. Place the mixer bowl on top of the saucepan to create a double boiler (be sure the bottom of the bowl does not touch the water). Whisking intermittently, heat the egg white mixture until it reaches 160°F (70°C) on a candy thermometer.

Carefully affix the mixer bowl to the stand mixer (it may be hot) and fit the mixer with the whisk attachment. Beat the egg white mixture on high for 8 to 10 minutes, or until it holds medium-stiff peaks and the outside of the bowl has returned to room temperature.

Turn the mixer down to low and add the vanilla. Add the butter a couple of tablespoons at a time, mixing until each is incorporated before adding the next. Stop the mixer and swap out the whisk for the paddle attachment.

Turn the mixer to medium-high and beat until the buttercream is silky smooth, 3 to 5 minutes.

ASSEMBLE THE CAKE

Place one cake layer on a cake board or serving plate. Fill a piping bag fitted with a plain round tip with the honey buttercream. Pipe a ring around the top edge of the cake to create a "dam." Fill the ring with half of the honey custard and smooth the top with an offset spatula or the back of a spoon. Top with a second cake layer and repeat; place the final cake layer on top.

Crumb coat the cake with the honey buttercream and chill in the refrigerator for 15 minutes.

DECORATE THE CAKE

Place the cake on a rotating cake stand. Smoothly frost the cake with a thin layer of buttercream.

To decorate the cake with the ruffle petal piping technique, fill a piping bag fitted with a petal tip (Wilton #104) with buttercream. Gently touch the tip to the cake, narrowed side facing down, about 1 inch (2.5 cm) from the bottom of the cake. Hold the piping bag at a 45-degree angle and pipe continuous swags of buttercream around the bottom of the cake. Each swag should be 1 to 2 inches (2.5 to 5 cm) wide. The bottom of each swag should graze the cake board or serving dish. Continue around the cake, slightly overlapping each row, until the sides are completely covered.

For the top, hold the piping bag at a 45-degree angle to the top of the cake. Keeping the narrowed side of the tip pointing away from the center of the cake, gently squeeze the piping bag as you move it out away from the center of the cake and back in. Continue piping concentric circles of petals around the top of the cake clockwise (or counterclockwise, if you are left handed), spinning the cake stand as you go. As you approach the center, tint the buttercream a soft peach color, or the color of your choice, to create a gentle ombré effect. Overlap the rows of petals and increase the angle of the piping bag until you reach the center. For the top of the cake, I find it most comfortable to pipe around the edge farthest from my body, gently spinning the cake stand as I go.

Loosely cover with plastic wrap or place in a cake box and chill in the refrigerator until 30 minutes before serving. Let come to room temperature for 30 minutes, then slice and serve.

Store leftovers loosely covered with plastic wrap or in a cake box in the refrigerator for up to 3 days.

Garden Cupcakes

FEATURED DECORATING TECHNIQUE:
BUTTERCREAM FLOWERS

Early in my career, I worked at a local bakery alongside veteran cake decorators. Every weekend, I'd watch in awe as our top decorator, Carol, would effortlessly pipe swoops and swirls on five-tier wedding cakes as I struggled to write "Happy Birthday" in my best chocolate cursive. My buttercream flowers are still not nearly as perfect as Carol's, but I will keep trying, experimenting with different designs and getting excited each time I transform a simple batch of cupcakes into an edible sugar garden.

My point is, it takes a lot of practice to be perfect, but don't put perfection over fun. Keep in mind that no flower in nature is perfectly symmetrical, so try not to let a few wonky petals keep you from enjoying the process. Thankfully it is just buttercream and you can always scrape it off and start again if you are not satisfied with your work. MAKES 14 TO 16 CUPCAKES

FOR THE SOUR CREAM VANILLA CUPCAKES:

½ cup (120 ml) whole milk

¼ cup (60 ml) sour cream

¾ cup (100 g) cake flour

¾ cup (95 g) all-purpose flour

1 teaspoon baking powder

¼ teaspoon baking soda

¼ teaspoon salt

½ cup (1 stick/115 g) unsalted butter, at room temperature

1 cup (200 g) granulated sugar

2 teaspoons pure vanilla extract

3 large egg whites

TO ASSEMBLE AND DECORATE:

1 large recipe Swiss Meringue Buttercream (page 262)

Gel food coloring

Sugar pearls

MAKE THE CUPCAKES

Preheat the oven to 350°F (175°C). Line two cupcake pans with paper liners.

In a small bowl or liquid measuring cup, mix together the milk and sour cream. In a separate bowl, sift together the flours, baking powder, baking soda, and salt.

In the bowl of a stand mixer fitted with the paddle attachment, beat the butter on medium speed for 2 minutes. Add the sugar and mix on medium-high until light and fluffy, 3 to 5 minutes. Stop the mixer and scrape down the bowl.

Turn the mixer to medium-low and add the vanilla. Add the egg whites one at a time, mixing until each is incorporated before adding the next. Mix until combined. Stop the mixer and scrape down the bowl.

Turn the mixer to low and add the flour mixture in three batches, alternating with the milk mixture, beginning and ending with the flour mixture. Mix on medium for no more than 30 seconds after the last streaks of the flour mixture are combined.

Using a disher or mechanical ice cream scoop, fill the cupcake liners about two-thirds of the way full with batter. Bake for 20 to 24 minutes, until a toothpick inserted into the center of a cupcake comes out clean. Let them cool in their pans for 5 to 10 minutes. Remove the cupcakes from their pans and allow to completely cool on a wire rack before frosting.

Decorate as described in the following pages and serve at room temperature.

Store cupcakes in a cake box or in a cake pan loosely covered with plastic wrap for up to 1 day at room temperature or up to 2 days in the refrigerator.

Rose Cupcake

Fill a piping bag fitted with a large round tip with about ¾ cup of the buttercream. Pipe a cone shape in the center of the cupcake; the cone should be a little less than 1 inch (2.5 cm) in diameter.

Fill a piping bag fitted with a petal tip (Wilton #104) with buttercream. Holding the piping bag at a 45-degree angle leaning in toward the cone, with the narrowed side of the tip facing up, pipe an inner petal that wraps around the tip of the cone to create the center bud.

For the inner row of petals, pipe three petals, equally spaced and slightly overlapping, around the center bud. Keeping the piping bag at a 45-degree angle leaning in toward the bud, with the narrowed side of the tip facing up, pipe arcs starting at the base and then up and partially over the center bud. Release the pressure on the bag after each petal before piping the next.

For the middle row of petals, pipe five petals around the cupcake. Keep the piping bag slightly leaning away from the center of the cupcake with the narrowed side of the tip always facing up.

For the outer petals, pipe seven or eight petals around the cupcake. Keep the piping bag at a 45-degree angle leaning away from the center of the cupcake. Continue to pipe arcs of buttercream to create the petal shapes.

Peony Cupcake

Fill a piping bag fitted with a large round tip with about ¾ cup of the buttercream. Pipe a flat disc shape, about 1 inch (2.5 cm) in diameter, in the center of the cupcake.

Fill a piping bag fitted with a large curved petal tip (Wilton #116) with buttercream. Keeping the narrowed side of the tip facing the center of the cupcake, pipe four fairly flat overlapping strips over the center of the cupcake. Release the pressure on the bag after each strip before piping the next.

Follow the instructions for the Rose Cupcake to create three rows of four, five, and six petals. The petals should be large and ruffly compared to those of the Rose Cupcake.

NOTES: An odd number of petals per row keeps the rose looking natural, and it's okay if they aren't perfectly spaced.

I find it easiest to keep the piping bag nearly still and instead rotate the cupcake around with my other hand. It is most comfortable to me to pipe with my right hand, piping the petals in a clockwise motion, toward my body, but feel free to pipe the petals in the opposite direction if that feels more natural.

Dahlia Cupcake

Fill a piping bag fitted with a large round tip with about ¾ cup of buttercream. Pipe a cone shape in the center of the cupcake. The cone should be a little less than 1 inch (2.5 cm) in diameter. Fill a piping bag fitted with a curved petal tip (Wilton #81) with buttercream. Holding the piping bag perpendicular to the top of the cupcake, pipe interlocking petals on the top of the cone, applying a small amount of pressure to the piping bag and gently pulling straight up for each petal and tapering off the pressure on the bag as you go. Release the pressure on the bag after each petal before piping the next.

Continue piping interlocking petals until the center of the cone is covered in five or six petals. Continue piping concentric circles of petals around the center of the cupcake. As the petals move farther away from the center of the cupcake, gradually angle the piping bag away from the center.

The outermost petals should be taller and may flare out around the edges. As the petals get taller, they have more of a tendency to flip or curl over, especially if the buttercream becomes too warm. The petals tend to support one another, so keep piping until the cupcake is completely full.

English Rose Cupcake

Fill a piping bag fitted with a small petal tip (Wilton #103) with buttercream. Angle the piping bag out so that it is nearly parallel with the top of the cupcake, with the narrowed side of the tip facing up. Starting in the center, pipe five ribbon-like loops evenly around the center.

Pipe a second row of loops directly around the first set and repeat until you have three layers of loops filling the center of the cupcake.

For the outer petals, pipe a row of five long petals around the cupcake. Keep the opening of the petal tip nearly perpendicular to the top of the cupcake, narrowed side facing up. Continue to pipe petals around the cupcake until the top is completely covered. Unlike the arced petals of the Rose Cupcake, these petals should be relatively straight.

For the outermost row of petals, angle the piping bag slightly away from the center to create a flared edge.

Yellow Blossom Cupcake

Fill a piping bag fitted with a petal tip (Wilton #104) with buttercream. Keeping the piping bag at a 45-degree angle away from the center of the cupcake, with the narrowed side of the piping tip facing away from the center of the cupcake, begin to pipe petals. Starting a little less than 1 inch (2.5 cm) from the edge of the cupcake, gradually apply pressure to the piping bag while moving it out from the center and then back in, tapering off the pressure as you return to the center. Continue to pipe petals around the outer edge of the cupcake.

Repeat to make a second row of petals, slightly overlapping the first row and angled in toward the center. Pipe a few center petals, as needed, until the top of the cupcake is completely covered. Sprinkle the center of the cupcake with sugar pearls.

YELLOW BLOSSOM CUPCAKE

Matcha White Chocolate Cake

FEATURED DECORATING TECHNIQUES: COMBED ICING, ROSETTE PIPING

One of my favorite ways to develop an original recipe is by introducing a fresh ingredient into a classic cake or pastry. So here I added Japanese matcha powder to a traditional Italian genoise sponge cake. Genoise sponge cakes are notoriously plain, which allows them to take on various flavorings. Here the complex, vegetal flavors of matcha tea are paired with creamy white chocolate buttercream for a not-too-sweet, delightful bite. MAKES ONE SIX-LAYER 6-INCH (15-CM) CAKE; SERVES 10 TO 12

FOR THE MATCHA GENOISE CAKE:

6 large eggs

1¼ cups (250 g) granulated sugar

1⅓ cups (165 g) all-purpose flour

2 tablespoons cornstarch

2 teaspoons matcha tea powder

4 tablespoons (½ stick/ 55 g) unsalted butter, melted and cooled

½ teaspoon pure vanilla extract

FOR THE WHITE CHOCOLATE BUTTERCREAM:

1 medium recipe Swiss Meringue Buttercream (page 262)

5 ounces (140 g) white chocolate, melted and cooled

FOR THE MATCHA SIMPLE SYRUP:

¾ cup (150 g) granulated sugar

1 tablespoon matcha tea powder

TO DECORATE:

Gel food coloring

Sugar pearls (optional)

MAKE THE MATCHA GENOISE CAKE

Preheat the oven to 350°F (175°C). Grease and flour three 6-inch (15-cm) cake pans and line the bottoms with parchment paper.

Put the eggs and sugar in the bowl of a stand mixer. Gently whisk by hand until just combined. In a medium saucepan, bring an inch or two (2.5 to 5 cm) of water to a simmer over medium-low heat. Place the mixer bowl on top of the saucepan to create a double boiler (be sure the bottom of the bowl does not touch the water). Heat the egg mixture, stirring intermittently, until warm to the touch or 100°F (38°C) on a candy thermometer.

Carefully affix the mixer bowl to the stand mixer (it may be hot) and fit the mixer with the whisk attachment. Whip the egg mixture on high speed until it triples in volume, about 8 minutes. When done, the mixture will be pale in color and slightly thickened. To test, stop the mixer and remove the whisk. Draw a figure eight with the batter dripping from the whisk. The batter should hold its shape just long enough for you to draw the "8."

Sift the flour, cornstarch, and matcha into the egg mixture. Gently fold until thoroughly combined.

In a separate bowl, stir together about 1 cup (240 ml) of the egg-flour mixture and the melted butter. Add the vanilla, pour the butter mixture back into the bowl with the remaining egg-flour mixture, and gently fold to thoroughly combine.

Evenly distribute the batter among the prepared pans, leaving at least ¾ inch (2 cm) of space from the top of the pans. Bake for 24 to 28 minutes, until the tops of the cakes spring back when gently touched with your fingertip and a toothpick inserted into the center of each cake comes out clean. Run a thin paring knife around the inside edges of the cake pans. Let

HOW TO DECORATE A
Combed Icing Cake

the cakes cool on a wire rack for 10 to 15 minutes before removing from the pans. Allow the cakes to cool completely, right-side up, on the wire rack before removing the parchment. Once cool, cut the cakes in half horizontally to create 6 even layers.

MAKE THE WHITE CHOCOLATE BUTTERCREAM

In the clean bowl of a stand mixer fitted with the paddle attachment, beat the buttercream until silky smooth. Add the melted white chocolate and mix on medium speed until combined.

MAKE THE MATCHA SIMPLE SYRUP

In a small saucepan, combine the sugar and ¾ cup (180 ml) water and bring to a simmer over medium-low heat. Turn the heat to low and add the matcha. Stir well. Remove from the heat. Allow to cool before using.

ASSEMBLE THE CAKE

Generously brush the cake layers with the matcha syrup. Place one cake layer on a cake board or serving plate. Spread on a thin layer of buttercream, about ⅓ cup (80 ml), with an offset spatula. Top with a second cake layer and repeat. Repeat with three additional cake layers and place the final layer on top.

Crumb coat the cake and chill it in the refrigerator for 15 minutes.

DECORATE THE CAKE

Set aside about 1 cup (240 ml) of the buttercream for the rosettes.

To decorate the cake with the combed icing technique, set the cake on a rotating cake stand. Smoothly frost the cake with the remaining buttercream. To create the buttercream stripe design, gently touch the edge of an icing comb to the side of the cake. Keeping the icing comb as parallel to the cake as possible, rotate the cake stand in a complete circle. The teeth of the comb should gently cut into the buttercream and make a stripe design. Repeat as needed. Use a small offset spatula to smooth the top of the cake.

Tint a small portion of buttercream green and fill a piping bag fitted with a small leaf tip (such as Wilton #352) with the green buttercream. Tint the remaining buttercream soft pink, or the color of your choice. Fill a piping bag fitted with a small star tip (such at Wilton #18) with the pink buttercream. To create the rosettes, hold the piping bag perpendicular to the surface of the cake and pipe tight spirals around the edges of the cake (see page 275). Pipe green leaves at various points inside and outside the ring of rosettes. Sprinkle with sugar pearls, if desired.

If eating the cake the same day as assembled, store it at room temperature until ready to serve. If assembled in advance, store in a cake box in the refrigerator overnight. Bring to room temperature for 30 minutes before serving. Store leftovers loosely covered with plastic wrap in the refrigerator for 3 to 4 days.

✻ ✻ ✻

NOTE: If the stripes are undefined or the buttercream begins to clump, try applying varying amounts of pressure to the icing comb or using a thinner layer of buttercream around the sides of the cake. The buttercream should be soft enough for the icing comb to create the pattern and not chilled.

Getting to Know
Genoise Sponge Cakes

* * *

1 LEAVENED WITH JUST WHIPPED EGGS, genoise cakes are extremely light and fluffy but not too delicate. They are mixed using the foaming method, where whole eggs and sugar are gently warmed before being whipped until thick and foamy, or the "ribbon stage."

2 ALBEIT A BIT BLAND ON THEIR OWN, they are extremely versatile and rely on syrups and soaks to flavor their tender crumbs. Used in everything from layer cakes, French entremets, and trifles, the beauty of this base cake comes from its simplicity.

3 SIMPLE IN FLAVOR AND STRUCTURE, YES, but genoise cakes can be finicky to put together. Unlike many other sponge cakes, genoise cakes typically call for the addition of melted butter. If the baked cake appears split with a dense, squishy, almost raw bottom and a springy top, then the butter was most likely not folded into the batter properly and sunk to the bottom of the pan while the cake was in the oven. To help remedy this problem without overmixing and deflating the whipped eggs, I mix a small portion of the batter with the melted butter first and then incorporate that into the batter in the mixer bowl.

4 LAYERED WITH CUSTARD, JAM, OR BUTTERCREAM AND SOAKED WITH FLAVORED SYRUPS, the genoise cake recipes in this book actually improve with time. Chilling the assembled cakes in the refrigerator for 4 to 8 hours allows the cakes to absorb the flavor and moisture from the fillings. Unlike other butter cakes, genoise cakes remain soft and tender even after refrigeration. Make sure to follow the serving instructions for each recipe to take the different frostings and finishes into account.

Almond Apricot Battenberg Cake

FEATURED DECORATING TECHNIQUES: CHECKERBOARD CAKE, COVERING A CAKE IN MARZIPAN

Working from home definitely has its advantages, but simultaneously entertaining a toddler can be challenging. Enter Emily—our real-life Mary Poppins. Straight from London, our lovely nanny helps care for Everett a couple of times a week. The pair is always taking off on their latest adventures full of sandcastles at the beach and trips on the train around the city. Around noon, they come bursting through the front door with stories, smiles, and curiosity about what I've been working on that day. The afternoon I was working on this Battenberg cake, Emily's response was priceless: "It looks just like the ones my nan makes!" Success!

Battenberg cakes, with their checkerboard interior, are commonplace in England and can be spotted everywhere from convenience stores to Nan's house. Made with a portion of almond flour, spread thin with jam (apricot, in this case), and covered with rolled marzipan, these slightly spongy, mildly sweet cakes pair perfectly with tea. SERVES 6 TO 8

1 cup (125 g) all-purpose flour

¾ teaspoon baking powder

¼ teaspoon salt

1 cup (200 g) granulated sugar

½ cup (60 g) almond flour

¾ cup (1½ sticks/170 g) unsalted butter, at room temperature, diced

2 tablespoons whole milk

3 large eggs

½ teaspoon pure vanilla extract

¼ teaspoon pure almond extract

Pink gel food coloring

½ cup (120 ml) apricot jam

7 ounces (200 g) marzipan

Preheat the oven to 350°F (190°C). Line two 8 by 4-inch (20 by 10-cm) loaf pans with parchment paper (if you do not have two loaf pans, see Note).

Sift the all-purpose flour, baking powder, and salt into the bowl of a stand mixer fitted with the paddle attachment. Add the sugar and almond flour. Stir to combine. Add the butter pieces and mix on medium speed until evenly distributed. Stream in the milk and mix until all the dry ingredients are moistened, about 1 minute. Stop the mixer and scrape down the sides and bottom of the bowl.

Whisk together the eggs, vanilla, and almond extract. Add the egg mixture to the flour mixture and mix on low until combined. Turn the mixer to medium and beat for about 1 minute.

Divide the batter between two medium bowls. Tint half of the batter with the pink gel food coloring. Pour the plain and pink batter into the two prepared loaf pans (see Note) and bake for 25 to 28 minutes, until a toothpick inserted into the center of each cake comes out clean. Let the cakes cool completely on a wire rack before removing from the pans. Remove the parchment.

To create the checkerboard cake pattern, trim each cake into two ¾ by ¾ by 8-inch (2 by 2 by 20-cm) blocks to make 4 blocks total. Spread a thin layer of apricot jam on one side of each pink cake block and sandwich each together with one of the plain cake blocks. Spread the top of one pair of cake blocks with more apricot jam and place the second pair of cake blocks on top, making sure the colors form a checkerboard pattern. No like-colored cake blocks should be touching each other.

Roll out the marzipan into an 8½-inch (22-cm) square. Spread a thin layer of jam on one of the long sides of the checkerboard cake and place it jam-side down on one edge of the marzipan. Spread a thin layer of jam on the remaining long edges of the cake and carefully roll up the cake in the marzipan. Press gently to seal and trim the marzipan and the cake as needed.

To serve, slice into 1-inch-thick (2.5-cm) pieces with a serrated knife.

Store leftovers well wrapped in plastic wrap at room temperature for up to 4 days.

✳   ✳   ✳

NOTES: If you do not have two loaf pans, use one 8-inch (20-cm) square pan. Fold a piece of foil so that it is three or four layers thick and trim it to fit inside the pan. Place the folded foil in the middle of the pan to divide the pan in half. Fill each side with the plain and pink cake batters and continue with the baking and assembling directions.

Marzipan is a soft and pliable dough made from sweetened almond paste. Similar to fondant, it rolls out smooth and can be used to cover and decorate cakes. Dust the marzipan with a bit of confectioners' sugar or roll out large amounts between two pieces of parchment paper to keep from sticking. When not using, cover marzipan with a piece of plastic wrap to keep it from drying out.

Meringue 101

*   *   *

From the pavlova on page 47 to the gems on page 224, meringue is a delicious component of several of the desserts in this book, and making it is an easy and useful skill to master. To get the most out of your meringue (i.e., create stable, voluminous whipped egg whites), be sure to follow these tips:

1   KEEP FREE FROM FATS: Make sure there are no drips of egg yolk in the mix and that all the equipment being used is free of grease. Plastic bowls are more porous, so I recommend using metal or glass bowls for whipping.

2   TEMPERATURE: Cold eggs are easier to separate, but room-temperature eggs whip up with more volume.

3   SPEED: Increase the mixer speed slowly. Start whipping the eggs on low speed. Once the egg whites begin to foam, slowly increase the speed and start adding the sugar.

4   SUGAR: Regular granulated sugar and superfine sugar both work, but in order to make sure the sugar fully dissolves into the meringue, it needs to be added very gradually as you increase the speed of the mixer. Depending on the size of your recipe, it should take at least a minute or two to add it all. Once all the sugar has been added, increase the speed to medium-high and mix until glossy, stiff peaks form.

5   STABILIZERS: Many meringue recipes call for the addition of cream of tartar, lemon juice, and/or vinegar. These ingredients act as stabilizers and strengthen the whipped whites. They won't necessarily increase the volume of the egg whites, but they help keep them from collapsing too quickly and aid in creating that coveted marshmallowy center of a baked meringue or pavlova.

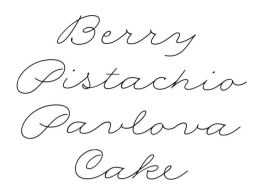

Berry Pistachio Pavlova Cake

FEATURED DECORATING TECHNIQUE: TEXTURED PIPING

I grew up with a mom who threw killer parties. Not too big, not too small, not too fancy, and not too long. Over the years, I remember an assortment of affairs being celebrated—from New Year's Eve to surprise birthdays, backyard BBQs to baby showers. Nothing was ever too formal, but my mom had hosting down to a science, from signature drinks to spectacular desserts.

Pavlova is one of my mom's favorite desserts and has made the occasional appearance at her parties and gatherings. With a pillow of crisp meringue filled with sweetened whipped cream and seasonal fruit, pavlova is definitely a crowd-pleaser any time of year. An easy way to elevate (literally and figuratively) a classic pavlova is to stack it, because two pavlovas are always better than one. My two-tier pavlova also stands out as a result of its textured piping, rose-scented whipped cream, and plump raspberries. Mom's parties might put mine to shame, but I think we can all agree that this recipe would be welcomed at any celebration. MAKES ONE TWO-TIERED PAVLOVA; SERVES 10 TO 12

FOR THE PAVLOVA:

5 large egg whites

1 cup (195 g) superfine sugar

2 teaspoons cornstarch

1 teaspoon distilled white vinegar

1 teaspoon pure vanilla extract

TO ASSEMBLE:

½ teaspoon rose water, or to taste

1 recipe Whipped Cream (page 263)

2 cups (250 g) fresh raspberries

1 cup (150 g) fresh strawberries, halved or quartered

¼ cup (30 g) shelled pistachios, chopped

MAKE THE PAVLOVA

Preheat the oven to 325°F (160°C). Line a baking sheet with parchment paper. Trace a 5-inch (13-cm) circle and a 7-inch (18-cm) circle onto the parchment to create two templates, then flip them over and place on the baking sheet.

In the bowl of a stand mixer fitted with the whisk attachment, whisk the egg whites on low speed until they begin to foam, form small, tight bubbles, and turn opaque. Over the course of about 3 minutes, very gradually increase the speed to medium while slowly adding the superfine sugar and cornstarch. Mix on medium-high until stiff peaks form. Add the vinegar and vanilla and mix for 30 to 60 seconds to combine.

Using the templates as a guide, dollop a portion of the meringue into the center of each circle. Use an offset spatula or the back of a spoon to spread the meringue to fill each circle. The smaller meringue should be thicker, about 1½ inches (4 cm), so it will bake evenly.

To decorate the pavlova with the textured piping technique, fill a piping bag fitted with a medium-large star tip (such as Wilton #1M) with the remaining meringue. Pipe strips of meringue all around the edge of one meringue disc: Starting at the base, apply pressure to the bag as you pull straight up from the baking sheet; release the pressure on the bag as you reach the top of the meringue disc and slightly pull the tip toward the center of the disc. Repeat until you've covered the outside of the meringue disc, then repeat with the second meringue disc.

Lower the oven temperature to 225°F (110°C). Bake the meringues for 1 hour 20 minutes to 2 hours, until the outsides are dry and crisp while the inside has a marshmallow-like texture. Turn the oven off, prop the oven door open, and allow the baked meringues to cool in the oven for 1 hour. If the meringue begins to brown, turn the oven down to 200°F (93°C).

ASSEMBLE THE PAVLOVA

Whisk the rose water into the whipped cream. Place the large meringue on a serving dish. Dollop about two-thirds of the whipped cream on top. Sprinkle half of the raspberries, strawberries, and pistachios over the whipped cream. Stack the smaller meringue disc on top. Spoon the remaining whipped cream on top and cover with the remaining berries and pistachios.

Serve within 30 minutes of assembling. If making in advance, store the baked meringues wrapped in plastic at room temperature. Store leftovers loosely covered in plastic wrap in the refrigerator for up to 2 days.

Blackberry Elderflower Vertical Layer Cake

FEATURED DECORATING TECHNIQUES: VERTICAL LAYER CAKE, SMOOTH FROSTING, CLOSED-STAR PIPING

I made my first vertical layer cake years ago. While it was visually striking, the cake resembled something closer to cardboard than a confection, and the filling was overly sweet and artificial. This cake, however, not only tastes of floral, sweet, and tart notes, it is delightful from the inside out. Blackberry and elderflower is the perfect pair for any springtime celebration. The flavor is light enough to take you all the way through the peak of summer when blackberries are plump and at their sweetest. It's a true showstopper even after it is sliced!

No, this is not an optical illusion. By flipping this jelly roll–style cake up on its side, each slice reveals vertical layers as opposed to horizontal ones. The naturally hued blackberry buttercream contrasts with the light cake to make the stunning stripes within. It is as delicious as it is dazzling!

MAKES ONE 6-INCH (15-CM) CAKE; SERVES 10 TO 14

FOR THE VANILLA SPONGE CAKE:

10 large eggs

1½ cups (300 g) granulated sugar

1¾ cups plus 2 tablespoons (235 g) all-purpose flour

2 tablespoons cornstarch

2 teaspoons baking powder

1 teaspoon salt

¼ cup (½ stick/55 g) unsalted butter, melted and cooled

2 teaspoons pure vanilla extract

Confectioners' sugar, for dusting

FOR THE ELDERFLOWER SYRUP:

½ cup (50 g) granulated sugar

¼ cup (60 ml) elderflower liqueur, such as St. Germain

2 tablespoons fresh lemon juice

FOR THE BLACKBERRY BUTTERCREAM:

1½ cups (210 g) fresh or frozen blackberries

Juice of 1 medium lemon

1 large recipe Whipped Vanilla Buttercream (page 261)

TO DECORATE:

Gel food coloring, optional

Sugar pearls

MAKE THE VANILLA SPONGE CAKE

Preheat the oven to 350°F (175°C). Grease two 13 by 18-inch (33 by 46-cm) pans and line the bottoms with parchment paper (see Notes).

In the bowl of a stand mixer fitted with the whisk attachment, beat the eggs and granulated sugar on medium-high speed until the mixture triples in volume, about 8 minutes. Stop the mixer and sift in the flour, cornstarch, baking powder, and salt. Using the mixer's whisk, stir the mixture by hand until combined.

In a separate bowl, stir together about 1 cup (240 ml) of the egg-flour mixture and the melted butter. Add the vanilla, pour the butter mixture back into the bowl with the remaining egg-flour mixture, and gently fold to thoroughly combine.

Evenly divide the batter between the prepared pans and bake for 12 to 15 minutes, until the surface springs back when gently touched. Rotate the pans halfway through baking. Do not overbake, or the cakes may crack.

Dust the warm cakes with a generous amount of confectioners' sugar. Place a clean tea towel on top of each cake. Carefully flip the pans upside down to release the cakes onto the towels. Peel off the parchment paper and dust the bottoms of the cakes with confectioners' sugar. While the cakes are still warm, roll them up in the towels, starting at the short ends. Set the cakes seam-side down and let cool completely in the towels, 30 to 45 minutes. Once cooled, carefully unroll the cakes, and remove the towels. Like muscle memory, the cake will "remember" to retain its curved shape once cooled.

MAKE THE ELDERFLOWER SYRUP

In a small saucepan, combine the sugar, elderflower liqueur, lemon juice, and 2 tablespoons water and bring to a boil. Reduce the heat to low and simmer for about 5 minutes. Remove from the heat and set aside to cool before use.

MAKE THE BLACKBERRY BUTTERCREAM:

In a small saucepan, combine the blackberries and lemon juice and bring to a simmer over medium heat, 5 to 10 minutes. Using a submersion blender, puree the cooked blackberries (be careful, as this can be messy). Alternatively, smash the blackberries with a potato masher or the back of a slotted spoon. Strain the mixture through a fine-mesh sieve set over a bowl. Press down on the puree with a rubber spatula to extract all the juice. Discard the solids in the strainer. Set the strained puree aside and cool before use.

With a handheld mixer or using a stand mixer fitted with the paddle attachment, beat together the buttercream and 4 to 6 tablespoons of the blackberry puree, a few tablespoons at a time. The buttercream should be soft and spreadable but not runny.

ASSEMBLE THE CAKE

To create the vertical layer cake, cut the cooled cakes in half lengthwise to create 4 long strips of cake. Generously brush the strips of cake with the elderflower syrup. Spread the blackberry buttercream on top of each strip of cake with a small offset spatula, using about ¾ cup (180 ml) of the buttercream per strip of cake. Gently roll up one strip to make a spiral. Turn the rolled strip on its side and begin wrapping the remaining cakes around the center spiral, setting the start of each strip at the end of the last one to create a large spiral of cake and filling. Place the cake on a cake board or serving plate. Crumb coat the cake with the buttercream and chill in the refrigerator for 15 minutes.

DECORATE THE CAKE

Set aside about ½ cup (120 ml) of the remaining buttercream. Remove the cake from the refrigerator and smoothly frost with the blackberry buttercream. Tint half of the reserved buttercream with a bit of the blackberry puree or gel food coloring to create two shades of purple.

To create the buttercream flowers, fill a piping bag fitted with a medium closed-star tip (such as Wilton #2B) with the two shades of remaining buttercream. Use a small offset spatula to place the two shades on either side of the piping bag (it is okay if they aren't perfectly divided—the swirl of color will give the piped flowers more dimension).

Holding the piping bag perpendicular to the surface of the cake, pipe clusters of flowers on the top and sides of the cake, or as desired. Use the same technique as piping a star (page 275). Place a sugar pearl in the center of each flower.

If eating the cake the same day as assembled, store it at room temperature until ready to serve. If assembled in advance, store in a cake box in the refrigerator overnight. Bring to room temperature for 30 minutes before serving. Store leftovers loosely covered with plastic wrap in the refrigerator for up to 3 days.

*　　*　　*

NOTE: If working with two cakes at the same time seems intimidating or you only have one large baking sheet, cut the cake recipe in half and bake them one at a time. Follow the images for the Yule Log Cake (page 249) for assembly.

Swedish Princess Cake

FEATURED DECORATING TECHNIQUES: COVERING A CAKE IN MARZIPAN, CREATING MARZIPAN FLOWERS

The summer of my twenty-first birthday, I embarked on a weeklong cruise through the Baltic Sea with my family. This was not a relax-by-the-pool-with-umbrella-drinks kind of cruise, but rather a wake-up-at-6-a.m.-and-explore-the-city-before-the-boat-departs situation. By the time we arrived in Stockholm, Sweden, our final destination, we were exhausted, so instead of participating in the ship's planned activities, we went rogue. We leisurely explored the city's neighborhoods, scoured the local grocery stores (a pastime I particularly enjoy while traveling), and participated in afternoon fika *(coffee break). And I spotted my first Swedish princess cake.*

The smooth, green marzipan and adorable pink roses were enough for me to fall in love with this cake, but the inside is just as delightful. Layers of light sponge cake are filled with jam and pastry cream before being covered in whipped cream. This version might not be exactly traditional (some are made with an almond cake base, while others skip the custard altogether), but I know you will love the fluffy layers of cake, my favorite vanilla bean pastry cream, and the tart yet sweet raspberry filling. Like other sponge cakes, the texture actually improves after it rests for a few hours and the flavors have a chance to mingle. MAKES ONE THREE-LAYER 8-INCH (20-CM) CAKE; SERVES 10 TO 12

FOR THE GENOISE CAKE:

6 large eggs

1¼ cups (250 g) granulated sugar

1⅓ cups (165 g) all-purpose flour

2 tablespoons cornstarch

¼ cup (½ stick/55 g) unsalted butter, melted and cooled

¼ teaspoon pure almond extract

TO ASSEMBLE AND DECORATE:

1 small recipe Vanilla Pastry Cream (page 264)

⅔ cup (160 ml) seedless raspberry jam

1 recipe Whipped Cream (page 263)

16 ounces (450 g) marzipan, plus 2½ ounces (70 g) more, separated

Green gel food coloring

Confectioners' sugar, for dusting

Pink gel food coloring

MAKE THE GENOISE CAKE

Preheat the oven to 350°F (175°C). Grease and flour three 8-inch (20-cm) cake pans and line the bottoms with parchment paper.

Put the eggs and sugar in the bowl of a stand mixer. Gently whisk by hand until just combined. In a medium saucepan, bring an inch or two (2.5 to 5 cm) of water to a simmer over medium-low heat. Place the mixer bowl on top of the saucepan to create a double boiler (be sure the bottom of the bowl does not touch the water). Heat the egg mixture, stirring intermittently, until warm to the touch or 100°F (38°C) on a candy thermometer.

Carefully affix the mixer bowl to the stand mixer (it may be hot) and fit the mixer with the whisk attachment. Whip the egg mixture on high speed until it triples in volume, about 8 minutes. When done, the mixture will be pale in color and slightly thickened. To test, stop the mixer and remove the whisk. Draw a figure eight with the batter dripping from the whisk. The batter should hold its shape just long enough for you to draw the "8."

Sift the flour and cornstarch into the egg mixture. Gently fold the mixture until thoroughly combined.

In a separate bowl, stir together about 1 cup (240 ml) of the egg-flour mixture and the melted butter. Add the almond extract and pour the butter mixture back into the bowl with the remaining egg-flour mixture. Gently fold to thoroughly combine.

Evenly distribute the batter among the three prepared pans. Bake the cakes for 20 to 22 minutes, until the tops of the cakes spring back when gently touched with your fingertip and a toothpick inserted into the center of each cake comes out clean. Run a thin paring knife around the inside edges of the cake pans. Let the cakes cool on a wire rack for 10 to 20 minutes before removing from the pans. Once cool, remove and discard the parchment paper.

ASSEMBLE THE CAKE

Whisk the pastry cream to loosen it. Place one cake layer on a cake board or serving plate. Spread half of the jam on top with a small offset spatula. Place half the pastry cream on top of the jam and carefully smooth it out with an offset spatula or the back of a spoon, making sure not to get too close to the edges. Top with a second cake layer and repeat; place the final cake layer on top.

Chill the cake in the refrigerator for 20 to 30 minutes.

Frost the top and sides with the whipped cream. Place a large dollop of whipped cream on top of the cake and smooth it out into a domed shape. Place the cake in the freezer for 30 to 60 minutes, or until it feels firm but not frozen through.

To cover the cake in marzipan, tint the 16 ounces of marzipan green and shape it into a large disc. Set aside about 2½ ounces (70 g) for the trim. Place the remaining marzipan in the center of a large piece of parchment and roll it out into a large circle about 18 inches (45 cm) in diameter. Remove the cake from the freezer. Keeping the marzipan attached to the parchment paper, carefully invert it and place the marzipan, parchment-side up, on top the cake. Peel off the parchment and gently smooth the marzipan over the top and sides of the cake. Press to seal any cracks and trim the marzipan around the bottom of the cake. Reserve a small amount of green marzipan for the leaves and roll any remaining green marzipan into a 24-inch-long (60-cm) "snake" and wrap it around the bottom edge of the cake. Dust the top of the cake with confectioners' sugar using a fine-mesh sieve.

DECORATE THE CAKE

Tint the 2½ ounces marzipan pink and divide it into three equal portions. Cover two of the portions with plastic wrap and set aside.

Roll a small piece of the uncovered marzipan between your fingertips into a small cone, less than 1 inch (2.5 cm) tall, and cover with plastic wrap. Roll the remaining marzipan into a log and cut it into 8 equal pieces. Roll each piece into a ball and set aside under the plastic wrap. Working with a few balls at a time, gently roll each out into a flat disc to form the petals. Taper one side of each disc so that the edge is slightly thinner than the base. This edge will become the top of the petal.

Take one marzipan disc and wrap it around the cone, with the thinner edge near the top of the cone, to create the center rose bud. Gently squeeze the base of the petal against the cone to secure. Take two more petals and wrap them around the center bud, overlapping them. Take the remaining five petals and evenly space them around the rose. The petals should overlap. Carefully manipulate the petals with your fingertips so they gently flare out around the flower. Pinch the base of the rose to secure and trim the bottom with a paring knife as needed. Set aside under plastic wrap.

Repeat with the remaining portions of marzipan to create 3 roses total.

Roll out any remaining green marzipan and use a paring knife to hand-cut leaves. Gently score the leaves down the center and pinch one end to shape. Place the marzipan leaves and roses on top of the cake.

Store the cake in the refrigerator, loosely covered in plastic wrap or in a cake box, until ready to serve. It is best served 4 to 8 hours after assembly, once the fillings have had a chance to soften the cake and mature. Store leftovers in the refrigerator for up to 2 days.

Marzipan roses may be made in advance and stored at room temperature in an airtight container for about a week. See page 44 for more tips on working with marzipan.

Almond Raspberry Celebration Cake

FEATURED DECORATING TECHNIQUES: SMOOTH FROSTING, SHELL BORDER,
STACKING A CAKE, WORKING WITH FRESH FLOWERS

This is an almond butter cake with raspberry jam and vanilla buttercream, but turned up a few notches. Don't let the lengthy ingredients list scare you away. No one flavor overpowers another; instead, they work in harmony to create a luxurious layer cake, ideal for any special occasion. Subtle aromatics— fresh lemon zest, vanilla bean, and cinnamon—elevate the almond cake, and replacing some of the butter in the frosting with creamy mascarpone makes it extra-silky and elegant.

I developed this two-tiered party cake for larger gatherings, although you can always downsize and make just one cake. I balanced a handful of macarons, meringues, and fresh flowers on each tier, but feel free to decorate as desired—perhaps with fresh raspberries to reflect the filling inside. Feel free to purchase a few macarons from your local bakery to use as decoration, or make a full batch at home and package the leftovers as take-away treats. MAKES ONE TWO-TIERED CAKE; SERVES 22 TO 30

FOR THE 6-INCH (15-CM) CAKE:

1½ cups plus 2 tablespoons (210 g) cake flour

1½ teaspoons baking powder

Heaping ¼ teaspoon baking soda

Heaping ¼ teaspoon salt

Heaping ¼ teaspoon ground cinnamon

6 tablespoons (45 g) almond flour

1¼ cups plus 1 tablespoon (260 g) granulated sugar

1 teaspoon finely grated lemon zest

¾ cup (1½ sticks/ 170 g) unsalted butter, at room temperature

¾ teaspoon vanilla bean paste or pure vanilla extract

½ teaspoon pure almond extract

3 large eggs

¾ cup (180 ml) buttermilk

FOR THE 8-INCH (20-CM) CAKE:

2½ cups (325 g) cake flour

2 teaspoons baking powder

½ teaspoon baking soda

½ teaspoon salt

½ teaspoon ground cinnamon

½ cup (60 g) almond flour

1 cup (2 sticks/225 g) unsalted butter, at room temperature

1¾ cups (350 g) granulated sugar

1½ teaspoons finely grated lemon zest

1 teaspoon vanilla bean paste or pure vanilla extract

¾ teaspoon pure almond extract

4 large eggs

1 cup (240 ml) buttermilk

FOR THE MASCARPONE BUTTERCREAM:

9 egg whites

3 cups (600 g) granulated sugar

1 tablespoon vanilla bean paste or pure vanilla extract

½ teaspoon pure almond extract

3¾ cups (7½ sticks/ 845 g) unsalted butter, at room temperature

1½ cups (345 g) mascarpone

½ teaspoon ground cinnamon

Pinch of salt

TO ASSEMBLE AND DECORATE:

1¼ cups (300 g) seedless raspberry jam

4 wooden cake dowels or thick plastic straws

Assorted decorations (such as macarons, meringues, and fresh flowers; see pages 99, 45, and 209)

MAKE THE 6-INCH (15-CM) CAKE

Preheat the oven to 350°F (175°C). Grease and flour three 6-inch (15-cm) cake pans and line the bottoms with parchment paper.

Sift together the cake flour, baking powder, baking soda, salt, and cinnamon into a large bowl. Stir in the almond flour.

In a small bowl, rub the sugar and lemon zest together between your fingertips until fragrant.

In the bowl of a stand mixer fitted with the paddle attachment, beat the butter on medium speed for 2 minutes. Add the sugar-zest mixture and mix on medium-high until light and fluffy, 3 to 5 minutes. Stop the mixer and scrape down the bowl.

Turn the mixer to medium-low and add the vanilla and almond extract. Add the eggs one at a time, mixing until each is incorporated before adding the next. Mix until combined. Stop the mixer and scrape down the bowl.

Turn the mixer to low and add the flour mixture in three batches, alternating with the buttermilk, beginning and ending with the flour mixture. After the last streaks of the flour mixture are combined, mix on medium for no more than 30 seconds.

Evenly divide the batter among the prepared pans. Bake for 25 to 28 minutes, until a toothpick inserted into the center of each cake comes out clean. Let the cakes cool on a wire rack for 10 to 15 minutes before removing from the pans. Allow the cakes to cool completely, right-side up, on the wire rack before removing the parchment. Level the tops of the cakes with a long serrated knife as needed.

MAKE THE 8-INCH (20-CM) CAKE

Preheat the oven to 350°F (175°C). Grease and flour three 8-inch (20-cm) cake pans and line the bottoms with parchment paper.

Make the batter using the same method as above. Evenly divide the batter among the prepared pans. Bake for 25 to 28 minutes, until a toothpick inserted into the center of each cake comes out clean. Let the cakes cool on a wire rack for 10 to 15 minutes before removing from the pans. Allow the cakes to cool completely, right-side up, on the wire rack before removing the parchment. Level the tops of the cakes with a long serrated knife as needed.

MAKE THE MASCARPONE BUTTERCREAM

Put the egg whites and sugar in the bowl of a stand mixer (see Notes). Gently whisk by hand until just combined. In a medium saucepan, bring an inch or two (2.5 to 5 cm) of water to a simmer over medium-low heat. Place the mixer bowl on top of the saucepan to create a double boiler (be sure the bottom of the bowl does not touch the water). Heat the egg mixture, stirring intermittently, until it reaches 160°F (70°C) on a candy thermometer.

Carefully affix the mixer bowl to the stand mixer (it may be hot) and fit the mixer with the whisk attachment. Beat the egg white mixture on high speed for 8 to 10 minutes, until it holds medium-stiff peaks and the outside of the bowl cools to room temperature.

Turn the mixer down to low and add the vanilla and almond extract. Add the butter a couple of tablespoons at a time, mixing until each is incorporated before adding the next. Add the mascarpone. Stop the mixer and swap out the whisk for the paddle attachment.

Add the cinnamon and salt and turn the mixer to medium-high. Beat until the buttercream is silky smooth, 3 to 5 minutes.

ASSEMBLE AND STACK THE CAKE

Place one 8-inch (20-cm) cake layer on a large cake board or serving plate. Fill a piping bag fitted with a plain round tip with mascarpone buttercream. Pipe a ring around the outer top edge of the cake to create a "dam." Fill the ring with ¾ cup (180 ml) of the buttercream and spread it out with an offset spatula or the back of a spoon. Spread on about ⅔ cup (80 ml) of the jam on top. Top with a second cake layer and repeat; place the final cake layer on top.

Crumb coat the 8-inch (20-cm) cake and chill in the refrigerator for about 15 minutes.

Meanwhile, place one 6-inch (15-cm) cake layer on a 6-inch (15-cm) cake board. If necessary, refill the piping bag fitted with the plain round tip and pipe a ring around the outer top edge of the cake to create a "dam." Fill the ring with ½ cup of the (60 ml) jam and smooth out the top with an offset spatula or the back of a spoon. Place about ½ cup (120 ml) of the buttercream on top and spread it out with an offset spatula. Top with a second cake layer and repeat; place the final cake layer on top.

Crumb coat the 6-inch (15-cm) cake and chill in the refrigerator for about 15 minutes.

Tint the remaining buttercream your color of choice, leaving about 1 cup (240 ml) untinted for piped details, if desired. Smoothly frost the 8-inch (20-cm) cake with the tinted buttercream. The top of the cake should be as level as possible. Repeat with the 6-inch (15-cm) cake.

To support the top tier, insert a wooden dowel or straw into the center of the 8-inch (20-cm) cake. Use a nontoxic edible writer to mark the dowel where it reaches the top of the cake. Remove the dowel and cut it at the mark so it will be flush with the top of the cake. Using that dowel as a guide, cut three more dowels to the exact same length. Place one dowel in the center of the cake and evenly space the remaining three around the cake, placing them within 1 inch (2.5 cm) of the edge of the cake.

Using a large offset spatula, carefully lift and place the 6-inch (15-cm) cake in the center of the bottom tier.

DECORATE THE CAKE

To decorate the cake with the shell border technique, fill a piping bag fitted with a small star tip with the reserved 1 cup (240 ml) buttercream. Pipe shell borders (see page 275) around the edges of the cake, especially where the two tiers meet. Decorate with macarons, meringues, fresh flowers, or as desired.

If eating the cake the same day as assembled, store it at room temperature until ready to serve. If assembled in advance, store in a cake box in the refrigerator overnight. Bring to room temperature for 30 minutes before serving. Store leftovers loosely covered with plastic wrap in the refrigerator for 3 to 4 days.

*   *   *

NOTES: A KitchenAid Professional 6-quart stand mixer will hold the entire batch of buttercream. If your mixer is smaller, make the buttercream in two batches.

Thick plastic straws may be used instead of wooden dowels.

Lavender Blackberry Cake

FEATURED DECORATING TECHNIQUES:
BUTTERCREAM FLOWERS, FLOWER CROWN

FOR THE LAVENDER MILK:

1 cup (240 ml) whole milk

2 teaspoons dried culinary lavender

FOR THE CAKE:

¼ cup (60 ml) sour cream

2½ cups (325 g) cake flour

1½ cups (300 g) granulated sugar

1 tablespoon baking powder

½ teaspoon salt

1 cup (2 sticks/225 g) unsalted butter, diced, at room temperature

1½ teaspoons pure vanilla extract

4 large eggs

FOR THE LAVENDER SYRUP:

½ cup (100 g) granulated sugar

1½ teaspoons dried culinary lavender

FOR THE CREAM CHEESE FROSTING:

1 cup (2 sticks/225 g) unsalted butter, at room temperature

4 ounces (115 g) cream cheese, at room temperature

5 to 6 cups (625 to 750 g) confectioners' sugar

3 to 4 tablespoons heavy cream or whole milk

2 teaspoons vanilla bean paste or pure vanilla extract

TO ASSEMBLE AND DECORATE:

½ to 1 cup (120 ml to 240 ml) blackberry jam

1 small recipe Swiss Meringue Buttercream (page 262)

Gel food coloring

Baking with lavender can be tricky. Even the most perfectly perfumed and slightly floral recipe is just one step away from tasting like fancy hand soap. In this recipe, I've gently infused the cake with lavender milk and a bath of lavender simple syrup. Paired with sweet blackberry jam and tangy cream cheese frosting, this cake is fresh, fruity, and floral. Using the reverse mixing method (see page 21), the cake layers are light, with a tight crumb, yet they hold up to the bold blackberry jam and thick cream cheese frosting. The ingredients can be found year-round, but I especially enjoy a slice of this cake in the late spring or early summer.

The flower crown is completely optional and one of the more complex decorations in the book. Instead of using the cream cheese frosting, the flowers are piped with a batch of Swiss meringue buttercream frosting for better stability. I found the subtle lavender and fruity blackberry filling in this cake to be the perfect match for this buttercream wreath, but simply topping this with fresh blackberries and sprigs of lavender would be equally chic and festive. MAKES ONE THREE-LAYER 8-INCH (20-CM) CAKE; SERVES 12 TO 16

MAKE THE LAVENDER MILK

In a small saucepan, slowly bring the milk to a simmer over low heat. Add the lavender and remove from the heat. Let steep for about 20 minutes. Strain the milk through a fine-mesh sieve set over a bowl and discard the lavender. Let cool completely.

MAKE THE CAKE

Preheat the oven to 350°F (175°C). Grease and flour three 8-inch (20-cm) cake pans and line the bottoms with parchment paper.

In a small bowl or liquid measuring cup, stir together ¾ cup (180 ml) of the lavender milk and the sour cream.

Sift together the flour, sugar, baking powder, and salt into the bowl of a stand mixer. Using the paddle attachment, beat the ingredients on low speed until just combined. Add the butter, vanilla, and about ½ cup (120 ml) of the lavender milk mixture. Mix on medium until evenly distributed and the dry ingredients are moistened, about 1 minute. Stop the mixer and scrape down the sides and bottom of the bowl.

Add the eggs to the remaining lavender milk mixture and stir to combine. With the mixer running on medium speed, add the egg mixture in three additions, mixing for about 15 seconds after each addition and stopping the mixer between additions to scrape down the sides and bottom of the bowl.

Evenly divide the batter among the prepared pans. Bake for 20 to 22 minutes, until a toothpick inserted into the center of each cake comes out clean. Let the cakes cool on a wire rack for 10 to 15 minutes before removing from the pans. Allow the cakes to cool completely, right-side up, on the wire rack before removing the parchment. Level the tops of the cakes with a long serrated knife as needed.

MAKE THE LAVENDER SYRUP

In a small saucepan, combine the sugar and ½ cup (120 ml) water and bring to a boil over medium-high heat. Reduce the heat to low and add the lavender. Simmer the syrup for 5 to 10 minutes. Remove from the heat and let steep until cool. Strain the syrup through a fine-mesh sieve set over a bowl and discard the lavender.

MAKE THE CREAM CHEESE FROSTING

In the bowl of a stand mixer fitted with the paddle attachment (or in a large bowl using a handheld mixer), beat the butter and cream cheese on medium until smooth. Meanwhile, sift the confectioners' sugar. With the mixer running on low, gradually add 5 cups (625 g) of the confectioners' sugar, 3 tablespoons of the cream, and the vanilla and mix until incorporated. Turn the mixer to medium-high and mix until fluffy, 3 to 5 minutes. Add the remaining 1 cup (125 g) confectioners' sugar, ½ cup (65 g) at a time, and/or the remaining 1 tablespoon cream until the desired consistency is reached. The frosting should be spreadable and creamy, not runny.

ASSEMBLE THE CAKE

Generously brush the cake layers with the lavender syrup. Place one cake layer on a cake board or serving plate. Place about ⅓ cup (80 ml) of the cream cheese frosting on top and spread it with an offset spatula. Fill a piping bag fitted with a plain round tip with some of the cream cheese frosting. Pipe a ring around the outer top edge of the cake to create a "dam." Pipe a second ring of cream cheese frosting a couple of inches in from the outer ring, to create a "bull's-eye."

Use a spoon to fill in the gaps between the rings of cream cheese frosting with ¼ to ½ cup (60 to 120 ml) of the blackberry jam. Top with a second cake layer and repeat; place the final cake layer on top.

Crumb coat the cake with the cream cheese frosting and chill in the refrigerator for 15 minutes.

DECORATE THE CAKE

Frost the cake with the remaining cream cheese frosting.

Tint a small amount of buttercream green for the leaves. Tint the remaining buttercream the colors of your choice for the flowers. Cut about thirty 2-inch (5-cm) squares of parchment paper. Dab a small amount of buttercream on a flower nail and secure a square of parchment on top. Fill piping bags fitted with various piping tips with the tinted buttercream. Pipe various buttercream flowers (page 276) on top of the parchment squares, then transfer the flowers on their parchment squares to a baking sheet or cutting board. Chill the piped flowers in the refrigerator until firm, at least 15 minutes.

To create the flower crown, pipe a ring of buttercream around the top of the cake, about 1 inch (2.5 cm) from the edge. Carefully peel the chilled flowers off their parchment squares and use a small offset spatula to arrange them on the ring of buttercream, angling them slightly in and away from the center of the cake.

Fill a piping bag fitted with a leaf tip with the green buttercream and pipe leaves to fill in any gaps between the flowers.

Loosely cover with plastic wrap or place in a cake box and chill in the refrigerator until 30 minutes before serving. Let come to room temperature for 30 minutes, then slice and serve. Store leftovers loosely covered with plastic wrap or in a cake box in the refrigerator for up to 3 to 4 days.

Decadent Desserts

When it's time to indulge, turn to these luscious desserts and exquisite cakes. While many are heavy with chocolate, smothered in ganache, or dripping with glaze and gold, they are well balanced and thoughtfully composed. Satisfy your chocolate cravings with a slice of Chocolate Millionaire's Cake or a sliver of the practically sinful Chocolate S'mores Tart. Explore the exotic flavors of the Vanilla Passion Fruit Caramel Cake that are equally luxurious. These recipes are perfect to serve at a dinner party or to celebrate a milestone birthday, but I'd be lying if I said I didn't treat myself to a Fancy-Pants Peanut Butter Chocolate Cupcake on the occasional weeknight.

Chocolate Millionaire's Cake

FEATURED DECORATING TECHNIQUES: SMOOTH FROSTING, GOLD PAINTING, CHOCOLATE DRIP, GOLD SPLATTER

When I think of decadent desserts, this is the type of cake that first comes to mind—a towering, velvety, deep chocolate cake, dripping with ganache and gold, with a flashy name that reveals the sinful treat that inspired it. Millionaire's shortbread is a cookie-confection hybrid that is traditionally composed of a tender shortbread cookie base, a chewy caramel filling, and a glossy chocolate topping. For the cake version, I crumble shortbread cookies and stuff them between layers of classic chocolate cake and homemade caramel sauce. Frosted in fudge and dripping with ganache, it's not just the gold splatters that make it truly worthy of such an elitist name. MAKES ONE FOUR-LAYER 8-INCH (20-CM) CAKE; SERVES 12 TO 16

FOR THE CLASSIC CHOCOLATE CAKE:

2½ cups (315 g) all-purpose flour

1 cup (95 g) unsweetened cocoa powder

2½ teaspoons baking powder

½ teaspoon baking soda

1 teaspoon salt

1 cup (240 ml) whole milk

½ cup (120 ml) sour cream

¾ cup (175 ml) grapeseed or canola oil

2 cups (400 g) granulated sugar

2 teaspoons pure vanilla extract

3 large eggs

1 cup (240 ml) strong-brewed coffee, hot

FOR THE FUDGE FROSTING:

1½ cups (3 sticks/340 g) unsalted butter, at room temperature

5 to 6 cups (625 to 750 g) confectioners' sugar, sifted if needed

½ cup (50 g) unsweetened cocoa powder

2 tablespoons black cocoa powder (or additional unsweetened cocoa powder)

1½ teaspoons pure vanilla extract

Pinch of salt

4 to 6 tablespoons (60 to 90 ml) whole milk

8 ounces (225 g) dark chocolate, melted and cooled

TO ASSEMBLE AND DECORATE:

1½ (5.3-ounce) boxes shortbread cookies, such as Walker

1 recipe Caramel Sauce (page 263), or 1 cup (240 ml) store-bought

Gold luster dust

Vodka or other clear alcohol

½ recipe Chocolate Drizzle (page 263)

Chocolate sprinkles

MAKE THE CLASSIC CHOCOLATE CAKE

Preheat the oven to 350°F (175°C). Grease and flour two 8-inch (20-cm) cake pans.

Sift together the flour, cocoa powder, baking powder, baking soda, and salt into a large bowl. In a small bowl or liquid measuring cup, stir together the milk and sour cream.

In the bowl of a stand mixer fitted with the paddle attachment (or in a large bowl using a handheld mixer), beat the oil and sugar on medium speed for 2 minutes. With the mixer running on low, add the vanilla. Add the eggs one at a time, mixing until each is incorporated before adding the next. Stop the mixer and scrape down the bowl.

Turn the mixer to low and add the flour mixture in three batches, alternating with the milk mixture, beginning and ending with the flour mixture. Stop the mixer and scrape down the bowl. With the mixer running on low, stream in the coffee. Mix on medium-low until just combined, no more than 30 seconds.

Evenly divide the batter between the prepared pans. Bake for 35 to 40 minutes, until a toothpick inserted into the center of each cake comes out clean. Let the cakes cool on a wire rack for 10 to 15 minutes before removing from the pans. Allow the cakes to cool completely, right-side up, on the wire rack. Level the tops of the cakes with a long serrated knife as needed, then cut the cakes in half horizontally to create 4 even layers.

MAKE THE FUDGE FROSTING

In the bowl of a stand mixer fitted with the paddle attachment (or in a large bowl using a handheld mixer), beat the butter until smooth and creamy. With the mixer running on low speed, gradually add 5 cups (625 g) of the confectioners' sugar, the cocoa powders, vanilla, and salt. Pour in 4 tablespoons (60 ml) of the milk and mix until incorporated. Turn the mixer up to medium-high and mix until the frosting is smooth and creamy. Stop the mixer and scrape down the bowl. Add the melted chocolate and mix until smooth. Add the remaining 1 cup (125 g) confectioners' sugar, ¼ cup (30 g) at a time, and/or the remaining 2 tablespoons milk until the desired consistency is achieved: The frosting should be soft and spreadable, not too stiff. The melted chocolate in the frosting may start to harden as it sits. If the frosting becomes too thick/stiff and difficult to spread at any point, gently rewarm it in the top portion of a double boiler (or in the mixer bowl set over a saucepan of simmering water; see page 14).

ASSEMBLE THE CAKE

Finely chop the shortbread cookies and set aside. Gently warm the caramel until it is slightly fluid and slowly drips off a spoon, but is not too hot.

Place one cake layer on a cake board or serving plate. Spread on a scant 1 cup (240 ml) of the fudge frosting with an offset spatula. Sprinkle on one-third of the chopped shortbread and gently press them down into the frosting with the palms of your hands. Drizzle about ⅓ cup (80 ml) of the caramel sauce over the shortbread crumbles. Top with a second cake layer and repeat; repeat with a third cake layer, then place the final cake layer on top.

Crumb coat the cake with the fudge frosting and chill in the refrigerator for 15 minutes.

DECORATE THE CAKE

Set aside about ¾ cup (180 ml) of the fudge frosting, then smoothly frost the cake with the remaining frosting. Chill the cake in the refrigerator for about 15 minutes to allow the frosting to form a slight crust.

To paint the cake in gold, mix a small amount of gold luster dust with a drop or two of vodka until it has a thin, paint-like consistency. Using a small pastry brush or clean, flat paintbrush, gently paint the gold mixture sporadically around the sides of the cake.

Gently warm the chocolate drizzle (in the microwave is fine) until it is fluid but not hot. Using a spoon, drip the chocolate drizzle around the edges of the frosted cake (see page 121). Fill a piping bag fitted with any size star tip with the reserved fudge frosting and pipe small spirals around the top border of the cake. If the fudge frosting is too stiff to pipe, stir in a bit of the leftover drizzle, 1 tablespoon at a time, until the desired consistency is achieved. Add chocolate sprinkles around the top edge of the cake. For the gold splatter technique, dip the brush back into the gold paint and, using your index finger, flick the end of the bristles to create paint splatters all over the cake. Add more or less vodka to create the right consistency and practice the splatters on a piece of parchment before splattering the cake.

If eating the cake the same day as assembled, store it at room temperature until ready to serve. If assembled in advance, store in a cake box in the refrigerator overnight. Bring to room temperature for 30 minutes before serving. Store leftovers loosely covered with plastic wrap in the refrigerator for 3 to 4 days.

HOW TO DECORATE A
Gold Painted Cake

Butterscotch Banana Cake

FEATURED DECORATING TECHNIQUES: ICING SWIRL, STAR PIPING

I met my husband, Brett, just after starting my cake decorating business. As it turns out, Brett was not only crushing on me but on my cakes, too. He has a huge sweet tooth and firmly believes that no dessert can be too decadent. He usually suggests flavor combinations involving caramel, peanut butter, and rich chocolate for me to try out (see the Chocolate Millionaire's Cake on page 66 and the Peanut Butter Lover's Chocolate Bombe cake in my first book, Layered). When I started toying around with a new banana cake recipe for this book, I just knew he would love the brown sugar butterscotch buttercream (sometimes made with a splash of bourbon), silky ganache, and flecks of dark chocolate that make this incredibly moist cake even more delicious. I hope you love it just as much as he does.

MAKES ONE THREE-LAYER 8-INCH (20-CM) CAKE; SERVES 12 TO 16

FOR THE BANANA CAKE:

4 very ripe bananas

2⅓ cups (290 g) all-purpose flour

1½ teaspoons baking powder

½ teaspoon baking soda

½ teaspoon ground cinnamon

½ teaspoon salt

¾ cup (1½ sticks/170 g) unsalted butter, at room temperature

1 cup (200 g) granulated sugar

¾ cup (165 g) packed brown sugar

2 teaspoons pure vanilla extract

3 large eggs

¾ cup (180 ml) sour cream, stirred

2 ounces (55 g) dark chocolate, finely chopped

FOR THE BUTTERSCOTCH:

6 tablespoons (¾ stick/85 g) unsalted butter

¾ cup (165 g) packed brown sugar

1 teaspoon corn syrup

½ teaspoon salt

¼ cup (60 ml) heavy cream, at room temperature

½ teaspoon pure vanilla extract

2 tablespoons bourbon (optional)

FOR THE BUTTERSCOTCH BUTTERCREAM:

1 large recipe Swiss Meringue Buttercream (page 262), using 2 cups (440 g) packed light brown sugar instead of the granulated sugar

FOR THE GANACHE:

4 tablespoons (½ stick/55 g) unsalted butter, diced

4 ounces (115 g) dark chocolate, chopped

TO DECORATE:

Chocolate sprinkles

MAKE THE BANANA CAKE

Preheat the oven to 350°F (175°C). Grease and flour two 8-inch (20-cm) cake pans.

Mash the bananas in a medium bowl. In a large bowl, sift together the flour, baking powder, baking soda, cinnamon, and salt.

In the bowl of a stand mixer fitted with the paddle attachment, beat the butter on medium speed for 2 minutes. Add both sugars and mix on medium-high until light and fluffy, 3 to 5 minutes. Stop the mixer and scrape down the bowl.

Turn the mixer to medium-low and add the vanilla. Add the eggs one at a time, mixing until each is incorporated before adding the next. Mix until combined. Stop the mixer and scrape down the bowl.

Turn the mixer to low and add the flour mixture in three batches, alternating with the sour cream. After the last streaks of the flour mixture are combined, mix on medium for no more than 30 seconds. Stop the mixer and fold in the mashed bananas and chocolate by hand.

Evenly divide the batter among the prepared pans. Bake for 28 to 35 minutes, until a toothpick inserted into the center of each cake comes out clean. Let the cakes cool on a wire rack for 10 to 15 minutes before removing from the pans. Allow the cakes to cool completely, right-side up on the wire rack. Level the tops of the cakes with a long serrated knife as needed, then cut the cakes in half horizontally to create 4 even layers.

MAKE THE BUTTERSCOTCH

In a heavy-bottomed saucepan, melt the butter over medium heat. Stir in the brown sugar, corn syrup, and salt. Raise the heat to medium-high and stir continuously with a wooden spoon for about 5 minutes, until the sugar has melted completely.

Remove from the heat and, while whisking, carefully pour in the cream. Return the pan to low heat and simmer, stirring continuously with a whisk, for about 8 minutes, until thick and bubbling. Pour the butterscotch into a heatproof container. Stir in the vanilla and bourbon (if using). Let cool at room temperature or in the refrigerator until thick and cool.

MAKE THE BUTTERSCOTCH BUTTERCREAM

Put the buttercream in the bowl of a stand mixer fitted with the paddle attachment. With the mixer on medium-low, slowly add ¾ cup (180 ml) of the cooled butterscotch a few tablespoons at a time and mix until combined. Taste and add more butterscotch if desired.

MAKE THE GANACHE

Put the butter and chocolate in the top portion of a double boiler (or in a heatproof bowl set over a saucepan of simmering water; see page 14). Heat until the butter and chocolate begin to melt. Remove from the heat and stir until smooth and well combined.

ASSEMBLE THE CAKE

Place one cake layer on a cake board or serving plate. Smear the top of the cake with a thin layer of ganache, 3 to 4 tablespoons. Spread ¾ cup (180 ml) of the buttercream over the ganache with an offset spatula. Top with a second cake layer and repeat; repeat with a third cake layer, then place the final cake layer on top.

Crumb coat the cake with the buttercream and chill in the refrigerator for 15 minutes.

DECORATE THE CAKE

Set aside a small portion of the buttercream for decorating, then frost the cake with the remaining buttercream. To create the icing swirl technique, place the cake on a rotating cake stand. Holding an offset spatula nearly parallel to the side of the cake, gently press the tip of the spatula into the bottom of the cake. Spin the cake stand while simultaneously bringing the tip of the spatula up the side of the cake. Smooth out the top edge of the cake with an offset spatula. Fill a piping bag fitted with a small star tip with the reserved buttercream and pipe stars on top of the cake (see page 275). Sprinkle with chocolate sprinkles.

If eating the cake the same day as assembled, store it at room temperature until ready to serve. If assembled in advance, store in a cake box in the refrigerator overnight. Bring to room temperature for 30 minutes before serving. Store leftovers loosely covered with plastic wrap in the refrigerator for 3 to 4 days.

Fancy-Pants Peanut Butter Chocolate Cupcakes

FEATURED DECORATING TECHNIQUE: SIMPLE SWIRL CUPCAKE FROSTING

This is the kind of party trick every host needs—a foolproof, back-pocket recipe for nearly any occasion that sweet treats are required (so basically, all of the time). There should be a permanent spot in your recipe box for these devil's food cupcakes. Made extra tender with the addition of butter and bit of instant espresso to intensify the chocolate, these cupcakes are topped with swirls of peanut butter buttercream. While you can dress them up or down depending on the occasion, here a crown of golden caramel popcorn elevates their otherwise simple flavor profile, making them the kings and queens of birthdays, bake sales, and backyard bashes. And if you need a quick cheat, I won't be mad if you opt for store-bought caramel corn. MAKES 20 TO 24 CUPCAKES

FOR THE DEVIL'S FOOD CUPCAKES:

4 ounces (115 g) dark chocolate, chopped

1¼ cups (300 ml) boiling water or hot coffee

¼ cup (25 g) unsweetened cocoa powder

1½ cups (190 g) all-purpose flour

1 teaspoon baking soda

½ teaspoon baking powder

½ teaspoon salt

1 tablespoon instant espresso powder (optional)

1 cup (2 sticks/225 g) unsalted butter, very soft

1 cup (200 g) granulated sugar

⅓ cup (75 g) packed brown sugar

1 teaspoon pure vanilla extract

3 large eggs

½ cup (120 ml) whole milk

FOR THE CARAMEL CORN:

6 cups (140 g) freshly popped popcorn (from about ¼ cup [50g] unpopped kernels)

½ cup (75 g) unsalted peanuts

1 recipe Caramel Sauce (page 263), cooled

FOR THE PEANUT BUTTER BUTTERCREAM:

1 cup (2 sticks/225 g) unsalted butter, at room temperature

⅓ cup (80 ml) smooth peanut butter

2½ to 3 cups (310 to 375 g) confectioners' sugar, sifted if needed

1 teaspoon pure vanilla extract

Pinch of salt

1 to 2 tablespoons whole milk

MAKE THE DEVIL'S FOOD CUPCAKES

Preheat the oven to 350°F (175°C). Line two cupcake pans with paper liners.

Put the chopped chocolate in a heatproof bowl and carefully pour in the boiling water. Add the cocoa powder and stir until everything is combined and melted.

Sift together the flour, baking soda, baking powder, salt, and espresso powder (if using) into a large bowl.

In the bowl of a stand mixer fitted with the paddle attachment (or in a large bowl using a handheld mixer), beat the butter and sugars on medium speed for about 2 minutes.

With the mixer running on low, add the vanilla and the eggs one at a time, mixing until each is incorporated before adding the next. Stop the mixer and scrape down the sides and bottom of the bowl.

With the mixer running on low, stream in the melted chocolate mixture and mix until combined. Add the flour mixture in three batches, alternating with the milk, beginning and ending with the flour mixture. After the last streaks of the flour mixture are combined, mix on medium for no more than 30 seconds.

Fill the cupcake liners about two-thirds of the way full and bake for 20 to 24 minutes, until a toothpick inserted into the center of a cupcake comes out clean. Let them cool in their pans for 5 to 10 minutes. Remove the cupcakes from their pans and allow to completely cool on a wire rack before frosting.

MAKE THE CARAMEL CORN

Preheat the oven to 250°F (120°C). Line a large rimmed baking sheet (or two smaller sheets) with parchment paper.

Stir together the popcorn and peanuts in a large bowl. Pour the cooled caramel sauce over the popcorn mixture. Quickly yet carefully stir the mixture with a rubber spatula until the popcorn mixture is evenly coated in caramel.

Tip the mixture out onto the prepared baking sheet(s) and spread it into an even layer. Bake for 45 to 60 minutes, stirring every 15 minutes. Let cool, then break into small chunks.

MAKE THE PEANUT BUTTER BUTTERCREAM

In the bowl of a stand mixer fitted with the paddle attachment (or in a large bowl using a handheld mixer), beat the butter and peanut butter until smooth and creamy. With the mixer running on low, gradually add 2½ cups (310 g) of the confectioners' sugar, the vanilla, and salt. Add 1 tablespoon of the milk and mix until incorporated. Turn the mixer up to medium-high and mix until the frosting is smooth and creamy. Add the remaining ½ cup (65 g) confectioners' sugar, ¼ cup (30 g) at a time, and/or the remaining 1 tablespoon milk until the desired consistency is achieved: The frosting should be soft and pipeable, but not runny.

ASSEMBLE THE CUPCAKES

To decorate with the simple swirl cupcake frosting technique, fill a piping bag fitted with a large round tip with the peanut butter buttercream. Swirl the buttercream on top of the cooled cupcakes (see page 273). Pile the cooled caramel corn on top of the buttercream.

Store the cupcakes covered loosely with plastic wrap or in a cake box for up to 1 day at room temperature or up to 4 days in the refrigerator. Serve at room temperature. Leftover caramel corn can be stored in an airtight container at room temperature for several days. If making in advance, top with caramel corn just before serving.

Triple-Coconut Cake

FEATURED DECORATING TECHNIQUE: SHREDDED COCONUT COATING

My grandfather grew up in the small town of Kahuku, Hawaii, so a large portion of my childhood was spent on the islands visiting family, leaping over waves at the local beach, and eating sticky shave ice with my cousins. If you've ever made the drive down Kamehameha Highway near Sunset Beach on the island of Oahu, then hopefully you've stopped for a slice of coconut cake at Ted's Bakery. In my version, I swapped the chiffon cake for a coconut butter cake and the whipped topping for coconut cream cheese, for an extra-creamy, decadent layer cake. Admittedly, my recipe is only a vague interpretation of the original, but if you can't make it to Hawaii, I hope you make plenty of birthday wishes over this cake at home. MAKES ONE THREE-LAYER 8-INCH (20-CM) CAKE; SERVES 12 TO 16

FOR THE TRIPLE-COCONUT CAKE:

1½ cups plus 2 tablespoons (205 g) all-purpose flour

1½ cups (195 g) cake flour

4 teaspoons baking powder

¾ teaspoon salt

¾ cup (1½ sticks/170 g) unsalted butter, at room temperature

⅓ cup (70 g) coconut oil, at room temperature

2 cups (400 g) granulated sugar

2 teaspoons pure vanilla extract

1 teaspoon pure coconut extract (optional)

3 large eggs

2 large egg yolks

1¼ cups (300 ml) full-fat coconut milk, stirred

3 ounces (1 cup/85 g) unsweetened shredded coconut

FOR THE COCONUT CREAM CHEESE FROSTING:

¾ cup plus 2 tablespoons (1¾ sticks/195 g) unsalted butter, at room temperature

3 ounces (90 g) cream cheese, at room temperature

5½ to 6 cups (690 to 750 g) confectioners' sugar, sifted if needed

3 tablespoons full-fat coconut milk

1 teaspoon pure vanilla extract

½ teaspoon pure coconut extract (optional)

TO ASSEMBLE:

2 to 3 cups (170 to 255 g) flaked or shredded coconut

MAKE THE TRIPLE-COCONUT CAKE

Preheat the oven to 350°F (175°C). Grease and flour three 8-inch (20-cm) cake pans and line the bottoms with parchment paper.

Sift together the flours, baking powder, and salt into a large bowl.

In the bowl of a stand mixer fitted with the paddle attachment, beat the butter and coconut oil on medium speed for 2 minutes. Add the sugar and mix on medium-high until light and fluffy, 3 to 5 minutes. Stop the mixer and scrape down the bowl.

Turn the mixer to medium-low and add the vanilla and coconut extract (if using). Add the eggs and egg yolks one at a time, mixing until each is incorporated before adding the next. Mix until combined. Stop the mixer and scrape down the bowl.

Turn the mixer to low and add the flour mixture in three batches, alternating with the coconut milk, beginning and ending with the flour mixture. Mix until just incorporated. Stop the mixer and fold in the shredded coconut by hand until well combined.

Evenly divide the batter among the prepared pans. Bake for 26 to 28 minutes, until a toothpick inserted into the center of each cake comes out clean. Let the cakes cool on a wire rack for 10 to 15 minutes before removing from the pans. Allow the cakes to cool completely, right-side up, on the wire rack before removing the parchment.

MAKE THE COCONUT CREAM CHEESE FROSTING

In the bowl of a stand mixer fitted with the paddle attachment (or in a large bowl with a handheld mixer), beat the butter and cream cheese on medium until smooth and creamy. With the mixer running on low, slowly add 5½ cups (690 g) of the confectioners' sugar, the coconut milk, vanilla, and coconut extract (if using). Turn the mixer up to medium-high and mix for 4 to 6 minutes, until the frosting is white, fluffy, and smooth. Add the remaining ½ cup (65 g) confectioners' sugar, ¼ cup (30 g) at a time, until the desired consistency is reached; the frosting should be soft and spreadable, but not runny.

ASSEMBLE THE CAKE

Place one cake layer on a cake board or serving plate. Spread on about 1 cup (240 ml) of the frosting with an offset spatula. Top with a second cake layer and repeat; place the final cake layer on top.

Crumb coat the cake and chill it in the refrigerator for 15 minutes.

To coat the cake in coconut shavings, set a rimmed baking sheet on the work surface and fill a bowl with the flaked coconut. Frost the cake with the remaining frosting. Before the frosting sets, carefully hold the cake in one hand and use the other to scoop and press the coconut around the sides and top of the cake. Let any unused coconut fall onto the baking sheet to be used again (see Note).

Loosely cover the cake with plastic wrap or store in a cake box in the refrigerator until 30 minutes before serving. Let the cake sit at room temperature for 30 minutes before serving. Store leftovers loosely covered with plastic wrap or in a cake box in the refrigerator for 3 to 4 days.

*   *   *

NOTE: Use the same technique for applying coconut shavings when applying other toppings such as sprinkles, chopped nuts, and decorative sanding sugar.

Vanilla Passion Fruit Caramel Cake

FEATURED DECORATING TECHNIQUE: OMBRÉ SHELL PIPING

I wanted to create a tropical cake that didn't remind me of a piña colada, so I decided to pair my favorite passion fruit buttercream with caramel for a more exotic and enticing combination. This might not be what first comes to mind when you think of "decadent desserts," but the complex flavors of the passion fruit caramel make this cake beyond luxurious. I studded the buttery cake with bits of caramelized white chocolate (see the Note about Valrhona Blond Dulcey, page 97) and spiked the buttercream with vibrant, mouth-puckering passion fruit concentrate. The passion fruit caramel sauce tastes exactly like it sounds—slightly bitter from the burnt sugar, tart, and fruity. Covered in candles, this is what I hope my next birthday cake will be. MAKES ONE FOUR-LAYER 8-INCH (20-CM) CAKE; SERVES 14 TO 18

FOR THE VANILLA BEAN CAKE:

- 3 cups plus 2 tablespoons (405 g) cake flour
- 1 tablespoon plus 2 teaspoons baking powder
- ¾ teaspoon salt
- 1 cup (2 sticks/225 g) unsalted butter, at room temperature
- 2 cups (400 g) granulated sugar
- 1 tablespoon vanilla bean paste or pure vanilla extract
- 4 large egg yolks
- 2 large eggs
- 1⅓ cups (320 ml) whole milk
- 3 ounces (85 g) Valrhona Blond Dulcey 32% chocolate or other white chocolate, finely chopped

FOR THE PASSION FRUIT BUTTERCREAM:

- 1 large recipe Swiss Meringue Buttercream (page 262)
- 6 to 8 tablespoons (90 to 120 ml) thawed frozen passion fruit concentrate

FOR THE PASSION FRUIT CARAMEL SAUCE:

- ¾ cup (150 g) granulated sugar
- 2 tablespoons corn syrup
- ¼ cup plus 1 tablespoon (75 ml) heavy cream
- 3 tablespoons thawed frozen passion fruit concentrate
- 2 tablespoons unsalted butter, diced
- Pinch of salt

TO DECORATE:

- Yellow gel food coloring (or color of your choice)

MAKE THE VANILLA BEAN CAKE

Preheat the oven to 350°F (175°C). Grease and flour two 8-inch (20-cm) cake pans and line the bottoms with parchment paper.

Sift together the cake flour, baking powder, and salt into a large bowl.

In the bowl of a stand mixer fitted with the paddle attachment, beat the butter on medium speed for 2 minutes. Add the sugar and mix on medium-high until light and fluffy, 3 to 5 minutes. Stop the mixer and scrape down the bowl.

Turn the mixer to medium-low and add the vanilla. Add the egg yolks and eggs one at a time, mixing until each is incorporated before adding the next. Mix until combined. Stop the mixer and scrape down the bowl.

Turn the mixer to low and add the flour mixture in three batches, alternating with the milk, beginning and ending with the flour mixture. After the last streaks of the flour mixture are combined, mix on medium for no more than 30 seconds. Stop the mixer and fold in the chocolate by hand.

Evenly divide the batter among the prepared pans. Bake for 28 to 35 minutes, until a toothpick inserted into the center of each cake comes out clean. Let the cakes cool on a wire rack for 10 to 15 minutes before removing from the pans. Allow the cakes to cool completely, right-side up, on the wire rack before removing the parchment. Level the tops of the cakes with a long serrated knife as needed, then cut the cakes in half horizontally to create 4 even layers.

MAKE THE PASSION FRUIT BUTTERCREAM

In the bowl of a stand mixer fitted with the paddle attachment, mix the buttercream until silky smooth. Add 6 tablespoons (90 ml) of the passion fruit concentrate a few tablespoons at a time and mix until combined, then taste and add the remaining passion fruit concentrate to your liking.

MAKE THE PASSION FRUIT CARAMEL SAUCE

In a small heavy-bottomed saucepan, stir together the sugar, corn syrup, and 2 tablespoons water. Heat over high heat, without stirring, until the mixture turns a medium amber color, 8 to 10 minutes. It will begin to rapidly boil before slowing down and darkening in color; the darker the color, the richer the caramel will taste. Remove the saucepan from the heat once the correct color is reached and the bubbles start to subside.

Slowly and carefully whisk in the cream and passion fruit concentrate. The mixture may foam up and sputter, so stand clear and keep whisking until combined.

Add the butter and salt and stir until combined. Pour the caramel into a heatproof container and let cool until it reaches the desired consistency (it will thicken as it cools) or refrigerate until ready to use, up to 10 days.

ASSEMBLE THE CAKE

Place one cake layer on a cake board or serving plate. Spread on about ¾ cup (180 ml) of the passion fruit buttercream with an offset spatula. Top with a second cake layer and repeat; place the final cake layer on top.

Crumb coat the cake with the buttercream and chill in the refrigerator for 15 minutes.

DECORATE THE CAKE

Smoothly frost the cake with a thin layer of buttercream.

To decorate the cake with the ombré shell piping, tint about ½ cup (120 ml) of the buttercream with food coloring in a small bowl. Fill a piping bag fitted with a small star tip (Wilton #18) with the tinted buttercream. Pipe a continuous row of shells around the bottom of the cake (see page 275). Stop after one row and empty the contents of the piping bag back into the small bowl. Stir in a few tablespoons of untinted buttercream to create a slightly lighter shade of yellow

(or the color you're using). Pipe another row of shells on top of the previous row and repeat, lightening the color of the buttercream with each row. Continue to pipe up the sides of the cake until you reach the top. Serve with a drizzle of the passion fruit caramel sauce.

If eating the cake the same day as assembled, store it at room temperature until ready to serve. If assembled in advance, store in a cake box in the refrigerator overnight. Bring to room temperature for 30 minutes before serving. Store leftovers loosely covered with plastic wrap in the refrigerator for 3 to 4 days.

Passion fruit caramel sauce may be made in advance. Store in an airtight container in the refrigerator for up to 2 weeks.

Pistachio Truffle Cake

FEATURED DECORATING TECHNIQUE:
WAVY RUFFLE PIPING

FOR THE WHIPPED GANACHE:

5 ounces (140 g) semisweet chocolate, chopped

¾ cup (180 ml) heavy cream

Pinch of salt

FOR THE PISTACHIO CAKE:

2¼ cups plus 2 tablespoons (310 g) cake flour

2½ teaspoons baking powder

¼ teaspoon salt

¾ cup (1½ sticks/170 g) unsalted butter, at room temperature

¾ cup (180 ml) pistachio paste, stirred

1¼ cups (250 g) granulated sugar

1¼ teaspoons vanilla bean paste or pure vanilla extract

3 large eggs

½ cup plus 2 tablespoons (150 ml) whole milk

FOR THE PISTACHIO BUTTERCREAM:

1 large recipe Swiss Meringue Buttercream (page 262)

⅔ cup (160 ml) pistachio paste, stirred

TO ASSEMBLE:

Chopped pistachios (optional)

The things I did not inherit from my father, but wish I had, include his organization, punctuality, and dishwashing skills. What I did get are his deep-set eyes, competitive nature, and affinity for salty snacks. As a child, I remember him ending each night with something salty—typically cashews, pretzel rods, or pistachios.

Pistachios are something I crave as well, in salty or sweet guises. Creamy, velvety, and luxurious, this Pistachio Truffle Cake is filled with lightened whipped ganache that perfectly complements the slightly nutty cake and buttercream. I like to think the delicate waves of this cake's exterior represent both my dad's orderly side and my slightly chaotic side, all lined up neatly, but slightly unruly around the edges. MAKES ONE THREE-LAYER 6-INCH (15-CM) CAKE; SERVES 10 TO 12

MAKE THE WHIPPED GANACHE

Put the chopped chocolate in a heat-safe bowl.

In a small saucepan, bring the cream just to a simmer over medium heat. Remove from the heat and pour over the chocolate. Let stand for 30 seconds, then whisk until smooth. Add the salt and stir to combine.

Let the ganache cool for about 2 hours, or until it is the consistency of very thick pudding.

MAKE THE PISTACHIO CAKE

Preheat the oven to 350°F (175°C). Grease and flour three 6-inch (15-cm) cake pans.

Sift together the flour, baking powder, and salt into a medium bowl.

In the bowl of a stand mixer fitted with the paddle attachment, beat the butter on medium speed for 2 minutes. Add the pistachio paste and sugar. Mix on medium-high until light and fluffy, 3 to 5 minutes. Stop the mixer and scrape down the bowl.

Turn the mixer to medium-low and add the vanilla. Add the eggs one at a time, mixing until each is incorporated before adding the next. Mix until combined. Stop the mixer and scrape down the bowl.

Turn the mixer to low and add the flour mixture in three additions, alternating with the milk, starting and ending with the flour mixture. After the last streaks of the flour mixture are combined, mix on medium for no more than 30 seconds.

Evenly divide the batter among the prepared pans. Bake for 25 to 28 minutes, until a toothpick inserted into the center of each cake comes out clean. Let the cakes cool on a wire rack for 10 to 15 minutes before removing from the pans. Allow the cakes to cool completely, right-side up, on the wire rack. Level the tops of the cakes with a long serrated knife as needed.

MAKE THE PISTACHIO BUTTERCREAM

In the bowl of a stand mixer fitted with the paddle attachment, mix the buttercream until silky smooth. Add the pistachio paste and mix until combined.

ASSEMBLE THE CAKE

After the ganache cools, scrape it into the mixer bowl or a large bowl with a hand mixer. Affix the mixer bowl to the stand mixer and fit the mixer with the whisk attachment. Whip the cooled ganache on medium-high speed for 30 to 60 seconds. Stop the mixer and whisk by hand with a balloon whisk until the ganache is thick enough to clump to the whisk and is lighter in color and texture. Do not overwhip or it will become grainy. Use immediately.

Place one cake layer on a cake board or serving plate. Fill a piping bag fitted with a plain round tip with the pistachio buttercream. Pipe a ring around the top edge of the cake to create a "dam." Fill the ring with ¾ cup (180 ml) of the whipped ganache and smooth out with an offset spatula or the back of a spoon. Top with a second cake layer and repeat; place the final cake layer on top.

Crumb coat the cake with the pistachio buttercream and chill in the refrigerator for 15 minutes.

DECORATE THE CAKE

Smoothly frost the cake with a thin coat of pistachio buttercream.

To decorate the cake with the wavy ruffle technique, fill a piping bag fitted with a petal tip (Wilton #104) with buttercream. Hold the piping bag nearly parallel to the side of the cake, with the opening of the tip facing down and the narrowed side pointing away from the cake. Starting at the bottom of the cake, pipe soft waves up the side of the cake, keeping even pressure on the piping bag. Release the pressure on the bag at the top of the cake before pulling the tip away. Pipe waves around the entire cake, loosely following the curves of the previous wave as you pipe the next. Smooth the top edges with a small offset spatula by gently pulling the tips of the waves in toward the center of the cake. Sprinkle the top of the cake with chopped pistachios, if desired.

If eating the cake the same day as assembled, store it at room temperature until ready to serve. If assembled in advance, store in a cake box in the refrigerator overnight. Bring to room temperature for 30 minutes before serving. Store leftovers loosely covered with plastic wrap in the refrigerator for 3 to 4 days.

Chocolate S'mores Tart

FEATURED DECORATING TECHNIQUE: WEAVE PIPING

If you are looking for an easy recipe that's guaranteed to be a crowd-pleaser, this is it. If the idea of sticky, gooey marshmallows between your fingertips and melted chocolate oozing everywhere makes you have heart palpitations, then try this twist on the campfire classic—all of your favorite nostalgic s'mores flavors in a shareable, sliceable tart! MAKES ONE 8- TO 9-INCH (20-CM TO 23-INCH) TART; SERVES 8 TO 10

FOR THE GRAHAM CRACKER CRUST:

1½ cups (180 g) graham cracker crumbs, from about 15 sheets

3 tablespoons granulated sugar

¼ teaspoon ground cinnamon

Pinch of salt

6 tablespoons (¾ stick/ 85 g) unsalted butter, melted

FOR THE GANACHE FILLING:

9 ounces (250 g) dark chocolate, chopped

2 tablespoons unsalted butter, diced

⅔ cup (160 ml) heavy cream

FOR THE SWISS MERINGUE TOPPING:

4 large egg whites

1 cup (200 g) granulated sugar

1 teaspoon pure vanilla extract

MAKE THE GRAHAM CRACKER CRUST

Preheat the oven to 350°F (175°C).

Combine the graham cracker crumbs, sugar, cinnamon, and salt in a medium bowl and stir to combine. Pour in the melted butter and stir until the crumbs are evenly moist. Tip the mixture into an 8- or 9-inch (20- or 23-cm) tart pan with a removable bottom. Starting with the sides, use the bottom of a drinking glass or dry measuring cup with straight sides to firmly and evenly press the mixture into the bottom and sides of the pan.

Bake for 10 to 12 minutes. Let the tart shell cool completely on a wire rack before filling.

MAKE THE GANACHE FILLING

Put the chocolate and butter in a heatproof bowl.

In a small saucepan, bring the cream just to a simmer over medium-low heat. Pour over the chocolate and butter. Let stand for 30 seconds, then slowly whisk from the center out, until the chocolate-butter mixture is completely melted and smooth.

Pour the ganache into the cooled tart crust. Smooth the top with an offset spatula as needed. Loosely cover with plastic wrap, making sure the plastic does not touch the surface of the ganache. (Alternatively, cover the tart with a large bowl turned upside down or a cake cloche.) Let stand at room temperature until the chocolate sets, about 4 hours or up to overnight.

MAKE THE SWISS MERINGUE TOPPING

Put the egg whites and sugar in the bowl of a stand mixer. Briefly whisk them together by hand until just combined. In a medium saucepan, bring an inch or two (2.5 to 5 cm) of water to a simmer over medium-low heat. Place the mixer bowl on top of the saucepan to create a double boiler (be sure the bottom of the bowl does not touch the water). Heat the mixture, whisking occasionally, until it registers 160°F (70°C) on a candy thermometer.

Carefully affix the bowl to the stand mixer (it may be hot) and fit the mixer with the whisk attachment. Beat the egg white mixture on high speed until glossy, medium-stiff peaks form, 8 to 10 minutes. Add the vanilla and mix until combined.

ASSEMBLE THE TART

Fill a piping bag fitted with a petal tip (Wilton #104) with the meringue. Follow the weave piping instructions on page 275 to pipe concentric circles on top of the ganache. Alternatively, dollop and swirl on the meringue. Gently toast the meringue with a culinary torch. If you don't have a culinary torch, brown the tart under the broiler, keeping a close eye on the meringue (don't walk away from the kitchen, as it browns quickly under the broiler).

Serve at room temperature the same day as assembling. Store leftovers loosely covered with plastic wrap in the refrigerator for up to 3 days.

Chocolate Stout Cake with Irish Cream

FEATURED DECORATING TECHNIQUES: RUSTIC OMBRÉ FROSTING, STAR PIPING

I recently got my first taste of a true Canadian winter. With near record-breaking temperatures, Vancouver remained frozen-over for months. The city is not used to such severe weather, but we got a small glimpse of what the other provinces deal with every year.

During the day, we bundled ourselves up in as many layers as possible to take the dog for a quick walk, and in the evening, I'd make soup and other comforting foods to warm our bellies. And after Everett went to bed, Brett and I would share a slice of this slightly boozy and extra-decadent cake under our thickest duvet. With notes of deep, malty chocolate and sweet, slightly nutty cream, this is exactly the type of cake you want to eat while bundled up next to the fire. A bit of chocolate swirled into the Irish cream buttercream also proves that fancy ombré cakes can take on a more masculine, food coloring–free appearance too. MAKES ONE THREE-LAYER 6-INCH (15-CM) CAKE; SERVES 10 TO 12

FOR THE CHOCOLATE STOUT CAKE:

1½ cups (190 g) all-purpose flour

1 teaspoon baking soda

1 teaspoon instant espresso powder (optional)

¾ teaspoon baking powder

½ teaspoon salt

½ cup (120 ml) sour cream

2 large eggs

1½ teaspoons pure vanilla extract

¾ cup stout beer

10 tablespoons (1¼ sticks/145 g) unsalted butter

½ cup (50 g) unsweetened cocoa powder

1½ cups (300 g) granulated sugar

FOR THE IRISH CREAM BUTTERCREAM:

1 medium recipe Whipped Vanilla Buttercream (page 261), using ¼ cup (60 ml), or to taste, Irish cream liqueur, such as Baileys, instead of the milk

TO ASSEMBLE:

2 ounces (55 g) dark chocolate, melted and cooled

2 tablespoons unsweetened cocoa powder

MAKE THE CHOCOLATE STOUT CAKE

Preheat the oven to 350°F (175°C). Grease and flour three 6-inch (15-cm) cake pans.

Sift together the flour, baking soda, espresso powder (if using), baking powder, and salt into a large bowl.

In a medium bowl, whisk together the sour cream, eggs, and vanilla.

In a medium-large saucepan, heat the stout and butter over medium heat until the butter has melted.

Whisk the cocoa powder and sugar into the stout mixture until well combined. Remove the saucepan from the heat and stir in the sour cream mixture. Whisk in the flour mixture until smooth.

Evenly distribute the batter among the prepared pans. Bake for 22 to 24 minutes, until a toothpick inserted into the center of each cake comes out clean. Let the cakes cool on a wire rack for 10 to 15 minutes before removing from the pans. Allow the cakes to cool completely, right-side up, on the wire rack. Level the tops of the cakes with a long serrated knife as needed.

MAKE THE IRISH CREAM BUTTERCREAM

In the bowl of a stand mixer fitted with the paddle attachment (or in a large bowl using a handheld mixer), prepare the buttercream. The frosting should be soft and spreadable, but not too thick.

ASSEMBLE THE CAKE

Place one cake layer on a cake board or serving dish. Spread on about ¾ cup (180 ml) of the buttercream with an offset spatula. Top with a second cake layer and repeat; place the final cake layer on top.

Crumb coat the cake with the buttercream and chill in the refrigerator for 15 minutes.

DECORATE THE CAKE

Put half of the remaining buttercream in a bowl and stir in the melted chocolate and cocoa powder until smooth.

To decorate the cake with the rustic ombré frosting technique, spread the dark chocolate buttercream around the bottom quarter of the cake with an offset spatula. Combine the remaining dark chocolate buttercream with a couple tablespoons of the plain buttercream to create a medium chocolate buttercream. Spread the medium chocolate buttercream around the cake directly above the dark chocolate layer.

Combine the remaining medium chocolate buttercream with a couple more tablespoons of the plain buttercream to create a light chocolate buttercream. Spread the light chocolate buttercream around the cake directly above the medium chocolate layer.

Dollop the remaining plain buttercream on top of the cake and smooth it out with an offset spatula.

Using an offset spatula, smooth out the buttercream on the sides of the cake so the colors blend together and create a chocolate ombré effect.

Fill a piping bag fitted with a star tip with any remaining buttercream and pipe a ring of stars around the top edge of the cake (see page 275).

If eating the cake the same day as assembled, store it at room temperature until ready to serve. If assembled in advance, store in a cake box in the refrigerator overnight. Bring to room temperature for 30 minutes before serving. Store leftovers loosely covered with plastic wrap in the refrigerator for 3 to 4 days.

Sticky Toffee Date Cake

FEATURED DECORATING TECHNIQUE: TOFFEE DRIP

Like the traditional English dessert, this layer cake version of sticky toffee pudding is soaked in warm, gooey toffee sauce. A date cake might not sound all that interesting, but trust me, it is bursting with flavor and is incredibly moist from all the chopped fruit. Between the layers of toffee-soaked cake is caramelized white chocolate buttercream. Is your mouth watering yet?

Basically, this is like buttery mashed potatoes or creamy macaroni and cheese—pure comfort food, but in dessert form. This recipe is one of the most popular cakes on my blog, Style Sweet, *and so I dedicate this recipe to all my blog readers. Thank you for your continuous support and passion for baking! Note that you need to make the toffee sauce while the cakes are baking so that both are warm when you pour the sauce over the cake.* MAKES ONE THREE-LAYER 8-INCH (20-CM) CAKE; SERVES 12 TO 16

FOR THE CARAMELIZED WHITE CHOCOLATE BUTTERCREAM (SEE NOTE):

4 ounces (115 g) white chocolate, chopped

Pinch of salt

1 small recipe Swiss Meringue Buttercream (page 262)

FOR THE DATE CAKE:

12 ounces Medjool dates

2 cups (480 ml) boiling water

1½ teaspoons baking soda

3 cups (375 g) all-purpose flour

4 teaspoons baking powder

¾ teaspoon salt

¾ cup (1½ sticks/170 g) unsalted butter, at room temperature

⅔ cup (135 g) granulated sugar

⅔ cup (145 g) packed brown sugar

2 teaspoons pure vanilla extract

4 large eggs

FOR THE TOFFEE SAUCE:

½ cup (1 stick/115 g) unsalted butter

1 cup (220 g) packed brown sugar

⅔ cup (160 ml) heavy cream

1 tablespoon bourbon (optional)

1 teaspoon pure vanilla extract

Pinch of salt

MAKE THE CARAMELIZED WHITE CHOCOLATE BUTTERCREAM

Preheat the oven to 250°F (120°C). Line a baking sheet with a silicone baking mat.

Sprinkle the chopped chocolate over the prepared baking sheet and bake for 30 to 40 minutes, stirring every 10 minutes. As the chocolate caramelizes, it may seem dry and clumpy. Keep stirring and smearing the chocolate with a heatproof rubber or metal offset spatula until it becomes a warm camel color and resembles smooth peanut butter. Remove from the oven, stir in the salt, and let cool slightly before using.

In the bowl of a stand mixer fitted with the paddle attachment, mix the buttercream until silky smooth. Add the caramelized white chocolate and mix until combined.

MAKE THE DATE CAKE

Preheat the oven to 350°F (175°C). Grease and flour three 8-inch (20-cm) cake pans and line the bottoms with parchment paper.

Pit and finely chop the dates. Place them in a heatproof bowl. Pour the boiling water over the dates and stir in the baking soda. Cover with a large plate and set aside for at least 10 minutes, as you prepare the batter.

Sift together the flour, baking powder, and salt into a medium bowl.

In the bowl of a stand mixer fitted with the paddle attachment, beat the butter on medium speed for 2 minutes. Add both sugars and mix on medium-high until light and fluffy, 3 to 5 minutes. Stop the mixer and scrape down the bowl.

Turn the mixer to medium-low and add the vanilla. Add the eggs one at a time, mixing until each is incorporated before adding the next. Mix until combined. Stop the mixer and scrape down the bowl.

With the mixer running on low, add half of the flour mixture and mix until incorporated. Carefully stream in most of the water from the date mixture and mix until combined. Add the remaining flour mixture. After the last streaks of the flour mixture are combined, mix on medium for no more than 30 seconds. Stop the mixer and fold in the dates and any remaining water by hand.

Evenly divide the batter among the prepared pans. Bake for 26 to 30 minutes, until a toothpick inserted into the center of each cake comes out clean.

Let the cakes cool in the pans on a wire rack for 10 to 20 minutes before removing from the pans. Remove the parchment paper and return the cakes to the pans.

MAKE THE TOFFEE SAUCE

While the cakes are baking, make the toffee sauce:

In a medium saucepan, melt the butter over medium-high heat. Add the brown sugar and cream. Whisk until combined. Cook, while whisking, until the sauce thickens slightly, 2 to 3 minutes.

Remove from the heat and stir in the bourbon (if using), vanilla, and salt.

Poke the tops of the cakes all over with a wooden skewer or chopstick. While the cakes and toffee sauce are both still warm, pour about ⅓ cup (80 ml) of the toffee sauce over the top of each cake. Let the sauce soak into the cakes for about 30 minutes before removing the cakes from their pans again. Wrap each layer well in plastic wrap and chill until ready to assemble, or assemble immediately.

Store toffee as directed.

ASSEMBLE THE CAKE

Place one cake layer on a cake board or serving plate. Spread on 1 cup (240 ml) of the buttercream with an offset spatula. Top with a second cake layer and repeat; place the final cake layer on top.

Crumb coat the cake with the buttercream and chill in the refrigerator for 15 minutes.

Spread the remaining buttercream on top of the cake and give the sides a semi-naked finish. To decorate with the toffee drip, be sure that the top edge of the cake is smooth for the toffee sauce to drip down. If needed, gently reheat the remaining toffee sauce. It should slowly drip off a spoon but not be hot. Pour the toffee sauce around the sides and top of the cake. Gently smooth the top of the cake as needed. Follow the same techniques as you would with chocolate drip (see page 120).

If eating the cake the same day as assembled, store it at room temperature until ready to serve. If assembled in advance, store in a cake box in the refrigerator overnight. Bring to room temperature for 30 minutes before serving. Store leftovers loosely covered with plastic wrap in the refrigerator for 3 to 4 days.

If baking the cake in advance, cut the toffee recipe in half—use half for the soaking and half for pouring over the finished cake, as reheating the toffee may cause it to split. If assembling the same day, make the toffee as directed—storing it at room temperature before pouring over the assembled cake.

Gently reheat at half power in the microwave at short intervals as needed.

*   *   *

NOTES: I find white chocolate to be a bit too sweet on its own, but by roasting it in the oven, the sugars caramelize as the cocoa butter melts and it turns into the most beautifully golden chocolate of your dreams. This technique was pioneered at the Valrhona Chocolate School. They also make a lovely Blond Dulcey 32% chocolate that you can purchase and use instead. In place of the white chocolate and salt, substitute 4 ounces (115 g) Valrhona Blond Dulcey 32% chocolate. Melt the chocolate and let cool, then add it to the buttercream and mix as directed.

The caramelized white chocolate may be made weeks in advance and stored in an airtight container at room temperature, but it will solidify as it cools. Gently reheat the chocolate, if needed, in the top portion of a double boiler (or in a heatproof bowl set over a saucepan of simmering water; see page 14) before using.

Macarons

DURING THE DAYS OF MY CAKE SHOP, I was devoted to making custom cakes. Although free time was always scarce, I still enjoyed other types of baking (in addition to cake) at home. While my husband was away on business one weekend, I decided to spend the whole time he was gone completely determined to master macarons. Spoiler alert: I did not achieve my goal that weekend. Did I learn a lot about the intricacies of *macaronage* (the term used for folding the macaron batter), that I actually didn't know how to make a proper French meringue at the time, and the importance of using a kitchen scale? Yes. Did I master macarons? No.

Those first few tries were somewhat of a disappointment. I made batch after batch of macaron shells and nearly every one was majorly flawed. Numerous batters that never stopped flowing, hollow centers, and lots of cracked shells later, I finally made a few passable macarons that somewhat resembled the dozens that had been served at our wedding the previous summer. After running out of egg whites and patience, I admitted defeat. Like most things in life, I accepted that macarons are not something most can master in just a day. However, just because they can be tricky to get a feel for at first doesn't mean they're impossible to make or shouldn't be given a second (or third) try.

After my first attempt almost a decade ago, I would later return to making macarons at several different times in my baking career, including a short stint at an exclusive macaron pâtisserie. Here's what I've learned . . .

THE ELUSIVE FRENCH MACARON

Walk into any French pâtisserie, or even the train station in Paris (where I first spotted them), and you'll see rows of dainty shells with a rainbow of fillings all lined up ready to be packaged into long rectangular boxes or served alongside afternoon tea. Those who have ever attempted making a macaron stare in awe at their perfection, while others marvel at their sheer cuteness and broad assortment of flavors. Biting into their crisp shells, discovering their incomparable texture, and tasting their flavorful centers will make your mouth sing every time. They are certainly not your run-of-the-mill sandwich cookie. But I have a secret: With a bit of practice and patience, you can indeed make these at home.

WHY ARE THEY ARE SO FINICKY?

It's no surprise that making macarons is considered an advanced pastry technique. They require a lot of attention to detail and patience. A few drips of egg yolk in your egg whites may mean your meringue whips up insufficiently and breaks your batter. Undermix, and the finished shells will be lumpy on top. On the other hand, folding the meringue and almond mixture just a handful too many times may cause a river of batter to come spewing from your piping bag as you try to pipe the shells.

Keep in mind that while each step is *very important*, none is exceedingly demanding on its own, and unless you burn the macarons to a crisp, they are probably going to still be worth eating. And when we nail a batch of macarons, we feel like culinary superstars!

MACARONS, TWO WAYS

If you break it down, macarons are little more than a combination of almond flour, confectioners' sugar, and meringue. Which type of meringue you decide to use and how you add the granulated sugar to your egg whites is a somewhat polarizing yet personal decision. Many will stand by the French meringue method because it's fast and doesn't require a candy thermometer. But did you know that macarons were actually first created by an Italian chef for Catherine de' Medici, who would shortly thereafter become the wife of French king Henry II back in the 1500s? Italian meringue does require a bit of extra work, with its boiling sugar and all, but it creates a more stable, more forgiving meringue in the end. Depending on your skill level and desires, I'll leave it to you to decide which to use.

Team French Method

You are confident in your French meringue–making and folding skills. You enjoy precision and efficiency, and despise washing extra dishes. You work hard for impeccable results, but won't be heartbroken or discouraged if your efforts end in a dud every now and then.

Team Italian Method

You aren't scared away by candy thermometers and are comfortable with boiling sugar, but you aren't as confident with your *macaronage* abilities. You've tried making macarons with the French method in the past, but with only average or inconsistent results. You aren't quite sure what the final batter should look or feel like, and would benefit from using a more forgiving meringue.

TIPS AND TRICKS

Weigh your ingredients: Using a kitchen scale is the most accurate way to measure for all recipes, but your macarons will really benefit if you weigh the ingredients. Eggs are the biggest variable, as each egg can contain a different amount of egg white.

Finely grind your almond flour: Even when using store-bought almond flour, I always pulse it, with the confectioners' sugar, in the food processor for a minute or so before sifting the mixture through a fine-mesh sieve. The confectioners' sugar keeps the almond flour from becoming almond butter.

Macaronage: Ideally, you will want to fold together the meringue with the almond flour mixture using the fewest number of strokes. However, unlike a genoise cake, you will want to knock out some of the air in the meringue as you go.

Start with a large bowl and a flexible rubber spatula. Add about one-third of the meringue to the almond flour mixture and begin to fold: Slide the spatula down the side of the bowl to the very bottom, then lift and rotate it over to bring the mixture from the bottom of the bowl up to the top. Give the mixture five to ten folds to get things going, rotating the bowl around as you go, then add the remaining meringue. Continue to fold. Every so often, after you flip the mixture to the top, smear it around the side of the bowl with the spatula to gently deflate the meringue. Periodically scrape the sides and bottom of the bowl to make sure all the dry ingredients get incorporated.

Take your time: A couple of folds too few or too many can make a drastic difference in your macarons. Once the batter becomes more uniform, begin evaluating the consistency after every couple of strokes.

Batter consistency: Knowing when to stop mixing the batter is crucial. The batter should have a "lava-like" consistency that flows very slowly off your spatula. When you lift your spatula and allow the batter to flow off, it should do so in ribbons that eventually, after several seconds, melt back into the batter in the bowl. If you use your spatula to scrape through the batter down the center of the mixing bowl like parting the Red Sea, the batter should very slowly ooze back into the center. If it floods, you've gone too far. If it is too stiff to pipe, then keep going.

Choosing a baking sheet: Pick quality or quantity here and use either two heavy-duty baking sheets or four inexpensive thinner ones. If you opt for the thinner ones, you will need to stack two on top of each other. In either case, you don't need to opt for nonstick, since you'll be using parchment paper or a silicone baking mat to line them.

Use a template: For round, even macarons, make a template: Trace a circle using a small round cookie cutter, about 1½ inches (4 cm) in diameter, as a guide, on a piece of parchment paper a little smaller than your baking sheet, covering the parchment with circles and leaving at least ½ inch (1½ cm) between them. Flip the parchment over and place it on the baking sheet before piping (you should still be able to see the circles through the parchment). If using a silicone baking mat, place the template underneath when piping, then slide it out before baking.

Piping macarons: Holding the piping bag straight down, pipe macarons using a plain round tip about ½ inch (1 cm) in diameter. Be sure to hover the tip slightly above the baking sheet as you pipe so there is room for the batter as it comes out of the bag. The batter will spread slightly, so pipe rounds of batter slightly smaller than the circles on the template. If the batter runs wild out of the piping bag or the macarons spread into one another, the batter was overmixed. If they have *small* peaks on top, that is okay!

Tapping the baking sheet: After the macarons are piped, tap the bottom of the baking sheet to remove any large air bubbles. You can hold one end of the baking sheet in each hand and rap the bottom on your counter a couple of times, but I prefer to hold the baking sheet with one hand and smack the bottom with the palm of my opposite hand, rotating the sheet as I go and giving a few taps in each corner. Any small peaks left over from piping should smooth out during this process. If they remain, the batter was probably undermixed. If so, give the remaining batter a few more folds before piping the next set of shells. Pop any obvious air bubbles with a toothpick at this time.

Resting the macarons: Set the piped macarons aside to dry at room temperature for 20 to 40 minutes before baking. This rest period allows a thin skin to form on the surface of the macaron batter. When baked, the base will rise under this skin, resulting in the signature "feet" around the bottom edges. Essentially, the air from the batter is escaping around the bottom instead of cracking through the top. The macarons are ready to be baked when they feel dry to the touch.

Checking for doneness: To determine if they are done baking, gently wiggle the top of the shell. It should feel secured to the feet but have a tiny bit of movement when nudged. Once cooled, a perfectly baked macaron shell should be easy to peel off the parchment or baking mat.

Maturation: Some recipes will call for the maturation of filled macarons overnight, but I often can't wait that long to dive in. In theory, allowing filled macarons to rest overnight creates a superior texture. This is especially true if you slightly overbaked your shells or if they end up being hollow. However, in my opinion an "immature" macaron is still tasty!

COMMON MACARON MISHAPS AND PROBABLE CAUSES

HOLLOW SHELLS:
batter was overmixed; meringue was broken and overwhipped; improper folding; underbaked (not enough structure to support itself as it cools)

CRACKED TOPS:
batter was overmixed; oven was too hot; batter was undermixed/too much air left in batter; baking pan too thin or not doubled; improper folding/batter not homogeneous; forgot to tap the baking sheet; batter was not rested

NO FEET:
oven was not hot enough; incorrect resting time (too long or too short); batter was too thin from underbeating the meringue or too much added liquid, like food coloring (use gel); batter was mixed too vigorously/meringue was deflated

PROTRUDING FEET:
oven was too hot; batter was overmixed

BUMPY TOPS WITH PEAKS:
dry ingredients were neither fine enough nor sifted; batter was undermixed; forgot to tap the baking sheet

UNEVEN SHELLS:
batter was overmixed; improper folding

BROWNED SHELLS:
oven was too hot or baked too close to heat source, overbaked; baking sheet too thin or not doubled

SHELLS STICK TO PARCHMENT:
undercooked; tried to remove from baking sheet while too warm

SPREADING/NOT HOLDING THEIR SHAPE:
overmixed batter or wet batter

SHELLS ARE BLOTCHY OR WRINKLY:
overwhipped or broken meringue, overmixed batter

French-Method Macarons

MAKES 30 TO 35 SANDWICHED MACARONS

1¼ cups plus 1½ tablespoons (158 g) almond flour

1¼ cups (158 g) confectioners' sugar

105 grams egg whites (from 3 or 4 eggs)

½ cup plus 1½ tablespoons (117 g) granulated sugar

Gel food coloring (optional)

Filling of your choice (such as buttercream or ganache)

1. Line two or three baking sheets with parchment paper templates or silicone baking mats set over the templates (see page 103). Fit a large piping bag with a plain round tip.

2. In a food processor, combine the almond flour and confectioners' sugar and process the mixture for 1 to 2 minutes, stopping once to scrape down the bowl, until the almond flour is finely ground. Sift the mixture through a fine-mesh sieve into a large bowl. Discard any large chunks left in the sieve or grind again until fine. If discarding a significant amount (more than a tablespoon or so), reweigh the mixture in the bowl and top it off with equal parts ground almond flour and confections' sugar until the mixture weighs 316 grams.

3. In the bowl of a stand mixer fitted with the whisk attachment, whisk the egg whites on low speed until they begin to foam, form small, tight bubbles, and turn opaque. Over the course of a couple of minutes, very gradually increase the speed to medium while slowly adding the granulated sugar. Mix on medium-high until stiff peaks form. Add gel food coloring (if using) during the last minute of mixing.

4. Using a flexible rubber spatula, scrape the meringue off the whisk attachment into the bowl with the almond mixture. Begin folding the meringue and almond mixture together, five to ten folds. Scrape in the meringue from the mixer bowl and continue the macaronage process. Continue folding the ingredients together, rotating the bowl as you go. Every so often, gently deflate the meringue by smearing the batter around the side of the bowl. Stop folding once the correct consistency is achieved: The batter should flow very slowly like lava.

5. Fill the prepared piping bag with the macaron batter. Holding the bag straight down, pipe the macarons. Once one baking sheet is full, tap the bottom of the sheet a few times in each corner with the palm of your hand. Set aside and repeat with the remaining prepared baking sheet(s). Set the piped macaron shells aside to rest for 20 to 40 minutes, until a skin forms over the shells and the tops feel dry to the touch.

6. Preheat the oven to 325°F (160°C) with a rack in the center position.

7. Bake the macaron shells one sheet at a time for 12 to 14 minutes, until the tops feel secured to the feet but wiggle very slightly when nudged.

8. Remove the baking sheet from the oven and place it on a wire rack. Let the macaron shells cool on the baking sheets for at least 5 minutes. Repeat to bake and cool the remaining shells.

9. Carefully remove the cooled shells from the baking sheets and set them on a clean baking sheet or cutting board. Match up the shells by size. Pipe prepared buttercream, ganache, or other filling of your choice over the bottom (flat side) of half the shells, staying within the edges of the shells. Top with a matching-size shell, flat-side down, and gently press together until the filling is pushed to the edges of the feet.

10. Store filled macarons in an airtight container in the refrigerator overnight to mature, or serve immediately once assembled.

Italian-Method Macarons

MAKES 30 TO 35 SANDWICHED MACARONS

1¼ cups (145 g) almond flour

1 cup plus 3 tablespoons (145 g) confectioners' sugar

105 grams egg whites (from 3 or 4 eggs)

⅔ cup plus 1 tablespoon (145 g) granulated sugar

Gel food coloring (optional)

Filling of your choice (such as buttercream or ganache)

1 Line two or three baking sheets with parchment paper templates or silicone baking mats set over the templates (see page 103). Fit a large piping bag with a plain round tip.

2 In a food processor, combine the almond flour and confectioners' sugar and process the mixture for 1 to 2 minutes, stopping once to scrape down the bowl, until the almond flour is finely ground. Sift the mixture through a fine-mesh sieve into a large bowl. Discard any large chunks left in the sieve or grind again until fine. If discarding a significant amount (more than a tablespoon or so), reweigh the mixture in the bowl and top it off with equal parts ground almond flour and confectioners' sugar until the mixture weighs 290 grams.

3 Gently whisk half of the egg whites by hand just to loosen them and pour into the bowl with the almond mixture. Stir until a thick paste forms. Place the remaining egg whites in the bowl of a stand mixer fitted with the whisk attachment.

4 In a small saucepan, combine the granulated sugar and 59 ml (¼ cup) water. Bring to a boil over high heat, without stirring, and cook until the mixture registers 238°F (115°C) on a candy thermometer. Meanwhile, begin whipping the egg whites on high speed until soft peaks form. Stop the mixer if the egg whites reach soft peaks before the sugar is hot enough.

5 Once the sugar syrup reaches 238°F (114°C), turn the mixer up to high and slowly stream the syrup into the whipped egg whites. Mix on high until stiff peaks form and the outside of the bowl cools to room temperature, 8 to 10 minutes. Add gel food coloring (if using) during the last minute of mixing.

6 From here, follow steps 4 to 10 from the French-Method Macarons.

Kids' Cakes and Party Treats

Whether you have children or are a kid at heart, it's hard not to gush over these delightful cakes and other treats. With whimsical designs and cheerful flavors like Brownie Sundae and Milk & Cookies, these treats are ready to party. The techniques embrace all skill levels, perfect for young and experienced bakers alike. Grab a stool and have your little one help pile on the cotton candy, cherries, and extra sprinkles, or make your own Rainbow No-Bake Cheesecake when you're feeling extra playful.

Sprinkle Surprise Cupcakes

FEATURED DECORATING TECHNIQUES:
SPRINKLE SURPRISE FILLING,
RUSTIC CUPCAKE FROSTING

It's true; becoming a mother is life changing. My son, Everett, was born exactly one week after I turned in the manuscript for my first book, and baking at home has never been the same. I remember icing cakes while wearing him in the carrier as a newborn and cleaning up showers of spilt flour after his early experiments in the kitchen. Now, he eagerly pulls up his own step stool to the counter, helps me carefully measure ingredients, and gives each cupcake we frost together an extra dose of sprinkles.

Our little Everett is sweet, silly, sensitive, and smart in equal measure. He is cautious and cuddly but also brave and curious. He looks before he leaps, but when he leaps, he soars! And just like Everett, these cupcakes are full of surprises. MAKES 8 EXTRA-LARGE CUPCAKES OR 14 TO 16 REGULAR CUPCAKES

1 recipe Sour Cream Vanilla Cupcakes (page 30)

FOR THE CAKE BATTER BUTTERCREAM:

¾ cup (1½ sticks/170 g) unsalted butter, at room temperature

2 tablespoons cream cheese, at room temperature

3 to 3½ cups (375 to 440 g) confectioners' sugar, sifted if needed

2 to 3 tablespoons heavy cream or whole milk

1 teaspoon pure vanilla extract

¼ teaspoon pure almond extract

TO ASSEMBLE AND DECORATE:

¾ to 1 cup (120 to 160 g) sprinkles

Gel food coloring

MAKE THE SOUR CREAM VANILLA CUPCAKES

Preheat the oven to 350°F (175°C). Line two regular cupcake pans with regular or extra-large paper liners.

Follow the method on page 30 for the sour cream vanilla cupcake batter.

Fill the cupcake liners about two-thirds of the way full. Bake until a toothpick inserted into the center of a cupcake comes out clean, 25 to 27 minutes for extra-large cupcakes or 20 to 22 minutes for regular ones. Let them cool in their pans for 5 to 10 minutes. Remove the cupcakes from their pans and allow to completely cool on a wire rack before filling and frosting.

MAKE THE CAKE BATTER BUTTERCREAM

In the bowl of a stand mixer fitted with the paddle attachment (or in a large bowl with a handheld mixer), beat the butter and cream cheese on medium speed until smooth and creamy. With the mixer running on low, slowly add 3 cups (375 g) of the confectioners' sugar, the cream, vanilla, and almond extract. Once incorporated, turn the mixer up to medium-high and mix for 2 to 3 minutes, until the buttercream is white, fluffy, and smooth. Add the remaining ½ cup (65 g) confectioners' sugar ¼ cup (30 g) at a time as needed and mix until the desired consistency is reached; the buttercream should be soft and spreadable, but not runny.

ASSEMBLE AND DECORATE THE CUPCAKES

Using an apple corer, an inverted large piping tip, or a small paring knife, gently cut the core out of each cupcake. Reserve the cores. Fill each cupcake with about 1 tablespoon of sprinkles. Trim the cupcake cores and replace the tops over the filled cupcake centers. Tint the buttercream, if desired. To decorate with the rustic cupcake frosting technique, use a metal spatula to dollop and swirl the buttercream onto filled cupcakes (see page 273). Roll the edges of the frosted cupcakes in sprinkles, if desired.

Store the cupcakes in a cake box or in a cake pan loosely covered with plastic wrap for up to 1 day at room temperature or up to 2 days in the refrigerator. Serve at room temperature.

Pink Lemonade Cake

FEATURED DECORATING TECHNIQUES: SMOOTH OMBRÉ FROSTING, MACARONS

If you had asked my six-year-old self, I would have requested a sheet cake decorated with plastic figurines and grocery store frosting for my birthday. Now I like to pretend that this is the type of cake I would have chosen as a child—so chic and sophisticated but with just enough whimsy. Better yet, I'd take this stunning cake today! The cake itself tastes like real strawberries and the lemon cream is in my top five fillings of all time. Any cake topped with macarons is a showstopper, in my opinion. Add a soft ombré of sunset-hued buttercream, and this might be the most charming cake of the book. I love this cake so much that I even made cute, frilly cupcakes (see page 115), which we also filled with lemon cream, to match. MAKES ONE THREE-LAYER 8-INCH (20-CM) CAKE; SERVES 12 TO 16

FOR THE STRAWBERRY PUREE:

2 cups (300 g) ripe strawberries, halved

1 tablespoon granulated sugar, or more to taste

1 teaspoon fresh lemon juice

Pinch of salt

FOR THE STRAWBERRY CAKE:

3¼ cups (425 g) cake flour

1 tablespoon baking powder

½ teaspoon baking soda

1 teaspoon salt

¾ cup (180 ml) whole milk

¼ cup (60 ml) sour cream

1 cup (2 sticks/225 g) unsalted butter, at room temperature

2 cups (400 g) granulated sugar

2 teaspoons pure vanilla extract

4 large eggs

Pink gel food coloring (optional)

FOR THE LEMON CREAM:

¾ cup (1½ sticks/170 g) unsalted butter, at room temperature

4 ounces (115 g) cream cheese, at room temperature

3 to 3½ cups (375 to 440 g) confectioners' sugar, sifted if needed

1 tablespoon whole milk

Finely grated zest of ½ lemon

2 tablespoons fresh lemon juice

TO ASSEMBLE AND DECORATE:

1 medium recipe Swiss Meringue Buttercream (page 262)

Gel food coloring

Lemon-Strawberry Macarons (page 115)

MAKE THE STRAWBERRY PUREE

Combine the strawberries, sugar, lemon juice, and salt in a small food processor and process until smooth. Taste and add more sugar as needed. Measure 1 cup (240 ml) of the puree and place in a medium-small saucepan. Place the saucepan over medium-high heat and bring the puree to a slow boil. Turn the heat down to a simmer and reduce the puree to ½ cup (120 ml), 25 to 30 minutes. Remove from the heat and allow to cool before using.

MAKE THE STRAWBERRY CAKE

Preheat the oven to 350°F (175°C). Grease and flour three 8-inch (20-cm) cake pans and line the bottoms with parchment paper.

Sift together the flour, baking powder, baking soda, and salt into a medium bowl. In a liquid measuring cup or small bowl, combine the reduced ½ cup (120 ml) strawberry puree with the milk and sour cream.

In the bowl of a stand mixer fitted with the paddle attachment, beat the butter on medium speed for 2 minutes. Add the sugar and mix on medium-high until light and fluffy, 3 to 5 minutes. Stop the mixer and scrape down the bowl.

Turn the mixer to medium-low and add the vanilla. Add the eggs one at a time, mixing until each is incorporated before adding the next. Mix until combined. Stop the mixer and scrape down the bowl.

Turn the mixer to low and add the flour mixture in three batches, alternating with the milk mixture, beginning and ending with the flour mixture. Tint the cake batter with food coloring, if desired. After the last streaks of the flour mixture are combined, mix on medium for no more than 30 seconds.

Evenly divide the batter among the prepared pans. Bake for 25 to 30 minutes, until a toothpick inserted into the center of each cake comes out clean. Let the cakes cool on a wire rack for 10 to 15 minutes before removing from the pans. Allow the cakes to cool completely, right-side up, on the wire rack before removing the parchment. Level the tops of the cakes with a long serrated knife as needed.

MAKE THE LEMON CREAM

In the bowl of a stand mixer fitted with the paddle attachment (or in a large bowl using a handheld mixer), beat the butter and cream cheese until smooth and creamy. With the mixer running on low, gradually add 3 cups (375 g) of the confectioners' sugar, the milk, lemon zest, and lemon juice. Turn the mixer up to medium-high and mix until the frosting is smooth and creamy. Add the remaining ½ cup (65 g) confectioners' sugar ¼ cup (30 g) at a time until the desired consistency is achieved; the filling should be soft and spreadable, but not runny.

ASSEMBLE THE CAKE

Place one cake layer on a cake board or serving plate. Fill a piping bag fitted with a plain round tip with buttercream and pipe a ring around the top edge of the cake to create a "dam." Fill the dam with half of the lemon cream and spread with an offset spatula or the back of a spoon. Top with a second cake layer and repeat; place the final cake layer on top.

Crumb coat the cake with buttercream and chill in the refrigerator for 15 minutes.

DECORATE THE CAKE

To decorate the cake with the smooth ombré frosting technique, place the cake on a rotating cake stand. Add a large dollop of plain buttercream on top of the cake and smooth it out with an offset spatula. There should be enough buttercream so that it slightly overhangs the sides of the cake. Set aside a small portion of the plain buttercream. Divide the remaining buttercream among three bowls and tint them pink, peach, and yellow, or the colors of your choice. Fill a piping bag fitted with a large round tip with the pink buttercream. Pipe a ring around the bottom of the cake. Mix the remaining pink buttercream with a portion of the peach buttercream. Fill the piping bag with the new color and pipe another ring around the cake, on top of the previous ring. Fill the piping bag with the peach buttercream and repeat. Mix the remaining peach buttercream with a portion of the yellow buttercream and pipe another ring around the cake. Repeat with the yellow buttercream. Finally, mix the remaining yellow buttercream with the reserved plain buttercream and pipe a final ring around the cake, near the top. The sides of the cake should be nearly covered in different shades of buttercream.

Hold an icing smoother so that it is gently touching the side of the cake, as perpendicular to the cake board as possible. Spin the cake stand so that it rotates one full time around. Clean off the icing smoother and repeat. Fill in any gaps with buttercream of the corresponding color. Smooth out the cake until an ombré effect is created. Using a small offset spatula, smooth out the top of the cake by gently dragging any raised edges toward the center of the cake. Top the finished cake with macarons, if desired.

If eating the cake the same day as assembled, store it at room temperature until ready to serve. If assembled in advance, store in a cake box in the refrigerator overnight. Bring to room temperature for 30 minutes before serving. Store leftovers loosely covered with plastic wrap in the refrigerator for 3 to 4 days.

*   *   *

NOTES: Reducing the strawberry puree makes for a more intense, real strawberry taste.

Lemonade Cupcakes

FEATURED DECORATING TECHNIQUE:
FRILLY TWO-TONE CUPCAKE FROSTING

MAKES ABOUT 24 CUPCAKES

FOR THE LEMON CUPCAKES:

1½ cups plus 2 tablespoons (205 g) all-purpose flour

1½ cups (195 g) cake flour

1 tablespoon baking powder

½ teaspoon baking soda

½ teaspoon salt

2 cups (400 g) granulated sugar

1 tablespoon finely grated lemon zest

1 cup (2 sticks/225 g) unsalted butter, at room temperature

2 tablespoons fresh lemon juice

1 teaspoon pure vanilla extract

3 large egg whites

2 large eggs

1¼ cups (300 ml) buttermilk

TO ASSEMBLE:

Lemon cream (page 111)

1 large recipe Swiss Meringue Buttercream (page 262)

Gel food coloring

MAKE THE LEMONADE CUPCAKES

Preheat the oven to 350°F (175°C). Line two cupcake pans with paper liners.

Sift together the flours, baking powder, baking soda, and salt into a large bowl. In a small bowl, rub the sugar and lemon zest together between your fingertips until fragrant.

In the bowl of a stand mixer fitted with the paddle attachment, beat the butter on medium speed for 2 minutes. Add the sugar-zest mixture and mix on medium-high until light and fluffy, 3 to 5 minutes. Stop the mixer and scrape down the bowl.

Turn the mixer to medium-low and add the lemon juice and vanilla. Add the egg whites and eggs one at a time, mixing until each is incorporated before adding the next. Mix until combined. Stop the mixer and scrape down the bowl.

Turn the mixer to low and add the flour mixture in three batches, alternating with the buttermilk, beginning and ending with the flour mixture. After the last streaks of the flour mixture are combined, mix on medium for no more than 30 seconds.

Fill the cupcake liners about two-thirds of the way full using a disher or mechanical ice cream scoop. Bake the cupcakes for 20 to 23 minutes, until a toothpick inserted into the center of a cupcake comes out clean. Let them cool in their pans for 5 to 10 minutes. Remove the cupcakes from their pans and allow to completely cool on a wire rack before filling and frosting.

ASSEMBLE AND DECORATE THE CUPCAKES

Using an apple corer, an inverted large piping tip, or a small paring knife, gently cut the core out of each cupcake. Reserve the cores. Pipe or spoon the lemon cream filling into the center of the cupcakes. Trim the cupcake cores and replace the tops over the filled cupcake centers.

To decorate with the frilly two-tone frosting technique, fit a piping bag with a large star tip. Divide the buttercream between two bowls and tint the colors of your choice. Fill two separate disposable piping bags with the tinted buttercreams. Snip the tips off the piping bags and carefully pipe the tinted buttercreams into the piping bag fitted with the star tip, one color on each side. Pipe the two-tone buttercream in a swirl formation on top of the cupcakes (see page 273).

Store the cupcakes in a cake box or in a cake pan loosely covered with plastic wrap for up to 1 day at room temperature or up to 2 days in the refrigerator. Serve at room temperature.

Lemon-Strawberry Macarons

MAKES ABOUT 30 TO 35 SANDWICHED MACARONS

1 recipe French- or Italian-Method Macarons, baked (pages 104–105)

½ recipe Lemon Cream (page 111)

Strawberry jam, for filling

ASSEMBLE THE MACARONS

Match the macaron shells by size and flip the bottoms upside down on a baking sheet. Fill a piping bag fitted with a medium-small round tip with the lemon cream. Pipe a ring of lemon cream around the edge of the bottom shells. Fill the centers with a small dollop of strawberry jam. Place the remaining shells on top and gently press together.

Use macarons to decorate the Pink Lemonade Cake or Lemonade Cupcakes, or store in an airtight container in the refrigerator for up to 1 week. Serve at room temperature.

Brownie Sundae Cake

FEATURED DECORATING TECHNIQUES: SMOOTH FROSTING, CHOCOLATE DRIP,
SPRINKLE COATING, ROSETTE PIPING

This cake is any child's dream! My nieces, Emmy and Ali, came to visit when I first created this recipe, and they absolutely loved it. In fact, we all did—adults included! With a chewy chocolate cake base similar to a brownie and all the toppings of an ice cream sundae, what's not to love? I've added sprinkles, chocolate sauce, whipped cream, chopped peanuts, and (of course) bright red cherries on top. Feel free to play around with any toppings that inspire you.

The brownie cake base is incredibly rich and decadent. I bet it would taste delicious with peanut butter frosting (page 74) or butterscotch buttercream (page 70) for an alternative, nearly sinful variation. Whatever the case, I highly recommend serving thin slices. MAKES ONE THREE-LAYER 8-INCH (20-CM) CAKE; SERVES 15 TO 20

FOR THE BROWNIE CAKE:

- 1 cup plus 6 tablespoons (2¾ sticks/310 g) unsalted butter, diced
- 10 ounces (280 g) dark chocolate, chopped
- 2⅓ cups (290 g) all-purpose flour
- ⅓ cup (30 g) unsweetened cocoa powder
- 1½ teaspoons baking powder
- 1 teaspoon salt
- 2⅔ cups (535 g) granulated sugar
- 5 large eggs
- 1 large egg yolk
- 1 teaspoon pure vanilla extract

FOR THE STRAWBERRY PUREE:

- ½ cup (75 g) ripe strawberries, halved
- 1 tablespoon granulated sugar, or more to taste
- 1 teaspoon fresh lemon juice
- Pinch of salt

FOR THE STRAWBERRY CREAM:

- ¾ cup (1½ sticks/170 g) unsalted butter, at room temperature
- 4 ounces (115 g) cream cheese, at room temperature
- 3½ to 4 cups (425 to 500 g) confectioners' sugar, sifted if needed

TO ASSEMBLE AND DECORATE:

- 1 small recipe Whipped Vanilla Buttercream (page 261)
- ½ to ¾ cup (80 to 120 g) sprinkles
- 1 recipe Chocolate Drizzle (page 263)
- ½ recipe Whipped Cream (page 263)
- Chopped peanuts, for sprinkling
- 14 to 16 cherries

MAKE THE BROWNIE CAKE

Preheat the oven to 350°F (175°C). Grease and flour three 8-inch (20-cm) cake pans and line the bottoms with parchment paper.

Put the butter and chocolate in a heatproof bowl. In a medium saucepan, bring an inch or two (2.5 to 5 cm) of water to a simmer over medium-low heat. Place the bowl with the butter-chocolate mixture on top of the saucepan to create a double boiler (be sure the bottom of the bowl does not touch the water). Heat the mixture until the butter and chocolate begin to melt. Remove from the heat and stir until smooth and well combined. Set aside to cool.

Sift together the flour, cocoa powder, baking powder, and salt into a large bowl.

In the bowl of a stand mixer fitted with the whisk attachment, beat the sugar, eggs, and egg yolk on medium-high until foamy and pale in color, about 5 minutes. Add the vanilla and mix to combine.

With the mixer running on low, gradually add the flour mixture to the egg mixture in two batches, stopping the mixer and scraping down the sides and bottom of the bowl between the additions.

Stop the mixer and add the melted butter-chocolate mixture. Fold the batter together until combined.

Evenly divide the batter among the prepared pans. Bake for 20 to 24 minutes, until the tops are slightly cracked and a toothpick inserted into the center comes out with a few moist crumbs attached. *Do not overbake.*

Let the cakes cool on a wire rack for 10 to 20 minutes before carefully removing from the pans. Allow the cakes to cool completely, right-side up, on the wire rack before removing the parchment.

MAKE THE STRAWBERRY PUREE

In a small food processor, combine the strawberries, sugar, lemon juice, and salt and process until smooth. Taste and add more sugar as desired (see Note, page 112).

MAKE THE STRAWBERRY CREAM

In the bowl of a stand mixer fitted with the paddle attachment (or in a large bowl using a handheld mixer), beat the butter and cream cheese together until smooth and creamy. With the mixer running on low, gradually add 3½ cups (425 g) of the confectioners' sugar and 3 tablespoons of the strawberry puree. Turn the mixer up to medium-high and mix until the filling is smooth and creamy. Add the remaining ½ cup (65 g) confectioners' sugar, ¼ cup (30 g) at a time, and/or 1 tablespoon strawberry puree until desired consistency is reached; the filling should be soft and spreadable, but not runny.

ASSEMBLE THE CAKE

Place one brownie cake layer on a cake board or serving plate. Spread on half of the strawberry cream with an offset spatula. Top with a second brownie cake layer and repeat; place the final cake layer on top.

Crumb coat the cake with buttercream and chill in the refrigerator for 15 minutes.

DECORATE THE CAKE

Frost the cake with the buttercream with a smooth finish. Set a rimmed baking sheet on your work surface and fill a small bowl with sprinkles. Carefully hold the cake in one hand and use the other to scoop and press the sprinkles around the bottom portion of the cake. Let any unused sprinkles fall onto the baking sheet to be used again. Chill the cake in the refrigerator for 15 to 30 minutes to set the buttercream before adding the chocolate drizzle.

To decorate the cake with the perfect chocolate drip, use a small spoon to carefully drip the cooled chocolate drizzle around the top edge of the cake. Pour the remaining drizzle onto the center of the cake and quickly smooth it out to the edge with a small offset spatula. See pages 120–121.

Fill a piping bag fitted with a star tip with the whipped cream. Pipe rosettes (see page 245) around the top edge of the cake and sprinkle with the chopped nuts. Place a cherry in the center of each rosette.

If eating the cake the same day as assembled, store it at room temperature until ready to serve. If assembled in advance, store in a cake box in the refrigerator overnight. Bring to room temperature for 30 minutes before serving. Store leftovers loosely covered with plastic wrap in the refrigerator for 3 to 4 days.

✳   ✳   ✳

NOTES: For a simpler version, use equal amounts of strained strawberry jam instead of the puree.

Tips for the Perfect
Chocolate Drip

*   *   *

1   CHILL THE FROSTED CAKE before you add the chocolate drips. The cold buttercream will help slow the drips for more control.

2   Make sure the chocolate drizzle is at the CORRECT TEMPERATURE. It should be fluid, but not warm or hot. Let it cool to room temperature or chill it in the refrigerator.

3   TEST THE DRIZZLE by making a practice drip or two on the back of the cake before adding it to the entire cake. The glaze should flow slowly and smoothly. If it slips right off the cake, it is too warm. If it clumps and does not drip, it is too cold.

4   CONTROL THE DRIPS. Instead of pouring the drizzle on top of the cake, add drips individually around the sides of the cake. I use a small spoon for this, while others prefer a squeeze bottle.

5   Once the sides are dripped, pour the remaining drizzle on top of the cake and GENTLY SMOOTH IT OUT with an offset spatula until it meets the edges. Again, make sure the drizzle is at the correct temperature. At this point, it may have cooled too much and you may have trouble smoothing it evenly. Gently reheat the drizzle as needed.

6   Once the top is smoothed, TAP THE CAKE on your work surface a few times to further smooth the top and release any air bubbles.

Milk & Cookies Cake

FEATURED DECORATING TECHNIQUES:
SMOOTH FROSTING, FLUFFY SHELL BORDER,
CHOCOLATE CHIP POLKA DOTS

FOR THE COOKIE DOUGH–INSPIRED FILLING:

¾ cup (1½ sticks/170 g) unsalted butter

2½ cups (310 g) confectioners' sugar

1 teaspoon pure vanilla extract

½ teaspoon fancy molasses

Pinch of salt

1 to 2 tablespoons whole milk, if needed

½ cup (90 g) mini chocolate chips

FOR THE WHITE CAKE:

¾ cup (180 ml) milk

¼ cup (60 ml) sour cream

2½ cups (325 g) cake flour

1½ cups (300 g) granulated sugar

1 tablespoon baking powder

½ teaspoon salt

¾ cup + 2 tablespoons unsalted butter, diced, at room temperature

1½ teaspoons pure vanilla extract

6 egg whites

FOR THE MASCARPONE BUTTERCREAM:

1 cup (2 sticks/225 g) unsalted butter, at room temperature

¼ cup (60 g) mascarpone or cream cheese, at room temperature

3½ to 4 cups (425 to 500 g) confectioners' sugar, sifted if needed

1 to 2 tablespoons whole milk

1 teaspoon pure vanilla extract

Gel food coloring

TO DECORATE:

Chocolate chips

With its playful, cookie dough–inspired filling and fluffy pink borders, there's no doubt that this cake would be a home run at a kid's birthday party. However, as with all the cakes in this chapter, the adults in the room will not be disappointed. In fact, I first made this cake for my husband on our sixth wedding anniversary because we go together like, well, milk and cookies!

I tried to keep most of the recipes in this chapter less fussy, but here, the browning of the butter really is important. It gives the filling a slightly nutty, caramel-like flavor that reminds me of cookie dough. I suggest using mini chips for the filling to make slicing easier, but regular chips look better for the design on the exterior. If you find it frivolous to buy two types of chocolate chips, go for the regular and coarsely chop them before adding to the filling. MAKES ONE THREE-LAYER 8-INCH (20-CM) CAKE; SERVES 12 TO 16

MAKE THE COOKIE DOUGH–INSPIRED FILLING

In a light-colored medium saucepan, melt the butter over medium-low heat. Increase the heat to medium-high and cook, stirring to keep the milk solids from sticking and burning at the bottom of the pan, for about 8 minutes, until the butter is very fragrant and nutty, and light-medium amber in color. There may be dark brown bits at the bottom of the pan. Strain the browned butter through a fine-mesh sieve into a heatproof container and discard any burnt milk solids. Chill the browned butter in the refrigerator until it has the consistency of room-temperature butter, about 1 hour.

In the bowl of a stand mixer fitted with the paddle attachment (or in a large bowl using a handheld mixer), beat the cooled browned butter on low speed until smooth. Slowly add the confectioners' sugar, vanilla, molasses, and salt. Once incorporated, turn the mixer to medium and mix for a couple of minutes, or until the filling is smooth and creamy. If the filling is too thick to spread, gradually add the milk, starting with 1 tablespoon. Stop the mixer and fold in the chocolate chips by hand.

MAKE THE WHITE CAKE

Preheat the oven to 350°F (175°C). Grease and flour three 8-inch (20-cm) cake pans and line the bottoms with parchment paper.

In a small bowl or liquid measuring cup, stir the milk and sour cream.

Sift the flour, sugar, baking powder, and salt into the bowl of a stand mixer. Using the paddle attachment, beat the ingredients on low speed until just combined. Add the butter, vanilla, and about ½ cup (120 ml) of the milk mixture. Mix on medium until the dry ingredients are evenly distributed and moistened, about 1 minute. Stop the mixer and scrape down the sides and bottom of the bowl.

Add the egg whites to the remaining milk mixture and stir to combine. With the mixer running on medium speed, add the egg mixture in three additions, mixing for about 15 seconds after each addition and stopping the mixer between additions to scrape down the sides and bottom of the bowl.

Evenly divide the batter among the prepared pans. Bake for 20 to 22 minutes, until a toothpick inserted into the center of each cake comes out clean. Let the cakes cool on a wire rack for 10 to 15 minutes before removing from the pans. Allow the cakes to cool completely, right-side up, on the wire rack before removing the parchment. Level the tops of the cakes with a long serrated knife as needed.

MAKE THE MASCARPONE BUTTERCREAM

In the bowl of a stand mixer fitted with the paddle attachment (or in a large bowl using a handheld mixer), beat the butter and mascarpone on medium speed until smooth and creamy. With the mixer running on low, slowly add 3½ cups (425 g) of the confectioners' sugar, the milk, and vanilla. Once incorporated, turn the mixer to medium-high and mix for 3 to 5 minutes, until the buttercream is white, fluffy, and smooth. Add the remaining ½ cup (65 g) confectioners' sugar ¼ cup (30 g) at a time and mix until the desired consistency is reached; the buttercream should be soft and spreadable, but not runny. Tint the buttercream using gel food coloring, if desired.

ASSEMBLE THE CAKE

Place one cake layer on a cake board or serving dish. Spread on half of the chocolate chip filling with an offset spatula. Top with a second cake layer and repeat. Place the final cake layer on top. Crumb coat the cake and chill it in the refrigerator for 15 minutes.

DECORATE THE CAKE

Fill a piping bag fitted with a star tip with 1 cup (240 ml) buttercream. Use the remaining buttercream to frost the cake with a smooth finish. For the fluffy shell border, use the filled piping bag to pipe buttercream around the top edge of the cake (see page 275).

To decorate the cake with chocolate chip polka dots, press the pointed tip of each chip into the frosted cake so the flat bottoms are facing out.

If eating the cake the same day as assembled, store it at room temperature until ready to serve. If assembled in advance, store in a cake box in the refrigerator overnight. Bring to room temperature for 30 minutes before serving. Store leftovers loosely covered with plastic wrap in the refrigerator for 3 to 4 days.

Rainbow No-Bake Cheesecake

FEATURED DECORATING TECHNIQUE: SHELL BORDER

Pretty pastels stun from inside and out in this light, airy, mousse-like cheesecake. When you can't stand to turn on your oven, sweet strawberries, tropical mangoes, and zesty limes make this summertime dessert a real treat. MAKES ONE 9-INCH (23-CM) CHEESECAKE; SERVES 12 TO 16

FOR THE GRAHAM CRACKER CRUST:

2 cups (240 g) graham cracker crumbs (from about 15 sheets)

2 tablespoons granulated sugar

Pinch of salt

½ cup (1 stick/115 g) unsalted butter, melted

FOR THE STRAWBERRY AND MANGO PUREES:

12 to 15 medium strawberries, hulled

2 to 4 tablespoons granulated sugar

3 or 4 mangoes, pitted and peeled

FOR THE STRAWBERRY LAYER:

3 tablespoons fresh lemon juice

2 teaspoons unflavored powdered gelatin

12 ounces (340 g) cream cheese, at room temperature

¾ cup (95 g) confectioners' sugar

1 teaspoon pure vanilla extract

Pink gel food coloring (optional)

½ cup (120 ml) heavy cream

FOR THE MANGO LAYER:

3 tablespoons fresh lemon juice

2 teaspoons unflavored powdered gelatin

12 ounces (340 g) cream cheese, at room temperature

¾ cup (95 g) confectioners' sugar

1 teaspoon pure vanilla extract

Yellow gel food coloring (optional)

½ cup (120 ml) heavy cream

FOR THE LIME LAYER:

¼ cup (60 ml) fresh lime juice

2 teaspoons unflavored powdered gelatin

12 ounces (340 g) cream cheese, at room temperature

¾ cup (95 g) confectioners' sugar

Finely grated zest of 2 limes

1 teaspoon pure vanilla extract

Lime green gel food coloring

1½ cups (360 ml) heavy cream

TO ASSEMBLE AND DECORATE:

½ recipe Whipped Cream (page 263)

Rainbow sprinkles (optional)

MAKE THE GRAHAM CRACKER CRUST

Fit a 9-inch (23-cm) springform pan with a collar: Cut a long strip of parchment paper, 28 inches (71 cm) in length and about 1 inch (2.5 cm) wider than the height of the pan (or use an acetate cake collar). Use a touch of baking spray or butter to lightly grease the back of the collar to help it stick to the pan and stay in place. Wrap the collar around the inside of the pan. Secure the ends with tape or a paperclip as needed. The collar is used to extend the height of the sides of the pan.

Combine the graham cracker crumbs, sugar, and salt in a medium bowl and stir to combine. Pour in the melted butter and stir until the crumbs are evenly moist. Tip the mixture into the prepared pan. Use the bottom of a drinking glass or dry measuring cup with straight sides to firmly and evenly press the mixture into the bottom of the pan. The crust should be tight and compact.

Chill the crust in the freezer for about 30 minutes before filling.

MAKE THE STRAWBERRY AND MANGO PUREES

Place the hulled strawberries in the bowl of a small food processor. Add 1 tablespoon of the sugar and blend until smooth. Taste and adjust the sugar as needed. The puree should be slightly sweet. Set aside 1 cup (240 ml) of the strawberry puree to use in the strawberry cheesecake layer. Rinse the food processor bowl and repeat with the mangoes and remaining sugar. Set aside 1 cup (240 ml) of the mango puree to use in the mango cheesecake layer.

MAKE THE STRAWBERRY LAYER

Put the lemon juice in heatproof container, like a glass measuring cup or a coffee mug, and sprinkle in the gelatin. Stir to combine and let bloom for about 5 minutes.

In the bowl of a stand mixer fitted with the paddle attachment, beat the cream cheese and confectioners' sugar on medium-low speed for several minutes, stopping and scraping down the bowl often, until smooth.

Zap the gelatin mixture in the microwave for 5 to 10 seconds to liquefy. Add the gelatin, 1 cup (240 ml) of the strawberry puree, and the vanilla to the cream cheese mixture. Mix on medium-low until combined. Add a drop or two of food coloring (if using) and mix to combine.

In a clean bowl of a stand mixer fitted with the whisk attachment (or in a large bowl using a handheld mixer), whip the cream on medium-high until it holds medium peaks. Gently fold the whipped cream into the strawberry mixture until fully combined.

Spoon the mixture into the prepared crust and gently spread with an offset spatula. Gently tap the bottom of the pan on the counter a couple of times. Chill in the freezer for 15 to 20 minutes as you prepare the mango layer.

MAKE THE MANGO LAYER

Follow the directions for the strawberry layer, substituting the mango puree for the strawberry. Spoon the mango mixture on top of the strawberry layer and gently it spread with an offset spatula. Gently tap the bottom of the pan on the counter a couple of times. Chill in the freezer for 15 to 20 minutes as you prepare the lime layer.

MAKE THE LIME LAYER

Follow the directions for blooming the gelatin in the strawberry layer but with the lime juice. In the bowl of a stand mixer fitted with the paddle attachment, beat the cream cheese, confectioners' sugar, and lime zest on medium-low speed for several minutes, stopping and scraping down the bowl often, until smooth. Add the gelatin, vanilla, and green gel food coloring and mix until combined.

Whip the cream following the directions for the strawberry layer, then fold into the lime-cream cheese mixture until fully combined. Spoon the lime mixture on top of the mango layer and gently spread it with an offset spatula. Gently tap the bottom of the pan on the counter a couple of times. Chill in the refrigerator for 1 to 2 hours until set.

ASSEMBLE AND DECORATE THE CHEESECAKE

Once set, carefully unlock the springform pan and remove the sides. Gently peel off the collar. Smooth out the sides of the cheesecake with an offset or straight spatula as needed.

Spread half of the whipped cream over the top of the cake with an offset spatula. Fill a piping bag fitted with a star tip with the remaining whipped cream and pipe a fluffy shell border around the top edge of the cake (see page 275). Add sprinkles, if desired.

Store loosely covered with plastic wrap or in a cake box in the refrigerator until ready to serve. To serve, warm a large chef's knife under hot water and wipe dry before slicing. Clean and warm the knife (as needed) between slices. Store leftovers in the refrigerator for up to 3 days.

*   *   *

NOTES: I prefer Ataulfo mangoes, but use whatever type is available to you.

Stir any leftover strawberry or mango puree into yogurt or serve with waffles!

The gelatin makes a super-stable cheesecake that will show off the clean layers when sliced. It also creates an airy texture similar to mousse.

The lime layer may be a bit thicker and fluffier than those made with fruit puree due to the additional whipped cream.

Blueberry Galaxy Cake

FEATURED DECORATING TECHNIQUE:
WATERCOLOR FROSTING

If it were up to my son, Everett, he would survive on blueberries alone, so I knew I had to include a blueberry cake in this book just for him. I tend to swirl on pink frosting or add buttercream flowers to dress up a cake, so I had extra fun designing this more masculine yet kid-friendly cake. The starry pattern on a background of space-hued swirls reminds me of a galaxy far, far away. MAKES ONE THREE-LAYER 8-INCH (20-CM) CAKE; SERVES 12 TO 16

FOR THE LEMON POPPY SEED CAKE:

1½ cups (195 g) cake flour

1½ cups plus 2 tablespoons (205 g) all-purpose flour

2 teaspoons baking powder

½ teaspoon baking soda

½ teaspoon salt

4 teaspoons poppy seeds

2 cups (400 g) granulated sugar

Finely grated zest of 1 large lemon

½ cup (120 ml) sour cream

¾ cup (180 ml) milk

1 cup (2 sticks/225 g) unsalted butter, at room temperature

1 teaspoon pure vanilla extract

6 egg whites, gently whisked to loosen

¼ cup (60 ml) fresh lemon juice

FOR THE VANILLA AND BLUEBERRY BUTTERCREAMS:

1 large recipe Whipped Vanilla Buttercream (page 261)

1 cup (145 g) fresh blueberries

Juice of 1 medium lemon

TO ASSEMBLE AND DECORATE:

Gel food coloring

½ cup (75 g) mixed fresh blueberries and blackberries

Gold and/or silver luster dust

Sugar pearls, dragées, and/or sanding sugar, for sprinkling

MAKE THE LEMON POPPY SEED CAKE

Preheat the oven to 350°F (175°C). Grease and flour three 8-inch (20-cm) cake pans and line the bottoms with parchment paper.

Sift together the flours, baking powder, baking soda, and salt into a large bowl. Stir in the poppy seeds. In a small bowl, rub the sugar and lemon zest together between your fingertips until fragrant. In a separate bowl or liquid measuring cup, combine the sour cream and milk.

In the bowl of a stand mixer fitted with the paddle attachment, beat the butter on medium speed for 2 minutes. Add the sugar-zest and mix on medium-high until light and fluffy, 3 to 5 minutes. Stop the mixer and scrape down the bowl.

Turn the mixer to medium-low and add the vanilla. Add the egg whites a little at a time, mixing until each addition is incorporated before adding the next. Add the lemon juice and mix until combined. Stop the mixer and scrape down the bowl.

Turn the mixer to low and add the flour mixture in two batches, alternating with the milk mixture, beginning and ending with the flour mixture. After the last streaks of the flour mixture are combined, mix on medium for no more than 30 seconds.

Evenly divide the batter among the prepared pans. Bake for 23 to 28 minutes, until a toothpick inserted into the center of each cake comes out clean. Let the cakes cool in their pans on a wire rack for 10 to 15 minutes before removing from the pans. Allow the cakes to cool completely, right-side up, on the wire rack before removing the parchment. Level the tops of the cakes with a long serrated knife as needed.

MAKE THE VANILLA AND BLUEBERRY BUTTERCREAMS

Put 2 cups (480 ml) of the buttercream into a medium bowl or the bowl of a stand mixer for the blueberry buttercream; set aside the remaining buttercream.

In a small saucepan, combine the blueberries and lemon juice and bring to a simmer over medium heat, 5 to 10 minutes. Strain the mixture through a fine-mesh sieve set over a bowl. Press down on the blueberries with a rubber spatula to extract all their juices. Discard the solids in the strainer. With a handheld mixer or using a stand mixer fitted with the paddle attachment, beat together the 2 cups (480 ml) buttercream and 2 tablespoons of the blueberry juice. Add another tablespoon of blueberry juice to deepen the color, if desired. The buttercream should be vibrant in color but not runny.

ASSEMBLE THE CAKE

Place one cake layer on a cake board or serving plate. Fill a piping bag fitted with a large round tip with vanilla buttercream. Pipe a ring around the top edge of the cake to create a "dam." Set aside about 3 tablespoons of the blueberry buttercream, then fill the ring with half of the remaining blueberry buttercream and smooth out with an offset spatula or the back of a spoon. Top with a second cake layer and repeat; place the final cake layer on top.

Crumb coat the cake with the plain vanilla buttercream and chill it in the refrigerator for 15 minutes.

DECORATE THE CAKE

Set aside ½ cup (30 ml) of the vanilla buttercream, then frost the cake with the remaining buttercream. The final coat does not need to be perfectly smooth. Divide the reserved ½ cup (30 ml) buttercream between two small bowls; tint one blue and the other lavender.

To decorate the cake with the watercolor frosting technique, use a small offset spatula to randomly add small dabs of the colored buttercreams, including the remaining blueberry buttercream, around the sides and top of the cake.

Hold an icing smoother so that it is gently touching the side of the cake, as perpendicular to the cake board as possible. Spin the cake stand so that it rotates one full time around. Clean off the icing smoother and repeat. Fill in any gaps with any remaining buttercream. Smooth out the cake until a watercolor effect is created. Using a small offset spatula, smooth out the top of the cake by gently dragging any raised edges toward the center of the cake. Gently place the edge of the icing smoother on top of the cake (see page 271) or an offset spatula held as flat as possible. Spin the cake stand and smooth out the top of the cake.

Using a pastry brush or clean paintbrush, brush the berries with the gold and silver luster dusts. Arrange the berries in a crescent shape around the top of the cake. Sprinkle with sugar pearls, dragées, and/or sanding sugar as desired.

If eating the cake the same day as assembled, store it at room temperature until ready to serve. If assembled in advance, store in a cake box in the refrigerator overnight. Bring to room temperature for 30 minutes before serving. Store leftovers loosely covered with plastic wrap in the refrigerator for 3 to 4 days.

*   *   *

NOTE: Stir any leftover blueberry juice into lemonade or drizzle over ice cream!

* * *

NOTE: Feel free to play around with different flavors of no-churn ice cream. Try adding different extracts like mint or rose. You may even try whisking in ¼ cup unsweetened cocoa powder or 2 teaspoons matcha tea powder into the condensed milk to make chocolate or green tea–flavored ice cream!

Ice Cream Macaron Sandwiches

FEATURED DECORATING TECHNIQUE: DIPPED SPRINKLES

Classic pastry meets fun, flirty, no-churn ice cream in these fancy-pants ice cream sandwiches made with extra-large macaron shells! Conveniently packaged as handheld, personal-size treats, these sandwiches are perfect for both little hands and large adult ones. The crisp yet chewy macarons are the ideal texture, even when frozen, for supporting the ice cream—in other words, the filling won't squish out with each bite. I encourage you to switch up the flavors (see Note), play around with different toppings, and change the colors to your heart's content. MAKES 10 TO 14 SANDWICHES

FOR THE NO-CHURN ICE CREAM:

2 cups (480 ml) cold heavy cream

1 (14-ounce/210-ml) can sweetened condensed milk

½ vanilla bean, split lengthwise and seeds scraped out

Pinch of salt

¼ teaspoon pure almond extract (optional)

FOR THE MACARONS:

Batter for 1 recipe French- or Italian-Method Macarons (page 99)

TO ASSEMBLE:

½ to ¾ cup (80 to 120 g) sprinkles

MAKE THE NO-CHURN ICE CREAM

In the bowl of a stand mixer fitted with the whisk attachment (or in a large bowl using a handheld mixer), beat the cream on high speed until it forms medium-soft peaks. In a separate bowl, whisk together the condensed milk, vanilla bean seeds, salt, and almond extract (if using).

Fold the whipped cream into the condensed milk mixture. Spread the mixture into a rimmed baking sheet and cover with a piece of waxed paper or parchment paper. Freeze until very firm, at least 4 hours or up to overnight.

MAKE THE MACARONS

Create a template by tracing 2½-inch (6-cm) round cookie cutters or the rim of a drinking glass on parchment paper, spaced 1 inch (2.5 cm) apart. Line two baking sheets with parchment paper templates flipped ink-side down or silicone baking mats set over the template.

Fill a large piping bag fitted with a plain round tip with the macaron batter. Holding the bag perpendicular to the baking sheet, pipe the macarons. Once you've filled one baking sheet, tap the bottom of the sheet with the palm of your hand a few times in each corner. Set aside and repeat with the remaining batter. Remove the parchment template if using under a silicone baking mat and discard. Let the piped macarons rest for 20 to 40 minutes, or until a skin has formed on the outside and the tops of the shells feel dry to the touch.

Preheat the oven to 325°F (160°C) with a rack in the center position.

Bake the macarons one sheet at a time for 16 to 20 minutes. When done, the tops of the macaron shells should feel secured to the feet but wiggle very slightly when nudged. Cool the shells per macaron instructions (page 99).

Carefully remove the cooled shells from the baking sheets and set them on a clean baking sheet or cutting board. Match up the shells by size.

ASSEMBLE THE SANDWICHES

Put a baking sheet in the freezer. Pour the sprinkles into a shallow dish.

Using a round cookie cutter the same diameter as the macarons, cut out a disc of the ice cream. Quickly place the ice cream disc between two macaron shells and gently press together. To decorate the macarons with the dipped sprinkles technique, roll the exposed edges of the ice cream in sprinkles and place on the baking sheet in the freezer. Repeat with the remaining ice cream and macaron shells. As the ice cream softens, you may need to refreeze it.

Freeze the assembled sandwiches for at least 1 hour before serving. Store leftovers wrapped in plastic wrap in the freezer for up to a few weeks.

Cotton Candy Cloud Cake

FEATURED DECORATING TECHNIQUES:
RUSTIC OMBRÉ FROSTING, MACARONS

This Cotton Candy Cloud Cake is pure fun. The whimsical cotton candy puffs and cloud-shaped macarons are enough to make anyone smile. At its core, it is a simple vanilla cake with whipped buttercream. But with a touch of food coloring, cotton candy flavoring, and a tiny bit of magic, the simple cake is transformed into something fit for any party or birthday celebration. The gentle pink watercolor buttercream hints at the ombré surprise inside. This recipe is slightly larger than the other buttermilk cakes in this book. Not into cotton candy but need to serve a crowd? Use this as your base recipe and change up the flavors and/or colors to suit all your party needs! MAKES
ONE FOUR-LAYER 8-INCH (20-CM) CAKE; SERVES 15 TO 20

FOR THE OMBRÉ CAKE:

2 cups + 2 teaspoons (265 g) all-purpose flour

2 cups (260 g) cake flour

5 teaspoons baking powder

1 teaspoon salt

1 cup + 6 tablespoons (2½ sticks + 2 tablespoons/ 305 g) unsalted butter, at room temperature

2½ cups (500 g) granulated sugar

1 tablespoon plus ½ teaspoon pure vanilla extract

5 large eggs

1¾ cups (420 ml) buttermilk

Gel food coloring

FOR THE CLOUD MACARONS:

Batter for ½ recipe French- or Italian- Method Macaron Shells (page 99)

FOR THE COTTON CANDY BUTTERCREAM:

1 large recipe Whipped Vanilla Buttercream (page 261)

½ teaspoon cotton candy flavoring, or to taste (see Notes)

TO DECORATE:

Gel food coloring

Cotton candy

MAKE THE OMBRÉ CAKE

Preheat the oven to 350°F (175°C). Grease and flour four 8-inch (20-cm) cake pans and line the bottoms with parchment paper.

Sift together the all-purpose flour, cake flour, baking powder, and salt into a large bowl.

In the bowl of a stand mixer fitted with the paddle attachment, beat the butter on medium speed for 2 minutes. Add the sugar and mix on medium-high until light and fluffy, 3 to 5 minutes. Stop the mixer and scrape down the bowl.

Turn the mixer to medium-low and add the vanilla. Add the eggs one at a time, mixing until each is incorporated before adding the next. Mix until combined. Stop the mixer and scrape down the bowl.

Turn the mixer to low and add the flour mixture in three batches, alternating with the buttermilk, beginning and ending with the flour mixture. Mix on medium until combined. Do not overmix.

Divide the batter among four bowls. Tint the batter dark pink, medium pink, and pale pink. Keep one portion white. Trying not to overmix, fold the batter until the color is evenly distributed.

Tip each color of batter into its own prepared cake pan and smooth the tops as needed. Bake for 23 to 28 minutes, until a toothpick inserted into the center of each cake comes out clean. Remove the cakes from the oven and reduce the oven temperature to 325°F (160°C). Let the cakes cool on a wire rack for 10 to 15 minutes before removing from the pans. Allow the cakes to cool completely, right-side up, on the wire rack before removing the parchment. Level the tops of the cakes with a long serrated knife as needed.

MAKE THE CLOUD MACARONS

Prepare a baking sheet with parchment paper or a silicone liner. Fill a piping bag fitted with a plain round tip with the macaron batter. To form a cloud shape, pipe two circles on top with three circles staggered underneath, making each circle about ¾ inch (2 cm) in diameter. The clouds will need to be symmetrical for sandwiching together. Let the piped macarons rest for 20 to 40 minutes, or until a skin has formed on the outside and the tops of the shells feel dry to the touch.

Bake for 15 to 18 minutes in the center rack of the oven, until the tops of the macaron clouds feel secured to the feet but wiggle very slightly when nudged. Remove the baking sheet from the oven and place it on a wire rack. Let the macaron clouds cool for at least 5 minutes on the baking sheet per macarons instructions (page 99).

Carefully remove the cooled cloud shells from the baking sheet and set them on a clean baking sheet or cutting board. Match up the cloud shells by size.

MAKE THE COTTON CANDY BUTTERCREAM

In the bowl of a stand mixer fitted with the paddle attachment, whip the buttercream until creamy. Add the cotton candy flavoring and mix until combined.

ASSEMBLE THE CAKE

Place the dark pink cake layer on a cake board or serving dish. Spread on ¾ to 1 cup (180 to 240 ml) of the cotton candy buttercream with an offset spatula. Top with the medium pink cake layer and repeat. Top with the pale pink cake layer and repeat. Place the plain cake layer on top.

Crumb coat the cake and chill it in the refrigerator for 15 minutes.

DECORATE THE CAKE

Reserve about 1 cup of buttercream to fill the macarons and set aside.

Frost the top of the cake with buttercream. Tint a small portion of the buttercream pink. To decorate the cake with the rustic ombré frosting technique, use the method from the Chocolate Stout Cake (page 90). Swipe the pink buttercream around the bottom of the cake with an offset spatula. Mix a small amount of pink buttercream with some of the plain buttercream to create a lighter shade of pink. Spread the light pink cream buttercream above the dark pink portion. Fill in the sides of the cake with the plain buttercream. Smooth out the buttercream with an offset spatula until the colors blend together.

Fill a piping bag fitted with a plain round tip with the remaining buttercream. Pipe the buttercream onto the bottom shells of the macarons and sandwich together with the tops. Top the cake with cotton candy and macarons just before serving (see Notes).

If eating the cake the same day as assembled, store it at room temperature until ready to serve. If assembled in advance, store in a cake box in the refrigerator overnight, without the cotton candy. Bring to room temperature for 30 minutes before serving. Store leftovers loosely covered with plastic wrap in the refrigerator for 3 to 4 days.

✴   ✴   ✴

NOTES: A little of the cotton candy flavoring goes a long way. It is easy to add more to taste. Look for brands online such as LorAnn oils. The cotton candy may begin to dissolve if it contacts moisture or humidity. To be safe, add the cotton candy just before serving.

Double-Vanilla Cake, Four Ways

FEATURED DECORATING TECHNIQUES: STRIPED BUTTERCREAM, PAINT SPLATTER, TEXTURED WATERCOLOR FROSTING, ZIGZAG PIPING

This easy vanilla cake comes together in just one bowl—no need to wait for butter to soften or be whipped with sugar. The light, springy texture pairs perfectly with fluffy vanilla buttercream. I've kept the cake recipe simple in order to show off even more ways to decorate with buttercream. I couldn't decide which design I liked best, so I'm sharing all four! MAKES ONE THREE-LAYER, 6-INCH (15-CM) CAKE; SERVES 10 TO 12

FOR THE VANILLA CAKE:

2¼ cups (280 g) all-purpose flour

1½ cups (300 g) granulated sugar

2½ teaspoons baking powder

½ teaspoon salt

1 cup (240 ml) buttermilk

3 large eggs

2 teaspoons pure vanilla extract

½ cup (1 stick/115 g) unsalted butter, melted and cooled

¼ cup (60 ml) canola or grapeseed oil

TO ASSEMBLE:

1 medium recipe Whipped Vanilla Buttercream (page 261); for the Zigzag Cake, use 1 large recipe

MAKE THE VANILLA CAKE

Preheat the oven to 350°F (175°C). Grease and flour three 6-inch (15-cm) cake pans.

Sift together the flour, sugar, baking powder, and salt into a large bowl. In a large measuring cup, whisk together the buttermilk, eggs, and vanilla. Create a well in the center of the flour mixture and pour in the buttermilk mixture. Whisk the ingredients together to combine. Pour in the melted butter and oil. Stir everything together until the batter is smooth. (If making the Paint-Splatter Cake, see below for instructions for tinting the batter before baking.)

Evenly divide the batter among the prepared pans. Bake for 26 to 30 minutes, until a toothpick inserted into the center of each cake comes out clean. Let the cakes cool on a wire rack for 10 to 15 minutes before removing from the pans. Allow the cakes to cool completely, right-side up, on the wire rack. Level the tops of the cakes with a long serrated knife as needed.

ASSEMBLE THE CAKE

Place one cake layer on a cake board or serving plate. Spread on ¾ cup (180 ml) of the buttercream with an offset spatula. Top with a second cake layer and repeat. Place the final cake layer on top.

Crumb coat the cake and chill in the refrigerator for 15 minutes.

Decorate using one of the options in the pages to follow.

All variations may be kept at room temperature until ready to serve. If assembled in advance, store the cake in a cake box in the refrigerator overnight. Bring to room temperature for 30 minutes before serving. Store leftovers loosely covered with plastic wrap in the refrigerator for 3 to 4 days.

STRIPED BUTTERCREAM CAKE

PAINT-SPLATTER CAKE

TEXTURED WATERCOLOR CAKE

ZIGZAG CAKE

Striped Buttercream Cake

Gel food coloring   ¼ cup (40 g) sprinkles

1 Set aside about ¾ cup (180 ml) of the buttercream. Divide the remaining buttercream in half and tint one portion the color of your choice. Fit two piping bags with round medium tips of the same size (or plastic couplers). Fill one with the plain buttercream and the other with the tinted buttercream.

2 Starting at the bottom of the cake, pipe a ring around the cake with the plain buttercream by holding the piping bag perpendicular to the side of the cake. Moving up the side of the cake, continue to pipe rings around the cake, alternating the colors.

3 Smooth the sides of the cake with an icing smoother to reveal the stripes. Only smooth the cake one full rotation at a time, cleaning the smoother between each rotation. Fill in any gaps with the coordinating color of buttercream and smooth again. The more the cake is smoothed, the more the stripes will blend together. Use an offset spatula to clean the top edge of the cake by pulling any excess frosting gently toward the center of the cake.

4 Fit a piping bag with a small star tip. Tint the reserved buttercream the color of your choice, then fill the piping bag. Pipe shell borders around the bottom and top of the cake (see page 275). Fill the center of the top of the cake with the sprinkles.

Paint-Splatter Cake

Gel food coloring   Canola oil, for thinning

4 ounces (115 g) Candy
 Melts of each color

1. Before baking the vanilla cake, evenly divide the batter among three bowls. Tint each bowl of batter a different color with gel food coloring. Pour a small amount of batter, one different color per pan, into the three prepared pans. Pour a second, different color into the center of each pan, on top of the first color. Repeat, making a bull's-eye effect, until all the batter has been used.

2. Use a wooden skewer or the tip of a paring knife to swirl the batter in each pan. Bake as directed.

3. Once assembled, smoothly frost the cake with the remaining buttercream.

4. For the paint-splatter design, put each color of Candy Melts in a separate bowl and microwave according to the directions on the package. Stir in a little bit of canola oil, ½ teaspoon at a time, to thin as needed.

5. Line your workspace with parchment paper. Dip a spoon into one of the melted candy coatings and swiftly fling the colored coating onto the cake. Create splatters of the various colors all around the top and sides of the cake.

*   *   *

NOTE: The harder you fling the splatters, the longer the streaks will be, but also the messier your work surface will become. Use caution when working around carpet. Once dry, the candy coating should scrape off most solid surfaces.

Textured Watercolor Cake

Gel food coloring

1 Smoothly frost the cake with a thin layer of buttercream and chill in the refrigerator for 15 minutes. Divide the remaining buttercream among three or four bowls and tint them various shades of coordinating colors.

2 Set the cake on a rotating cake stand. Load the edge of an icing smoother with a bit of colored buttercream. Gently press the buttercream-coated edge to the side of the cake and use the cake stand to spin the cake as you smear on the buttercream. Use the icing smoother and buttercream like spackling paste, adding and smearing on small amounts of the buttercream in layers. Continue until the entire cake is covered. Use an offset spatula to fill in any gaps and clean up the top edge of the cake. Repeat the process on the top of the cake, holding the icing smoother nearly perpendicular to the top of the cake. Keeping the cake cold will create the layered, textured effect. Chill the cake between layers of buttercream as needed.

Zigzag Cake

1 Place a small dollop of buttercream on top of the cake and smooth it with an offset spatula. Using the edge of an icing smoother or the back of a paring knife, gently score the sides of the crumb-coated cake in roughly 1-inch (2.5-cm) intervals.

2 Fill a piping bag fitted with a small star tip (Wilton #18) with buttercream. Holding the piping bag perpendicular to the side of the cake, use even pressure to pipe zigzags back and forth between the scored lines. Start at the bottom of the cake and work your way up. Continue around the cake until the sides are covered.

Classic Cakes with a Twist

Mixing traditional pastry techniques with modern designs is my favorite way to create new recipes. A contemporary Cannoli Cake boasts flavors of the classic pistachio and ricotta pastry, while a traditional tiramisu is transformed into a show-stopping Chocolate Tiramisu Cake, complete with homemade ladyfingers. Using fresh, flirty flavors like matcha and passion fruit update the century-old French Opera Cake in this chapter full of mouthwatering revitalized treats.

Chocolate Tiramisu Cake

FEATURED DECORATING TECHNIQUE: CHOCOLATE PETALS

Traditional tiramisu was my dad's favorite dessert—until I made this. The thin layers of chocolate genoise cake are soaked in rum-coffee syrup and layered with an eggless whipped mascarpone cream that is basically heaven. Homemade ladyfingers encase the cake, and dramatic chocolate petals take the presentation over the top.

This recipe makes just enough ladyfingers to go all the way around the cake, so try not to snack on too many before assembling the cake. Trust me, it will be difficult not to—they are so good! However, the recipe is super easy, so you should probably go ahead and just make a second batch while you're at it.

MAKES ONE FOUR-LAYER 8-INCH (20-CM) CAKE; SERVES 12 TO 16

FOR THE LADYFINGERS:

4 large eggs, separated

1 cup (200 g) granulated sugar

½ teaspoon vanilla bean paste, or seeds from ½ vanilla bean

1⅓ cups (165 g) all-purpose flour

1 tablespoon cornstarch

Confectioners' sugar, for dusting

FOR THE CHOCOLATE GENOISE CAKE:

6 large eggs

1¼ cups (250 g) granulated sugar

1 cup (125 g) all-purpose flour

¼ cup plus 2 tablespoons (35 g) unsweetened cocoa powder

2 tablespoons cornstarch

1 teaspoon instant espresso powder

4 tablespoons (½ stick/ 55 g) unsalted butter, melted and cooled

FOR THE RUM-COFFEE SOAK:

½ cup (100 g) granulated sugar

2 teaspoons instant espresso powder

⅓ cup (80 ml) dark rum (see Notes)

FOR THE WHIPPED MASCARPONE CREAM:

1¼ cups (290 g) mascarpone

1¼ cups (300 ml) heavy cream

⅓ cup (65 g) granulated sugar

1 teaspoon vanilla bean paste, or seeds from ½ vanilla bean

TO ASSEMBLE AND DECORATE:

½ recipe Whipped Cream (page 263)

About 1½ cups (360 ml) chocolate petals (see page 152)

MAKE THE LADYFINGERS

Preheat the oven to 350°F (175°C). Line two baking sheets with parchment paper. Fit a piping bag with a ½-inch (12-mm) round tip.

In the bowl of a stand mixer fitted with the whisk attachment, whisk the egg whites on low speed until they begin to foam, form small, tight bubbles, and turn opaque. Over the course of about 1 minute, gradually increase the speed to medium-high while slowly adding ¼ cup (50 g) of the granulated sugar. Mix on medium-high until stiff peaks form. Stop the mixer and scrape the whipped egg whites into a clean bowl.

Put the egg yolks, the remaining ¾ cup (150 g) granulated sugar, and the vanilla bean paste in the mixer bowl (no need to wash it). Whip on high until the mixture is pale in color and thick, 3 to 4 minutes. Stop the mixer and gently fold the whipped egg whites into the egg yolk mixture by hand.

Once the egg mixtures are combined, sift the flour and cornstarch into the bowl. Gently fold until the batter is combined. Try not to deflate or overmix the batter.

Spoon the batter into the prepared piping bag. Pipe the batter onto the prepared baking sheets into 4-inch-long (10-cm) "fingers," spaced about 1 inch (2.5 cm) apart. Sift the confectioners' sugar over the piped batter.

Bake for 12 to 15 minutes, until the ladyfingers are firm to the touch. Set the baking sheets on wire racks and let the ladyfingers cool completely before carefully removing them from the parchment paper. If not using immediately, store in an airtight container or zip-top bag at room temperature for up to 3 days.

MAKE THE CHOCOLATE GENOISE CAKE

Preheat the oven to 350°F (175°C). Grease and flour two 8-inch (20-cm) cake pans and line the bottoms with parchment paper.

Put the eggs and sugar in the bowl of a stand mixer. Gently whisk by hand until just combined. In a medium saucepan, bring an inch or two (2.5 to 5 cm) of water to a simmer over medium-low heat. Place the mixer bowl on top of the saucepan to create a double boiler (be sure the bottom of the bowl does not touch the water). Heat the egg mixture, stirring intermittently, until warm to the touch or 100°F (38°C) on a candy thermometer.

Carefully affix the mixer bowl to the stand mixer (it may be hot) and fit the mixer with the whisk attachment. Whip the egg mixture on high speed until it triples in volume and is pale in color and thick, about 8 minutes. To test, stop the mixer and remove the whisk. Draw a figure eight with the batter dripping from the whisk. The batter should hold its shape for just long enough for you to draw the "8."

Sift the flour, cocoa powder, cornstarch, and espresso powder into the egg mixture. Gently fold to thoroughly combine.

In a separate bowl, stir together about 1 cup (240 ml) of the egg-flour mixture and the melted butter. Pour the butter mixture back into the bowl with the remaining egg-flour mixture and gently fold to thoroughly combine.

Evenly divide the batter between the prepared pans and bake for 18 to 20 minutes, until the tops of the cakes spring back when gently touched and a toothpick inserted into the center of each cake comes out clean. Run a thin paring knife around the inside edges of the cake pans and let the cakes cool on a wire rack for 10 to 15 minutes before removing from the pans. Allow the cakes to cool completely, right-side up, on the wire rack before removing the parchment. Carefully cut the cakes in half horizontally with a long serrated knife to create 4 even layers.

MAKE THE RUM-COFFEE SOAK

In a small saucepan, combine the sugar, espresso powder, and ½ cup (120 ml) water and bring to a boil. Reduce the heat to low and simmer for about 5 minutes. Remove from the heat and stir in the rum.

MAKE THE WHIPPED MASCARPONE CREAM

In a large bowl using a handheld mixer or in the bowl of a stand mixer fitted with the whisk attachment, whip the mascarpone, cream, sugar, and vanilla on high speed until the cream holds soft peaks. Turn the mixer off and finish whisking by hand with a balloon whisk until thick. Do not overmix or the cream may become grainy.

ASSEMBLE AND DECORATE THE CAKE

Generously brush the cake layers with the rum soak. Place one cake layer on a cake board or serving plate. Spread ¾ to 1 cup (180 to 240 ml) of the mascarpone cream on top with an offset spatula. Top with the second cake layer and repeat with the remaining layers of cake. Use the remaining whipped mascarpone cream to crumb coat the cake. Wrap in plastic wrap and chill in the refrigerator for 4 to 8 hours.

Before serving, carefully trim the bottoms of the ladyfingers with a serrated knife so that they are all equal in length. They should be slightly longer than the height of the filled cake. Gently press the ladyfingers to the sides of the crumb-coated cake, with the cut-side ends on the cake board or serving plate.

Fill a piping bag fitted with a medium or large star tip with the whipped cream. Pipe rosettes on top of the cake. Finish the cake with a mound of chocolate petals in the center (see Notes and page 152).

Store leftovers covered with plastic wrap or in a cake box in the refrigerator for up to 3 days. Serve within 30 minutes of removing from the refrigerator..

*   *   *

NOTES: The soak can be made without the rum. For a plain coffee soak, increase the water and sugar to ¾ cup each (180 ml water and 150 g sugar) and the instant espresso powder to 2½ teaspoons.

Add the chocolate petals just before serving, after the cake has set up in the refrigerator. "Practice" or leftover chocolate petals can be saved in a zip-top plastic bag for your next baking project that calls for melted chocolate.

Working with Chocolate

* * *

TO MAKE CHOCOLATE PETALS: Hold a large block of milk chocolate or gianduja (see Note, page 168) in one hand. Using the sharp edge of a round metal cookie or biscuit cutter (2 to 3 inches/5 to 7.5 cm in diameter), scrape along the length of the block of chocolate, pulling toward your body and applying a bit of pressure. It may take a few tries using various amounts of pressure. The chocolate will begin to curl. The petals will be quite delicate, so consider creating them directly over the top of the finished cake for maximum volume and minimal breakage. If needed, carefully manipulate the curls with your fingertips to create tighter petals/curls.

If the chocolate does not curl and only breaks, gently heat it in the microwave at 50% power in 15-second intervals, testing it after each, until it is soft enough to form curls.

TO MAKE CHOCOLATE SHAVINGS: Hold a block of chocolate in one hand. With your other hand, use a bench scraper to firmly press/scrape away from your body along the length of the block. If the chocolate is too hard, gently microwave it at 50% power in 15-second intervals, testing after each, until soft enough to form fine shavings. Do not melt the chocolate. (See page 177.)

FOR SOMETHING IN BETWEEN SIMPLE SHAVINGS AND VOLUMINOUS PETALS, run a vegetable peeler down the length of a bar of chocolate to make chocolate curls. Warm the chocolate bar as you would for making chocolate shavings or as needed.

Coffee Cheesecake

FEATURED DECORATING TECHNIQUE:
CHOCOLATE PIPING

I am so lucky that not only does my brother happen to be one of my dearest friends, but he also lives down the street. Being related, I guess it's no surprise that he shares my affinity for sweet treats. We spend many afternoons together, whether on the hunt for the best chocolate chip cookie, driving around town looking for the perfect slice of pie, or exploring new cafés and consuming large amounts of coffee. On the days that we don't have time to fight traffic, there is usually something sweet that I've just baked up for us to enjoy at home—this chocolate-glazed coffee cheesecake is one of his favorites

MAKES ONE 9-INCH (23-CM) ROUND CHEESECAKE;
SERVES 12 TO 16

Ingredients

FOR THE CHOCOLATE COOKIE CRUST:

2 cups (8 oz/240 g) chocolate wafer cookie crumbs

6 tablespoons (¾ stick/ 85 g) unsalted butter, melted and cooled

2 tablespoons brown sugar

FOR THE COFFEE CHEESECAKE:

2 pounds (900 g) cream cheese, at room temperature

1⅓ cups (265 g) granulated sugar

½ teaspoon salt

2 teaspoons instant espresso

2 tablespoons coffee liqueur

2 teaspoons vanilla bean paste or pure vanilla extract

3 large eggs, at room temperature

1 large egg yolk, at room temperature

1½ cups (360 ml) sour cream, at room temperature

4 to 6 cups (960 ml to 1.4 L) boiling water for the pan

FOR THE CHOCOLATE GANACHE GLAZE:

7 ounces (200 g) semisweet chocolate, chopped

6 tablespoons (¾ stick/ 85 g) unsalted butter, diced

¼ cup (60 ml) heavy cream

2 tablespoons corn syrup

TO DECORATE:

1 ounce (28 g) white chocolate

1 ounce (28 g) milk chocolate

MAKE THE CHOCOLATE COOKIE CRUST

Preheat the oven to 325°F (160°C).

In a medium bowl, stir together the cookie crumbs, melted butter, and brown sugar until uniformly moist. Tip the mixture into a 9-inch (23-cm) springform pan. Use the bottom of a flat measuring cup or drinking glass to evenly and firmly press the mixture into the bottom of the pan. The crust should be tight and compact.

Bake for 12 minutes. Let cool completely on a wire rack before filling.

MAKE THE COFFEE CHEESECAKE

Turn the oven up to 350°F (175°C).

In the bowl of a stand mixer fitted with the paddle attachment (or in a large bowl using a handheld mixer), beat the cream cheese on medium-low speed for 6 to 8 minutes. You will need to mix this batter for longer than feels natural. Stop the mixer every few minutes to scrape down the sides and bottom of the bowl. Add the sugar and salt. Mix for 4 to 5 minutes more, until the mixture is completely smooth. Stop the mixer and scrape down the bowl.

Meanwhile, stir the instant espresso into the coffee liqueur to dissolve. If needed, microwave the mixture for about 10 seconds, then stir until smooth.

With the mixer running on low, add the vanilla to the cream cheese mixture. Slowly add the eggs and egg yolk one at a time, mixing until each is incorporated before adding the next. Incorporating them slowly will help the cheesecake avoid cracking after baking.

With the mixer running on medium-low, add the sour cream and espresso mixture. Mix for 2 to 3 minutes, until the mixture is smooth.

Spoon the cheesecake into the cooled crust and smooth the top with an offset spatula. Wrap a double layer of foil, shiny side facing out, around the sides of the pan to keep the cheesecake from browning too quickly.

Place a roasting pan on the bottom rack of the oven. Carefully pour the boiling water into the pan, making sure it does not overflow. Set a rack on the next rung above the roasting pan and place the cheesecake on the rack. Bake for 1 hour, without opening the oven. At 1 hour, open the oven and carefully jiggle the pan. The cheesecake is done when the sides are puffed and cooked, but there is still movement in the center. If it isn't, bake for 5 to 10 minutes more, until done.

To cool the cheesecake without cracking, turn off the oven and prop the door open with a wooden spoon. Let the cheesecake cool in the oven for 1 hour. Remove the cheesecake from the oven and let cool on the counter for 30 to 60 minutes. Wrap the cheesecake in plastic wrap and refrigerate for at least 2 hours or up to overnight.

Carefully run a thin knife around the inside of the pan before unlocking and removing the springform ring.

MAKE THE CHOCOLATE GANACHE GLAZE

Put the chocolate, butter, cream, and corn syrup in the top portion of a double boiler (or in a heatproof bowl set over a saucepan of simmering water; see page 14). Heat until the chocolate and butter begin to melt. Remove from the heat and stir until smooth and well combined. Use the ganache glaze while it is still warm.

ASSEMBLE THE CHEESECAKE

Place the cooled cheesecake on a wire rack set over a baking sheet. Pour the warm glaze over the top of the cheesecake. Use an offset spatula to carefully spread the glaze on the top and on the sides as needed. Use as few strokes as possible. Gently rap the wire rack on the counter a few times to smooth the glaze and pop any air bubbles. Let the glaze set for about 30 minutes.

DECORATE THE CHEESECAKE

In separate bowls, gently melt both the white and milk chocolates in the microwave at 50% power in 20-second intervals until smooth. Pour them into separate disposable piping bags. Snip the ends of the piping bags to create very small openings. To decorate the cheesecake with the chocolate piping technique, use quick motions to pipe the melted chocolate across the cheesecake. The faster you move the piping bag, the straighter the lines will be. Practice on a piece of parchment paper, if needed. Continue to pipe organic lines until your desired design is achieved.

Serve within 30 minutes of assembling. To slice, warm a large chef's knife under hot water and wipe dry before cutting into the cheesecake. Clean and warm the knife (as needed) between slices. Store leftovers loosely covered in plastic wrap in the refrigerator for up to 3 days.

Cannoli Cake

FEATURED DECORATING TECHNIQUE: LOOPY RUFFLE PIPING

The crunch of a freshly filled cannoli is incredibly satisfying, but the extra equipment and frying involved makes re-creating them at home difficult. This cake takes all those great cannoli flavors and turns them into a layered beauty that you can easily make in your own kitchen. Ricotta keeps the cake layers extra moist and the filling perfectly tangy. This cake is missing that freshly fried crunch, but it more than makes up for it with cloud-like milk chocolate Swiss meringue buttercream. MAKES ONE FOUR-LAYER 8-INCH (20-CM) CAKE; SERVES 12 TO 16

FOR THE RICOTTA CREAM FILLING

1⅓ cups (325 g) full-fat ricotta, drained, if needed (see Notes)

5 ounces (145 g) cream cheese, at room temperature

4 to 4½ cups (500 to 565 g) confectioners' sugar, sifted if needed

6 tablespoons (¾ stick/ 85 g) unsalted butter, at room temperature

2 teaspoons pure vanilla extract

Pinch of ground cinnamon, or to taste

FOR THE CANNOLI CAKE

3 cups plus 2 tablespoons (390 g) all-purpose flour

2 teaspoons baking powder

½ teaspoon baking soda

½ teaspoon salt

½ teaspoon ground cinnamon

1 cup (245 g) full-fat ricotta, drained if needed (see Notes)

1 cup (240 ml) whole milk

2 cups (400 g) granulated sugar

Finely grated zest of 1 orange

1 cup (2 sticks/225 g) unsalted butter, at room temperature

2 teaspoons pure vanilla extract

3 large eggs

½ cup (65 g) finely chopped pistachios

3 ounces (85 g) dark chocolate, finely chopped (½ cup)

FOR THE MILK CHOCOLATE BUTTERCREAM:

1 medium recipe Swiss Meringue Buttercream (page 262)

5 ounces (140 g) milk chocolate, melted and cooled

TO DECORATE:

Chocolate sprinkles (optional)

MAKE THE RICOTTA CREAM FILLING

In a food processor, combine the ricotta and cream cheese and process until smooth. Add 2 cups (250 g) of the confectioners' sugar and process until thick.

In the bowl of a stand mixer fitted with the paddle attachment, beat the butter until smooth. Add the ricotta mixture and mix on medium-low speed until smooth. Add 2 cups (250 g) of the confectioners' sugar, the vanilla, and cinnamon. Mix on medium-low until combined. Add the remaining ½ cup (65 g) confectioners' sugar as needed, ¼ cup (30 g) at a time, and mix until thick and creamy. The ricotta cream filling will be slightly looser than a whipped buttercream frosting. Chill in the refrigerator until it is thick and spreadable, at least 1 hour.

MAKE THE CANNOLI CAKE

Preheat the oven to 350°F (175°C). Grease and flour two 8-inch (20-cm) cake pans.

Sift together the flour, baking powder, baking soda, salt, and cinnamon into a large bowl. In a small bowl or liquid measuring cup, combine the ricotta and milk.

In a small bowl, rub the sugar and orange zest together between your fingertips until fragrant.

In the bowl of a stand mixer fitted with the paddle attachment, beat the butter on medium speed for 2 minutes. Add the sugar-zest mixture and mix on medium-high until light and fluffy, 3 to 5 minutes. Stop the mixer and scrape down the bowl.

Turn the mixer to medium-low and add the vanilla. Add the eggs one at a time, mixing until each is incorporated before adding the next. Mix until thoroughly combined. Stop the mixer and scrape down the bowl.

Turn the mixer to low and add the flour mixture in three batches, alternating with the milk mixture, beginning and ending with the flour mixture. After the last streaks of the flour mixture are combined, mix on medium for no more than 30 seconds. Stop the mixer and fold in the pistachios and chocolate.

Evenly divide the batter between the prepared pans. Bake for 35 to 40 minutes, until a toothpick inserted into the center of each cake comes out clean. Let the cakes cool on a wire rack for 10 to 15 minutes before removing from the pans. Allow the cakes to cool completely, right-side up, on the wire rack. Level the tops of the cakes with a long serrated knife as needed, then cut the cakes in half horizontally to create 4 even layers.

MAKE THE MILK CHOCOLATE BUTTERCREAM

In the bowl of a stand mixer fitted with the paddle attachment, whip the buttercream until silky smooth. Add the melted chocolate and mix until combined.

ASSEMBLE THE CAKE

Place one cake layer on a cake board or serving plate. Fill a piping bag fitted with a plain round tip with the milk chocolate buttercream. Pipe a ring around the top edge of the cake to create a frosting "dam." Fill the dam with one-third of the ricotta cream and spread with an offset spatula or the back of a spoon. Top with a second cake layer and repeat. Repeat with the third cake layer, then place the final layer on top.

Crumb coat the cake with buttercream and chill in the refrigerator for 15 minutes.

DECORATE THE CAKE

Frost the top of the cake with buttercream. To decorate the cake with the loopy ruffle piping technique, fill a piping bag fitted with a petal tip (Wilton #104) with the buttercream. Hold the piping bag at a slight angle, narrowed side of the tip pointing away from the cake. Starting at the bottom of the cake, pipe loops of buttercream by moving the piping bag in a spiral motion all the way up the side of the cake. Overlapping the continuous loops will create the ruffled effect. Continue to pipe columns of spiral ruffles all the way around the cake. Be sure that the buttercream is not too soft or it will not hold its shape as well. For more consistent piping, aim for the same number of loops in each column. Finish the top of the cake with chocolate sprinkles, if desired.

Place in a cake box and chill in the refrigerator for at least 1 hour for the filling to set up. Before serving, let come to room temperature for 30 minutes, then slice and serve. Store leftovers loosely covered with plastic wrap or in a cake box in the refrigerator for up to 3 to 4 days.

NOTES: Depending on the brand of ricotta you use, it may need to be drained of excess liquid. To drain the ricotta, line a sieve with cheesecloth or paper towels and set it over a bowl. Put the ricotta in the sieve and refrigerate for 4 to 8 hours. Discard the liquid that collects in the bowl.

Adding the ricotta to the food processor first helps smooth it out without making the filling too runny.

Peanut Butter Éclairs

FEATURED DECORATING TECHNIQUES:
CHOCOLATE GLAZE, GILDED CHOCOLATE PEARLS,
CHOCOLATE PIPING

*My husband Brett's favorite dessert of all time
is a Long John doughnut. If you are like me and
frying yeasted dough isn't your strong suit, then
try making éclairs! Similar to a cream-filled
doughnut, an éclair has a higher ratio of custard
to dough and is baked, not fried, to perfection.
Pâte à choux, the thick batter used to make éclairs
and cream puffs, is a classic example of French
pastry, which I have given a more American flavor
profile here.* MAKES ABOUT 20 ÉCLAIRS

FOR THE PEANUT BUTTER PASTRY CREAM:

¼ cup plus 2 tablespoons (90 ml) creamy peanut butter (not natural)

2 tablespoons unsalted butter, diced

1½ cups (360 ml) whole milk

1 tablespoon plus ⅓ cup (75 g) granulated sugar

3 large egg yolks

2 tablespoons cornstarch

1 tablespoon all-purpose flour

1 teaspoon pure vanilla extract

Pinch of salt

FOR THE ÉCLAIR SHELLS:

½ cup (1 stick/115 g) unsalted butter, diced

½ cup (120 ml) whole milk

¾ teaspoon salt

1 teaspoon granulated sugar

1 cup (125 g) all-purpose flour

4 or 5 large eggs

FOR THE CHOCOLATE GLAZE:

4 ounces (115 g) dark chocolate, chopped

4 tablespoons (½ stick/ 55 g) unsalted butter, diced

1 tablespoon corn syrup

TO DECORATE:

2 ounces (55 g) white chocolate, melted and cooled

Crispy chocolate pearls

Gold luster dust

MAKE THE PEANUT BUTTER PASTRY CREAM

Follow the method for Vanilla Pastry Cream (page 264) using the quantities listed here (omit the vanilla bean), adding the peanut butter to the butter in a heatproof bowl in the first step, and adding 1 tablespoon of the sugar to the milk mixture. Add the salt with the vanilla extract at the end.

MAKE THE ÉCLAIR SHELLS

Preheat the oven to 350°F (175°C). Line two baking sheets with parchment paper or silicone baking mats.

In a medium saucepan, combine the butter, milk, salt, sugar, and ½ cup (120 ml) water. Bring to a boil over medium-high heat and cook until the butter has melted completely. Remove from the heat.

Dump all the flour into the butter mixture and stir vigorously with a wooden spoon. Place the saucepan back over medium heat and cook, stirring continuously, until the batter balls up in the center and a film forms on the bottom of the pan, 3 to 5 minutes.

Transfer the batter to the bowl of a stand mixer fitted with the paddle attachment. Mix on low speed until the batter is just barely warm to the touch. Meanwhile, whisk 4 of the eggs together in a separate bowl.

Once the batter has cooled, turn the mixer to medium-low and slowly add the eggs in about three additions, allowing each addition to be completely incorporated before adding the next.

Stop the mixer and check the batter. Use the tip of the paddle attachment to scoop up a small portion of the batter and then lift it out of the bowl. A "V" of batter should hang off the tip of the paddle. The batter should be thick, smooth, and pipeable. If it is too thick, whisk the remaining egg in a small bowl, then add half to the batter and mix until completely incorporated. Check the consistency again; if needed, add the remaining ½ egg and repeat.

Fill a piping bag fitted with a medium-large star tip (Wilton #88) with the batter. Holding the piping bag at a 45-degree angle, pipe 4- to 5-inch-long (10- to 13-cm) "fingers" of batter onto the prepared baking sheets, spacing them about 1 inch (2.5 cm) apart. If the batter is sticky and won't release from the end of the piping bag, use kitchen shears to cleanly snip the batter from the piping tip. Use a clean, damp finger to pat down any tails that may have formed.

Bake for 30 to 35 minutes, rotating the baking sheets at the 20-minute mark. When done, remove one sheet at a time and quickly poke the ends of each éclair shell with a wooden skewer. Turn the oven off and place the baking sheets back in the oven. Prop open the door with a wooden spoon and let the éclair shells cool in the oven for 15 minutes.

When done baking, they will be deep golden in color and the centers should be dry and hollow.

FILL THE ÉCLAIRS

Stir the chilled pastry cream to loosen. Fill a piping bag fitted with a Bismarck tip (or a small round tip) with the pastry cream. Insert the tip into the bottom of an éclair shell near one of the ends. Angle the tip toward the center of the éclair and gently squeeze the piping bag to fill the éclair. You will feel the éclair expanding in your hand as it fills up. Take out the tip and repeat in the center and opposite end of the éclair until it is full of pastry cream. Chill the filled eclairs in the refrigerator as you make the chocolate glaze.

MAKE THE CHOCOLATE GLAZE

Put the dark chocolate, butter, and corn syrup in the top portion of a double boiler (or in a heatproof bowl set over a saucepan of simmering water; see page 14). Heat until the chocolate and butter begin to melt. Remove from the heat and stir until smooth and well combined. Place the glaze in a shallow dish, wide enough for an éclair to fit inside.

Submerge the top of an éclair in the glaze so the glaze comes halfway up the side of the shell. Lift the éclair up and tip it upright, allowing the excess glaze to drip off smoothly. Use a clean finger to wipe the edges. Place glaze-side up on a cutting board or piece of parchment paper. Repeat with the remaining éclairs. Rewarm the glaze as needed.

DECORATE THE ÉCLAIRS

For the chocolate piping, fill a disposable piping bag with the melted white chocolate. Snip off the tip of the bag and pipe diagonal lines across the bottom half of each éclair. The faster you pipe, the straighter the chocolate lines (see Coffee Cheesecake, page 154). To make the gilded chocolate pearls, place the crispy chocolate pearls in a small bowl and sprinkle in the luster dust. Gently shake the bowl around until the pearls are covered in gold. Using your fingers or clean tweezers, place the gold crispy pearls on top of the éclairs.

Serve immediately or chill loosely covered in plastic in the refrigerator. Éclairs are best eaten within a few hours of assembly. The shells and pastry cream may be made ahead of time and stored separately. The shells will stay crisp in an airtight container at room temperature for a couple of days. The pastry cream can be stored in the refrigerator for up to 3 days.

Pâte à Choux

*   *   *

MADE FROM STAPLES LIKE MILK, BUTTER, EGGS, AND FLOUR, the soft, velvety batter is piped and then baked. Pâte à choux contains a significant amount of liquid (from the milk and eggs), and once these liquids hit the heat of the oven, they steam and "puff" up the batter. At the same time, the proteins in the eggs uncoil, stretch, and help support the signature hollow centers found in cream puffs and éclairs.

THE NUMBER OF EGGS IN A PÂTE À CHOUX IS NOT ALWAYS SET. Why, you ask? Just like adding water to pie dough, the absorption of the eggs depends on the brand of flour, humidity, and the actual size of the eggs being used. The goal is to add as many eggs as the batter will accommodate and still be able to hold its shape when piped. Remember, it's okay to not use the last egg.

THE ONLY REAL DIFFERENCE BETWEEN CREAM PUFFS AND ÉCLAIRS IS THEIR SHAPE. To make cream puffs, pipe the batter into puffy, 2-inch (5 cm) wide mounds and bake and cool as directed for the éclairs, reducing the baking time to 25 to 30 minutes. One batch of pâte à choux and one large recipe Vanilla Pastry Cream (page 264) will yield 12 to 14 large cream puffs. Assemble and store the same as the éclairs.

IN ADDITION TO ÉCLAIRS AND CREAM PUFFS, PÂTE À CHOUX IS USED FOR A VARIETY OF OTHER DESSERTS, TOO! Piped into rings and fried, it becomes French crullers. Mix the batter with cheese and you get gougères. Cut and fill puffs with ice cream and cover in chocolate drizzle (page 120) for classic profiteroles. Or glue mini cream puffs together with caramel to create a show-stopping croquembouche!

French Opera Cake, Two Ways

French opera cakes are small individual cakes made of soaked sponge, ganache, and buttercream. Traditionally, the cakes are flavored with chocolate and coffee, but I've given new life to the century-old classic by using passion fruit and matcha in two different modern variations. They do take a bit of time to assemble, but the end results are certainly impressive and delicious. **MAKES 16 INDIVIDUAL CAKES**

FOR THE SPONGE CAKE:

4 large eggs

⅔ cup (85 g) confectioners' sugar

1 teaspoon pure vanilla extract

1 cup (115 g) almond flour

½ cup (65 g) all-purpose flour

1 teaspoon baking powder

⅛ teaspoon salt

2 tablespoons unsalted butter, melted and cooled

4 large egg whites

¼ cup (50 g) granulated sugar

1 teaspoon cream of tartar

MAKE THE SPONGE CAKE

Preheat the oven to 375°F (190°C). Grease an 18 by 13-inch (46 by 33-cm) pan and line it with parchment paper, letting the paper overhang the edges by a couple of inches.

In the bowl of a stand mixer fitted with the whisk attachment, beat together the eggs, confectioners' sugar, and vanilla on medium-high speed for about 5 minutes, until thick, pale ribbons form. Stop the mixer and sift in the flours, baking powder, and salt. Fold in by hand until thoroughly combined. Stir in the melted butter. Transfer the batter to a separate bowl and set aside.

Clean and thoroughly dry the mixer bowl. Fit the mixer with the whisk attachment and begin beating the egg whites on medium-low until they begin to foam, form small, tight bubbles, and turn opaque. Over the course of a couple of minutes, gradually increase the speed to high while slowly adding the granulated sugar and cream of tartar. Mix on high until medium-stiff peaks form.

Carefully but deliberately fold the egg whites into the batter.

Pour the batter into the prepared pan and evenly spread it out with an offset spatula. The layer of batter will be quite thin. Bake for 8 to 10 minutes, until the cake springs back to the touch. Let cool in the pan on a wire rack for about 10 minutes, then carefully use the overhanging parchment paper to remove the cake from the pan.

Fill, assemble, and decorate as described in the variations on the following pages.

If eating the cake the same day as assembled, store it at room temperature until ready to serve. If assembled in advance, store in a cake box in the refrigerator overnight. Bring to room temperature for 30 minutes before serving. Store leftovers loosely covered with plastic wrap in the refrigerator for 3 to 4 days.

Cake may be baked in two 9 by 13-inch (23 by 33 cm) pans. Dimensions of cut cake slices will differ.

Passion Fruit French Opera Cake

**FOR THE GIANDUJA
GANACHE:**

8 ounces (225 g) gianduja
(see Note on page 167),
chopped

4 ounces (115 g) dark
chocolate, chopped

⅔ cup (160 ml) heavy
cream

**FOR THE PASSION FRUIT
BUTTERCREAM:**

1 medium recipe Swiss
Meringue Buttercream
(page 262)

4 to 6 tablespoons (60
to 90 ml) thawed
frozen passion fruit
concentrate, or to taste

**FOR THE COFFEE SIMPLE
SYRUP:**

½ cup (120 ml) brewed
coffee

2 tablespoons granulated
sugar

MAKE THE GIANDUJA GANACHE

Place the chocolates in a heatproof bowl.

In a small saucepan, bring the cream just to a simmer
over medium heat. Pour the cream over the chocolate.
Let stand for 30 seconds, then slowly whisk until
smooth and well combined. Let cool, either at room
temperature or in the refrigerator, stirring often,
until thick and spreadable, about 2 hours at room
temperature or 30 minutes in the refrigerator.

MAKE THE PASSION FRUIT BUTTERCREAM

In the bowl of a stand mixer fitted with the paddle
attachment, mix the buttercream until silky smooth.
Add 4 tablespoons (60 ml) of the passion fruit
concentrate and mix until combined. Taste and add
the remaining 2 tablespoons passion fruit concentrate,
or to taste.

MAKE THE COFFEE SIMPLE SYRUP

In small saucepan, stir together the coffee and sugar
over medium heat until the sugar has dissolved. Allow
to cool before using.

ASSEMBLE THE CAKE

Cut the cooled cake into three even rectangles, 5½ by
12 inches (14 by 30 cm) each. Brush the simple syrup
over each cake. Place one cake layer on a cutting
board. Spread on ½ cup (120 ml) of the ganache with
an offset spatula. Chill in the refrigerator for 5 minutes
to set. Spread 1 cup (240 ml) of the buttercream over
the ganache with an offset spatula. Top with a second
cake layer and repeat. Place the final cake layer on
top and spread on the remaining ganache. Chill in the
refrigerator for about 30 minutes before slicing.

Use a long chef's knife to cut the cake into 16 even
slices, about 1¼ by 3 inches (3 by 8 cm) each. If
needed, between cuts, run the blade under hot water,
dry it, and then slice.

DECORATE THE CAKE

Fill a piping bag fitted with a small petal tip (such as
Wilton #103) with the remaining buttercream. Hold
the piping bag so the opening of the tip is parallel with
the short side of one slice of the cake, narrowed side
of the tip facing out. Pipe rows of overlapping ruffles
on top of the cake slices (see page 275), or decorate
as desired.

*   *   *

NOTE: Gianduja is a creamy Italian chocolate
made from dark chocolate and hazelnut paste.
Look for it at Whole Foods, European or
specialty grocery stores, or online. Substitute
equal parts milk chocolate and semisweet
chocolate if it's unavailable.

Matcha French Opera Cake

FOR THE DARK CHOCOLATE GANACHE:

9 ounces (255 g) dark chocolate, finely chopped

¾ cup (180 ml) heavy cream

FOR THE MATCHA BUTTERCREAM:

2 to 3 tablespoons matcha tea powder, or to taste

2 to 3 tablespoons warm water

1 medium recipe Swiss Meringue Buttercream (page 262)

FOR THE VANILLA SIMPLE SYRUP:

½ cup (100 g) granulated sugar

½ teaspoon vanilla bean paste

MAKE THE DARK CHOCOLATE GANACHE

Put the chopped chocolate in a heatproof bowl.

In a small saucepan, bring the cream just to a simmer over medium heat. Remove from the heat and pour the cream over the chocolate. Let stand for 30 seconds, then slowly whisk until smooth and well combined. Let cool, either at room temperature or in the refrigerator, stirring often, until thick and spreadable, about 2 hours at room temperature or 30 minutes in the refrigerator.

MAKE THE MATCHA BUTTERCREAM

In a small bowl, dissolve the matcha in the warm water, stirring to form a paste.

In the bowl of a stand mixer fitted with the paddle attachment, mix the buttercream until silky smooth. Add the matcha paste and mix until combined.

MAKE THE VANILLA SIMPLE SYRUP

In a small saucepan, combine the sugar and ½ cup (120 ml) water. Heat over medium heat, stirring, until the sugar has dissolved and the mixture is warmed through. Remove from the heat and stir in the vanilla. Allow to cool before using.

Assemble the cake as directed in the Passion Fruit variation, opposite.

DECORATE THE CAKES

Fill a piping bag fitted with a small star tip (Wilton #18) with the buttercream. Pipe interlocking shells in a "V" pattern down the length of the top of the cake slices (follow the weave piping instructions on page 275, but use a small star tip, not a petal tip), or decorate as desired.

＊ ＊ ＊

NOTE: If the ganache splits and/or appears oily, stir in a bit of warmed cream, a teaspoon at a time, until the ganache is silky smooth. If that does not work, warm a couple tablespoons of corn syrup in the microwave for 10 seconds. Add a tablespoon of the "broken" ganache into the hot corn syrup and stir until smooth. Continue adding in small amounts of the broken ganache until smooth and shiny.

Mix-and-Match Meringues

FEATURED DECORATING TECHINQUES: STAR, KISS, AND ROSETTE PIPING

Whether balanced on an elaborate cake or served on their own, meringues are mystical little treats. It is amazing how the incredibly simple ingredients transform into airy, slightly sweet, crispy gems. They are possibly the lightest of all cookies and pastries. I love how cute these two-bite meringues are, but you can bake them in sizes ranging from mini-kisses to clouds as big as your head. Once you master making French meringue (an important skill for many recipes), you'll enjoy mixing and matching these melt-in-your-mouth delights using various colors, flavors, and textures. MAKES ABOUT 36 MERINGUES

3 large egg whites

¾ cup (150 g) granulated sugar

¼ teaspoon cream of tartar

½ teaspoon vanilla bean paste or pure vanilla extract

Preheat the oven to 225°F (110°C). Line two baking sheets with parchment paper.

In the bowl of a stand mixer fitted with the whisk attachment, begin beating the egg whites on low speed until they begin to foam, form small, tight bubbles, and turn opaque. Over the course of 1 to 2 minutes, gradually increase the speed to medium while slowly adding the sugar and cream of tartar. Turn the mixer to medium-high and beat until glossy, stiff peaks form. Add the vanilla and mix until incorporated.

Fill a piping bag fitted with the piping tip of your choice with the meringue. Pipe the meringue onto the prepared baking sheets as kisses, rosettes, or small clouds (see page 136). Garnish as desired and bake for 1 hour to 1 hour 15 minutes, until the meringues are crisp on the outside and easily peel off the parchment paper.

Store in an airtight container at room temperature for up to 5 days.

Variations

FLAVOR ADD-INS: Add ½ teaspoon vanilla bean seeds, grated citrus zest, almond extract, or rose extract at the end of mixing, or sift 3 to 4 tablespoons unsweetened cocoa powder and fold into the finished meringue before baking.

CRUNCHY TOPPERS: Sprinkle chopped pistachios, crispy chocolate pearls, sprinkles, freeze-dried raspberries, or chopped chocolate on top of the piped meringue before baking.

SWIRLS: Dollop ½ teaspoon berry jam on top of the piped meringue and swirl with a toothpick before baking.

STRIPED KISSES: Before adding the meringue to the piping bag, partially invert the piping bag and paint stripes on the inside using a clean paintbrush and gel food coloring. Fill the bag with meringue, pipe, and bake.

GOLD SPLATTERS: Mix gold luster dust with a tiny bit of vodka or other clear alcohol to create a thin paste. Dip a clean paintbrush into the gold mixture and flick it over the baked meringues (see page 69).

Tuxedo Checkerboard Cake

FEATURED DECORATING TECHNIQUES: CHECKERBOARD CAKE, SMOOTH FROSTING, SHELL PIPING

This unassuming cake with its modest exterior and subtle piping has a secret. The real party is inside the cake! The two-toned tuxedo cake is made up of contrasting white and dark chocolate cake. When served, each slice reveals a dramatic checkerboard of cake and buttercream that is equally whimsical as it is elegant. From Mad Hatter tea parties to black-tie events, this cake is sure to amaze.

This ornate cake is way easier to assemble than you might think. You won't need a degree in architecture or any special cake pans, but you'll look like a culinary wizard! The same technique would work with any two cake recipes, as long as the cakes are trimmed to the same height, share a similar texture, and are different colors. MAKES ONE FOUR-LAYER 8-INCH (20-CM) CAKE; SERVES 15 TO 20

FOR THE WHITE CHOCOLATE CAKE:

¾ cup (180 ml) whole milk

¼ cup (60 ml) sour cream

2½ cups (325 g) cake flour

1⅓ cups (265 g) granulated sugar

1 tablespoon baking powder

½ teaspoon salt

½ cup plus 6 tablespoons (1¾ sticks/200 g) unsalted butter, at room temperature

2 teaspoons pure vanilla extract

4 large eggs

4 ounces (115 g) white chocolate, melted and cooled

FOR THE CLASSIC CHOCOLATE CAKE:

2½ cups (315 g) all-purpose flour

1 cup (95 g) unsweetened cocoa powder

2½ teaspoons baking powder

½ teaspoon baking soda

1 teaspoon salt

1 cup (240 ml) whole milk

½ cup (120 ml) sour cream

¾ cup (180 ml) grapeseed or canola oil

2 cups (400 g) granulated sugar

2 teaspoons pure vanilla extract

3 large eggs

1 cup (240 ml) hot strong-brewed coffee

TO ASSEMBLE:

1 large recipe Swiss Meringue Buttercream (page 262)

MAKE THE WHITE CHOCOLATE CAKE

Preheat the oven to 350°F (175°C). Grease and flour two 8-inch (20-cm) cake pans and line the bottoms with parchment paper.

In a small bowl or liquid measuring cup, stir together the milk and sour cream.

Sift together the flour, sugar, baking powder, and salt into the bowl of a stand mixer. Using the paddle attachment, beat on low speed until just combined. Add the butter, vanilla, and about ½ cup (120 ml) of the milk mixture. Mix on medium until evenly distributed and the dry ingredients are moistened, about 1 minute. Stop the mixer and scrape down the sides and bottom of the bowl.

Add the eggs to the remaining milk mixture and stir to combine. With the mixer running on medium speed, add the egg mixture in three additions, mixing for about 15 seconds after each and stopping the mixer between additions to scrape down the sides and bottom of the bowl. Stop the mixer and fold in the melted chocolate by hand until combined.

Evenly divide the batter between the prepared pans. Bake for 28 to 32 minutes, until a toothpick inserted into the center of each cake comes out clean. Let the cakes cool on a wire rack for 10 to 15 minutes before removing from the pans. Allow the cakes to cool completely, right-side up, on the wire rack before removing the parchment.

MAKE THE CLASSIC CHOCOLATE CAKE

Preheat the oven to 350°F (175°C). Grease and flour two 8-inch (20-cm) cake pans.

Sift together the flour, cocoa powder, baking powder, baking soda, and salt into a large bowl. In a small bowl or liquid measuring cup, stir together the milk and sour cream.

In the bowl of a stand mixer fitted with the paddle attachment (or in a large bowl using a handheld mixer), beat the oil and sugar on medium speed for 2 minutes. With the mixer running on medium, add the vanilla. Add the eggs one at a time, mixing until each is incorporated before adding the next. Stop the mixer and scrape down the bowl.

Turn the mixer to low and add the flour mixture in three batches, alternating with the milk mixture, beginning and ending with the flour mixture. Stop the mixer and scrape down the bowl. With the mixer running on low, stream in the coffee. Mix on medium-low just until combined, no more than 30 seconds.

HOW TO DECORATE A
Checkerboard Cake

Evenly divide the batter between the prepared pans. Bake for 30 to 40 minutes, until a toothpick inserted into the center of each cake comes out clean. Let the cakes cool on a wire rack for 10 to 15 minutes before removing from the pans. Allow the cakes to cool completely, right-side up, on the wire rack.

ASSEMBLE THE CAKE

Once all four cakes are completely cool, carefully level them so they are the exact same height, about 1 inch (2.5 cm) tall. To create the checkerboard cake pattern, use 2-inch (5-cm) and 4-inch (10-cm) round cookie cutters and a 6-inch (15-cm) cake pan to score the tops of each cake to create four concentric rings, each about 1 inch (2.5 cm) wide, in a bull's-eye pattern. Using a paring knife or the cookie cutters, carefully cut out the rings and separate them.

On a cake board, place a 2-inch (5-cm) chocolate round. Set a 4-inch (10-cm) white ring around it. Set a 6-inch (15-cm) chocolate ring around the white ring. Finally set an 8-inch (20-cm) white ring as the outermost ring of the cake layer. Repeat on a second cake board to make an identical cake layer, then repeat to make two layers in the opposite pattern (with white centers and chocolate edges).

Making sure the rings stay in place, put one cake layer with chocolate edges on a cake board or serving plate. Spread 1 cup (240 ml) of the buttercream on top with an offset spatula. Carefully place one cake layer with white chocolate edges on top and repeat. Continue to fill and stack the layers, alternating the edge colors.

Crumb coat the cake with the buttercream and chill in the refrigerator for 15 minutes.

DECORATE THE CAKE

Smoothly frost the cake with the buttercream. Fill a piping bag fitted with a small star tip (Wilton #18) with the remaining buttercream and pipe swags and shells around the cake (see page 275). Gently score the edges of the cake before piping the swags to ensure even placement.

If eating the cake the same day as assembled, store it at room temperature until ready to serve. If assembled in advance, store in a cake box in the refrigerator overnight. Bring to room temperature for 30 minutes before serving. Store leftovers loosely covered with plastic wrap in the refrigerator for up to 3 days.

Chocolate Banana Pie

FEATURED DEDORATING TECHNIQUE:
CHOCOLATE SHAVINGS

This pie needs little introduction. The photo speaks for itself: crispy, flaky piecrust; decadent chocolate custard; sticky toffee sauce; fresh banana slices; and mounds of whipped cream covered in chocolate shavings. Sometimes the simplest accessories are all you need, like a generous shower of chocolate on top of an unapologetic, mile-high pie. If that doesn't make you want to face-plant right into the whipped cream, then I don't know what will.

Inspired by a classic "banoffee" pie with its chewy toffee filling, bananas, and whipped cream, this version swaps out the toffee filling for the most succulent, mouthwatering chocolate custard you have ever tasted. Don't worry—there is still plenty of toffee left for drizzling on each slice. Grab a spoon and dig in! MAKES ONE 9-INCH (23-CM) PIE; SERVES 10 TO 12

FOR THE PIECRUST:

1 single-crust recipe All-Butter Pie Dough (page 183), chilled

FOR THE CHOCOLATE CUSTARD:

3 ounces (85 g) bittersweet chocolate (70% cacao), finely chopped

2 tablespoons unsalted butter, diced

2¼ cups (540 ml) whole milk

½ cup (120 ml) heavy cream

¾ cup plus 2 tablespoons (160 g) granulated sugar

5 large egg yolks

⅓ cup (45 g) cornstarch

2 tablespoons unsweetened cocoa powder

2 teaspoons pure vanilla extract

¼ teaspoon salt

FOR THE TOFFEE SAUCE:

½ cup (1 stick/115 g) unsalted butter

1 cup (220 g) packed brown sugar

⅔ cup (160 ml) heavy cream

1 tablespoon bourbon (optional)

1 teaspoon pure vanilla extract

Pinch of salt

FOR THE BROWN SUGAR WHIPPED CREAM:

2 tablespoons cream cheese, at room temperature

1½ cups (360 ml) heavy cream

3 tablespoons light brown sugar

1 teaspoon pure vanilla extract

TO ASSEMBLE AND DECORATE:

4 ripe but firm bananas

Block of chocolate for shavings (see page 152)

MAKE THE PIECRUST

Let the chilled dough sit at room temperature for about 10 minutes.

On a lightly flour-dusted surface, roll out the pie dough until it is ⅛ to ¼ inch (3 to 6 mm) thick and 12 to 13 inches (30 to 33 cm) in diameter. Carefully fit the dough into a 9-inch (23-cm) pie pan and trim the edges, leaving a 1-inch (2.5-cm) overhang. Tuck the edges under and press to the rim of the pie pan to secure. Crimp the edges (see page 195) and chill in the refrigerator for at least 20 minutes.

Preheat the oven to 400°F (200°C).

Line the chilled pie dough with parchment paper and fill with pie weights or dried beans. Bake for 15 to 20 minutes, until the edges begin to turn light golden brown. Remove from the oven (leave the oven on) and carefully remove the parchment paper and weights. Return the crust to the oven and bake until it is completely golden, 10 to 15 minutes more. Let the piecrust cool completely before filling.

MAKE THE CHOCOLATE CUSTARD

Put the chopped chocolate and butter in a large heatproof bowl. Set a fine-mesh sieve over the bowl.

In a medium saucepan, combine the milk, cream, and 2 tablespoons of the granulated sugar. Slowly bring the mixture to a simmer over medium-low heat. Remove from the heat.

In a medium bowl, whisk together the remaining ¾ cup (150 g) of the sugar and egg yolks until smooth. Whisk the cornstarch and cocoa powder into the egg mixture until smooth.

While whisking, stream about half of the hot milk mixture into the egg mixture to temper the egg yolks (this slowly raises the temperature of the eggs so they don't curdle). Pour the tempered egg mixture into the saucepan with the remaining hot milk mixture and heat over medium-low heat, stirring continuously, until the custard thickens and slow, large bubbles start to pop on the surface. Whisk for 1 minute more, then remove from the heat.

Pour the custard through the sieve into the bowl with the chocolate and butter. Add the vanilla and salt. Stir until the chocolate has melted and the mixture is fully incorporated. Spoon the custard directly into the piecrust. Cover loosely with a piece of plastic wrap and chill in the refrigerator until set, at least 1 hour, until ready to assemble and serve.

MAKE THE TOFFEE SAUCE

In a saucepan, melt the butter over medium-high heat. Add the brown sugar and cream. Whisk until combined. Cook, whisking, until the sauce thickens slightly, 2 to 3 minutes.

Remove from the heat and stir in the bourbon (if using), vanilla, and salt. Pour the toffee into a heatproof container and let cool to room temperature. It will thicken as it cools.

MAKE THE BROWN SUGAR WHIPPED CREAM

In a large bowl using a handheld mixer or in the bowl of a stand mixer fitted with the whisk attachment, beat the cream cheese until smooth. Add the heavy cream, brown sugar, and vanilla and whisk on high speed until medium peaks form.

ASSEMBLE AND DECORATE THE PIE

Once the chocolate custard has set, slice the bananas into ½-inch (12-mm) coins. Place half of the sliced bananas on top of the chocolate custard. Drizzle a few tablespoons of cooled toffee sauce over the banana slices. Top with the remaining banana slices, creating a mound on top. Dollop the whipped cream on top and shave the chocolate directly onto the pie (see page 152).

Serve just after assembling to keep the bananas from turning brown. Serve with extra toffee sauce, if desired. Store leftovers loosely wrapped in plastic wrap in the refrigerator for 2 to 3 days.

ALL ABOUT
Pie

STUDY ONE THING EXCLUSIVELY FOR WEEKS ON END, and you will undoubtedly discover little nuances that you probably wouldn't have noticed before. When I baked and decorated cakes full-time for years, certain things became second nature to me. I knew when the butter-cream was done whipping from across the room just by hearing the slapping sound it made in the commercial mixer. Sitting in my office, the smell of nearly baked chocolate cake could wake me from whatever email I was tackling and send me back into the kitchen just before the timer went off almost every time.

My first experiences with pie started later in my baking journey. The patience needed for lattice work and weaving braids of pastry came pretty naturally. But as I became more committed to making pies, not only was it important for me to develop recipes that created consistent results, but I also wanted to know *why* they worked.

For several weeks straight, I made pie dough nightly. I'd note the subtle changes I made to the short ingredient list in order to see which recipe was the easiest to roll out and which yielded the most flakes and crispiest edges. I studied thickeners and discovered which worked best with my Rosy Rhubarb Strawberry Pie as opposed to the stone fruit in my Cinnamon Peach Apricot Pie. I noticed that the coarse turbinado sugar that I liked to sprinkle on top browned quickly, but was still wonderfully crunchy and golden when added 10 minutes before the pie was done. By the end, muscle memory took over the rolling and crimping, and I could visually determine how flaky a crust would bake up based on the marbling of the butter.

Like with most crafts, practice made for better, more consistent results. The pies in this book are based on my own personal pie philosophy, but as you read you will see how you can adapt and alter my theories for your own needs.

PRETTY VS. FLAKY

The good news is that you can have both! Kind of. Let's rewind just a bit. Flaky pie crust is the result of irregularly incorporated chunks of cold butter. When cutting butter into the flour, the butter should range in size—from the size of a pea to a walnut. As the dough is mixed, these large, uneven chunks of butter begin to marbleize throughout the mixture. Once rolled out and baked, the butter melts in the heat of the oven and the water content is released as steam, creating air pockets throughout and resulting in a super-flaky, crisp crust. In my opinion, this is the most ideal, tastiest situation. However, this type of dough is difficult to manipulate when it comes to decorative designs.

As a general rule, the more the butter is uniformly worked into the dough, the more malleable it will be, but the less flaky upon baking. I hate to sacrifice texture for looks, but sometimes a compromise results in a pie that is both pretty and delicious. A slightly mealier pie dough isn't necessarily inferior to a flaky pie dough, as long as it is not overworked. When attempting skinny braids or other highly decorative designs, instead of craggy, walnut-shaped chunks of butter, aim for all peas.

My personal pie theory is this: I toe the line between flaky and mealy pie dough. I work the dough as little as possible to keep it tender and exercise as much patience as I can muster to weave detailed designs. I like to ensure that a few larger butter chunks remain, especially for the bottom crust, even if this results in a few wonky braids or puffy cut-outs. I know the designs would stay more intact after baking if I kneaded the dough just a tad longer, but that's where I compromise in order to have the best of both worlds.

DESIGN VS. DIFFICULTY

I'm sure I've mentioned this before, but just because something requires time and patience doesn't always mean the task itself is difficult. This applies to pie making as well. You might think the roses on the Apple Blackberry Pie (page 232) are extremely difficult to create, when they are actually made with a round cookie cutter. Sure, they took half a morning to roll, but it was calming, satisfying, simple work.

In the end, you do you. If you think it's fun and relaxing to weave braids out of pie dough, then go for it! If you think that a pie should just be humble and rustic, then that's fine too. A solid top crust or classic lattice pie with crunchy sugar and all its imperfections are still gorgeous and delicious to me.

TIPS AND TECHNIQUES

Temperature: Cold! From your butter and your water to your tools and even yourself, keep everything very cold. While the dough is coming together, cold water and butter are important for keeping those chunks of butter from fully combining. On extra-warm days, try freezing your butter, either diced or whole, and then grating it into the flour.

Chill the dough between every step. Not only will this make the dough easier to handle and roll out along the way, but chilling a finished pie will help keep its shape while baking.

Handling the dough: While you can make pie dough in the food processor, I prefer to make it by hand. Not only do I find it relaxing and enjoy feeling the butter and flour coming together between my fingertips, I find that you have much more control. Plus, fewer dishes! In order to keep the butter from warming up, work quickly yet deliberately. Start by smushing and smearing bits of butter between your thumbs, index, and middle fingers until the butter is in pieces ranging between the size of a pea and a walnut. Quickly dip your hands back into the bowl and smear the flour-covered butter bits between the palms of your hand to create sheets of butter throughout the mixture. Don't overthink and definitely don't overwork it. If you have exceptionally warm hands, try using a pastry cutter or a pair of forks to cut in the butter.

When adding the water, simply stir the dough with your fingertips to evenly moisten. After this step, the dough will appear quite shaggy at first. Instead of kneading, use a bench scraper to help fold the dough to keep the butter marbleized. Overmixing will strengthen the gluten and create a less tender crust.

Handling the dough too much may result in shrinking and tough crusts; this goes for when it's time to roll and decorate, too. Again, keeping the dough chilled will help with this.

Water content: You'll notice the recipe calls for a vague amount of water. The less water, the better, so only use as much as you need for the shaggy dough to come together. Most of the dough should come together when given a tight squeeze, but it's okay if there are some dry bits left behind. Once you begin to fold the dough, if you feel that it is still too dry, sprinkle on a bit more water with your fingertips. The range of water needed will be affected by the humidity, the age and brand of your flour, and how much the butter was worked into the dough. Be careful that no bits of ice fall into the bowl.

Taste: The ingredient list for my All-Butter Pie Dough (page 183) is quite short. I've tried recipes with lemon juice, apple cider vinegar, vodka, and cream cheese that are said to help the crust stay tender and not overworked. In my research, I found that several of these theories actually contradicted one another. In the end, the mixing technique is far more important than these subtle additives. European butter has less water content, so I definitely recommend saving it for pie dough and tart crusts rather than cake or buttercream.

As for the filling, always taste your fruit (except raw rhubarb) and adjust accordingly. Use the best fruit you can find. It shouldn't be overly ripe or soft—if you wouldn't eat it plain, it's probably not worth all your efforts to turn it into a subpar pie. Add more or less sugar as needed, keeping in mind that the more sugar you add, the juicier the pie may be.

Baking the pie: Bake the pie on the bottom rack of your oven. The heat source in most ovens is at the bottom, so this will help brown the bottom of the pie. I typically bake my pies with the pie pan set on a baking sheet to keep any escaping juices from burning on the floor of the oven.

For extra-golden pies, bake at a high temperature for the first 20 to 25 minutes, then turn the oven temperature down and continue baking as directed in the recipe. If the crust begins to brown too quickly, cover it with a pie shield or foil. The type of sugar and egg wash you choose will also cause more or less browning. I like my pies extra-golden and crisp, and typically opt to give them a second sprinkle of chunky turbinado sugar during the last 10 minutes of baking.

The pie is done when the juices are steadily bubbling between the vents. This is important when using corn or tapioca starch as a thickener, because they need to be heated to a certain temperature to activate. You can also slip the tip of a paring knife between the lattices to check if the fruit inside is tender.

Pie pans: As pretty as ceramic pie plates can be, I prefer to use metal or glass. I find they conduct heat better and more evenly. Say no to soggy-bottomed crusts! If you are new to pie baking, go for a glass pan where you can literally see if the bottom has browned or not. In either case, try to choose a pan that has a lip around the rim to help the crimped edges stick and keep the dough from slumping. If you are baking a pie from frozen, please use a metal pie pan only. The quick temperature change may cause ceramic and glass pans to shatter in the oven.

Freezing pie: The pie dough may be wrapped well in plastic and then placed in a freezer bag and stored in the freezer for 2 to 3 months. Let thaw in the refrigerator overnight before using.

You can also freeze a filled, unbaked pie, too! I prefer to chill it first to make sure the crimped edges and any decorations are firm before being wrapped in a couple layers of plastic and placed in the freezer. Bake from frozen, adding the egg wash before it goes into the oven. Increase the bake time by about 30 minutes or as needed. Do not freeze unbaked pies in ceramic or glass pie pans, as the heat change may cause them to shatter.

Egg Washes for Pie

For enhanced browning and shine, brush an egg wash over the assembled pie before it enters the oven. Essentially, proteins contribute to the browning effects of baking the crust in the oven while fats promote shine. I prefer a wash made up of a whole egg and a splash of milk, but let's take a closer look at a few other options:

Egg whites only: **subtle shine and not much color**

Whole eggs: **rich and golden color**

Egg yolks (with or without water): **glossy and golden brown**

Whole eggs with milk: **dark, golden brown with a touch of shine**

Cream: **crisp crust, but not much color**

None: **matte and dull**

Egg washes also act as "glue" for sticking on decorative elements!

All-Butter Pie Dough

SINGLE CRUST

MAKES ONE DISC, ENOUGH FOR ONE 9-INCH (23-CM)
SINGLE-CRUST PIE OR TART

1⅓ cups plus 2 tablespoons (180 g) all-purpose flour

1½ teaspoons granulated sugar

¼ teaspoon salt

9 tablespoons (130 g) unsalted butter, diced, very cold

¼ cup (60 ml) ice plus ½ cup (120 ml) water

DOUBLE CRUST

MAKES TWO DISCS, ENOUGH FOR ONE 9-INCH (23-CM)
DOUBLE-CRUST OR LATTICE PIE

2¾ cups plus 2 tablespoons (360 g) all-purpose flour

1 tablespoon granulated sugar

½ teaspoon salt

1 cup plus 2 tablespoons (2¼ sticks/250 g) unsalted butter, diced, very cold

¼ cup (60 ml) ice plus ¾ cup (180 ml) water

1 In a large bowl, combine the flour, sugar, and salt. Add the butter. Using your fingertips, a pastry cutter, or a pair of forks, cut the butter into the flour mixture. Continue by rubbing the butter into the flour between your fingertips until the butter ranges in size from small peas to the size of a walnut. Do not overmix.

2 Create a small well in the center of the bowl. Add about half of the ice water and stir with your fingertips. Continue adding water, 1 tablespoon at a time, until most of the dough sticks together when given a firm squeeze with one hand. (You'll use about 6 tablespoons [90 ml] ice water total for the single crust or about 8 tablespoons [120 ml] for the double crust.)

3 Dump the dough onto a clean work surface, gently gather it, then flatten it out into a rectangular shape with the palms of your hands, with one narrow side facing you. Using a bench scraper, scoop under the top third of the dough and fold it to the center. Repeat with the bottom third to make a tri-fold (like a business letter). Don't worry if the dough is rather crumbly at this point. Rotate the dough 180 degrees and repeat two or three more times. Flatten the dough into one disc for the single crust or divide into two discs for the double crust, wrap well in plastic wrap, and refrigerate for at least 1 hour or up to 3 days.

Pie dough can be wrapped well in plastic wrap and stored in the refrigerator for 2 to 3 days or in the freezer for up to 2 months. Thaw frozen pie dough in the refrigerator overnight before rolling or using.

Rustic Bakes and Cakes

The natural beauty of a blushing apricot on a tart or crystallized sugar on a flaky pie crust is enough to make me swoon. A bit casual and carefree, these rustic bakes and cakes don't need gold flakes or extra sprinkles to be gorgeous. Seasonal fruit and natural adornments take center stage. Looking for something a bit deconstructed and unfussy? Try a semifrosted cake or seasonal hand pie!

Caramel Apple Pear Pie

I was never the child with flour-dusted cheeks standing on tiptoe in her grandmother's kitchen and learning all her baking secrets—except for one cherished day. It was Christmas, the year I turned five, that I remember my grandma taught me how to make my first apple pie. She handed me a small pie tin, leftover pie dough, and sliced apples to work with. I can't recall a single other time we all made apple pie at Christmas, but I distinctly remember this occasion.

In honor of that very first dessert I ever made, I created this incredibly flaky and slightly spiced pie with a classic lattice top and an updated filling. It uses a combination of seasonal apples and pears, topped off with a cinnamon-infused caramel sauce. I find that apples and pears bake at different rates, so be sure to slice the apples thinner for a more harmonious texture when baked. MAKES ONE 9-INCH (23-CM) PIE; SERVES 8 TO 12

FOR THE CINNAMON CARAMEL:

⅔ cup (160 ml) heavy cream

2 cinnamon sticks (see Note)

¾ cup (150 g) granulated sugar

2 tablespoons corn syrup

2 tablespoons unsalted butter, diced

1 teaspoon pure vanilla extract

½ teaspoon salt

¼ teaspoon ground cinnamon, or to taste

FOR THE PIE:

1 recipe double-crust All-Butter Pie Dough (page 183), chilled

Juice of ½ lemon

4 or 5 ripe firm pears (Bosc, Anjou, Bartlett, or a combination)

3 medium apples (Honeycrisp, Gala, Granny Smith, or a combination)

¼ cup (55 g) packed brown sugar

¼ cup (30 g) all-purpose flour

2 teaspoons ground cinnamon

2 teaspoons pure vanilla extract

½ teaspoon salt

¼ teaspoon freshly grated nutmeg

TO ASSEMBLE:

1 large egg

1 tablespoon whole milk

Granulated or turbinado sugar, for sprinkling

MAKE THE CINNAMON CARAMEL

Put ½ cup (120 ml) of the cream and the cinnamon sticks in a small saucepan and bring to a simmer over medium heat. Remove from the heat and let cool for about 10 minutes. Transfer the cream and cinnamon sticks to a lidded container and infuse in the refrigerator for about 8 hours or overnight.

Remove the cinnamon sticks and discard. Re-measure the cream and top it off until it reaches ½ cup (120 ml). Set aside to bring to room temperature or gently heat in the microwave until lukewarm.

Put the sugar, corn syrup, and 2 tablespoons water in a small saucepan. Swirl to combine. Without stirring, bring the mixture to a boil over high heat. Cook until the caramel turns medium amber in color, then immediately remove from the heat. Carefully whisk in the cream. The mixture may begin to fizz, but keep whisking.

Add the butter, vanilla, salt, and ground cinnamon and stir to combine. Pour the caramel into a heat-safe container and let cool before use.

MAKE THE PIE

Let one disc of the chilled pie dough soften at room temperature for about 10 minutes.

On a lightly floured surface, roll out the pie dough until it is ⅛ to ¼ inch (3 to 6 mm) thick and 12 to 13 inches (30 to 33 cm) in diameter. Gently roll half the dough onto the rolling pin, lift, and unroll it into a 9-inch (23-cm) pie pan. Fit the dough into the bottom and up the sides of the pie pan. Trim the excess dough with a paring knife or kitchen shears, leaving a 1-inch (2.5-cm) overhang all around, then chill in the refrigerator as you prepare the filling.

Put the lemon juice in a large bowl. Peel and core the pears and cut them into ½-inch-thick (12-mm) slices. Put the pear slices in the bowl and toss with the lemon juice. Repeat with the apples, cutting them into thin slices (thinner than the pear slices). Add the apples to the bowl and toss. Add the brown sugar, flour, cinnamon, vanilla, salt, and nutmeg and toss to combine and coat the pears and apples.

Remove the second disc of chilled pie dough from the refrigerator and let it soften at room temperature for about 10 minutes.

Tightly pack half of the pear and apple slices (leaving any juices behind in the bowl) into the bottom of the pie pan, layering the slices in concentric circles. Pour about ⅓ cup (80 ml) of the caramel sauce over the top of the filling. (The caramel sauce should be cool, but if it is too thick to pour, gently reheat it in the microwave in 15-second intervals until it is roughly room temperature and pourable.) Add the remaining pear and apple slices, gently mounding them on top. Pour on another ⅓ cup (80 ml) of the caramel sauce. Chill the filled pie in the refrigerator as you prepare the lattice.

Roll out the second disc of pie dough into an oval about 13 by 11 inches (33 by 28 cm) and ⅛ to ¼ inch (3 to 6 mm) thick. Using a paring knife or pastry cutter, cut 8 long strips of dough, about 1½ inches (4 cm) wide. The longest strips in the center should be 10 to 11 inches (25 to 27.5 cm) long.

Remove the filled pie from the refrigerator and create a lattice top with the dough strips (see How to Weave a Classic Lattice Crust, page 190). Trim the ends of the strips with a paring knife or kitchen shears, leaving about ½ inch (1.5 cm) overhanging all around.

Fold the overhanging dough from the bottom crust up and over the ends of the lattice strips and press to seal. Crimp the edges (see How to Crimp a Pie, page 195) and secure them to the rim of the pie plate. Chill in the refrigerator for at least 30 minutes.

Preheat the oven to 425°F (220°C) with a rack in the lowest position.

FINISH THE PIE

When ready to bake, gently whisk together the egg and milk to make an egg wash. Brush the egg wash over the pie with a pastry brush and sprinkle the pie with sugar. Place the pie on a rimmed baking sheet and bake for 25 minutes. Lower the oven temperature to 375°F (190°C) and bake for 30 to 40 minutes more, until the crust is golden brown, the juices are bubbling, and the tip of a paring knife easily pierces through the fruit (in between the lattice).

Let the pie cool completely before slicing, at least 4 hours. Serve with the remaining cinnamon caramel sauce. Store leftovers covered with foil or plastic wrap at room temperature for up to 2 days or in the refrigerator for up to 3 days.

*   *   *

NOTE: I like the depth of flavor the cinnamon sticks add to the caramel. If you are in a pinch, skip the infusion and increase the amount of ground cinnamon to taste.

Make a Classic Lattice Pie

*   *   *

1   Cut 8 strips of dough or as many as directed in the recipe. Evenly place 4 strips across the filled pie, all going the same direction.

2   Fold the 1st and 3rd strips halfway back. Place a 5th strip of dough on top of the 2nd and 4th strips, perpendicular to the first set. Unfold the 1st and 3rd strips so that they are lying on top of and perpendicular to the 5th strip.

3   Fold the 2nd and 4th strips halfway back on the opposite side of the pie from the 5th strip. Place a 6th strip of dough on top of the 1st and 3rd strips, parallel to the 5th strip. Unfold the 2nd and 4th strips so they are lying on top of and perpendicular to the 6th strip.

4   Repeat the same folding actions with the remaining dough strips until the top of the pie is covered.

HOW TO WEAVE A

Classic Lattice Crust

Rosy Rhubarb Strawberry Slab Pie

FEATURED DECORATING TECHNIQUES: CLASSIC LATTICE, CRIMPED EDGES

Make nearly anything in a sheet pan, and it instantly becomes easier to assemble, cut, serve, and transport. This slab pie is no exception and is perfect for potlucks, picnics, and backyard BBQs. With a hint of rose and a dash of cardamom, this Rosy Rhubarb Strawberry Slab Pie is a little sweet, a little tart, and slightly floral—a wonderful way to welcome the summer season. The vibrant pink filling speaks to how bright and fresh this pie truly is. MAKES ONE 9 BY 13-INCH (23 BY 33-CM) SLAB PIE; SERVES 12 TO 16

3 recipes single-crust All-Butter Pie Dough (page 183)

1¼ pounds (560 g) fresh rhubarb stalks, cut into ½-inch (1.5-cm) pieces

2½ cups (300 to 375 g) fresh strawberries, halved

1 cup (200 g) granulated sugar

Finely grated zest and juice of ½ large lemon

Pinch of salt

2 teaspoons pure rose extract or 2 tablespoons rose water

2 tablespoons plus 1 teaspoon cornstarch

3 tablespoons all-purpose flour

Pinch of ground cardamom

TO ASSEMBLE:

1 large egg

1 tablespoon whole milk

Granulated or turbinado sugar, for sprinkling

Let 1½ discs of the chilled pie dough soften at room temperature for 10 to 20 minutes.

On a lightly floured surface, roll out the pie dough to an 11 by 15-inch (28 by 38-cm) rectangle, ⅛ to ¼ inch (3 to 6 mm) thick. Sliding your forearms under the dough, carefully lift and place it in a 9 by 13-inch (23 by 33-cm) jelly-roll or quarter sheet pan. Fit the dough into the pan. Trim the excess dough, leaving a 1-inch (2.5-cm) overhang on all sides.

Let the remaining 1½ discs of the pie dough soften at room temperature for about 10 minutes.

Put the rhubarb and strawberries in a large bowl and toss with the sugar, lemon zest, lemon juice, salt, and rose extract. Add the cornstarch, flour, and cardamom and stir until combined. Tip the mixture into the dough-lined pan. Leave about a ½-inch (1.5-cm) gap between the top of the filling and the rim of the pan to keep the juices from overflowing.

On a lightly floured surface, roll the remaining pie dough into a large oval about the same size as the pan and ¼ inch (6 mm) thick; the longest section of the oval should be 15 inches (38 cm) long. Using a pastry cutter or paring knife, cut 13 strips of dough, about 1 inch (2.5 cm) wide and of various lengths. Cut 6 skinny strips; working with 3 skinny strips at a time, pinch the strips together at the top and gently braid them to create a pair of long braids.

Following the directions on page 190, create a lattice over the top of the pie. Start by laying the longest pieces across from corner to corner. Use the braids in place of 2 strips in the classic lattice. Fold the overhanging dough of the bottom crust up and over the ends of the lattice strips and crimp to secure. Chill in the refrigerator for at least 30 minutes.

Preheat the oven to 425°F (220°C) with a rack in the lowest position.

BAKE THE PIE

When ready to bake, gently whisk together the egg and milk to make an egg wash. Brush the egg wash over the pie with a pastry brush and sprinkle the pie with sugar. Place the pie on a baking sheet and bake for 25 minutes. Lower the oven temperature to 375°F (190°C) and bake for 25 to 30 minutes more, until the crust is golden brown and the juices are bubbling.

Let the pie cool completely before slicing, at least 2 hours. Store leftovers covered with foil or plastic wrap at room temperature for up to 2 days or in the refrigerator for up to 3 days.

NOTE: To serve an even larger crowd, try baking the pie in an 18 by 13-inch (46 by 33-cm) sheet pan. Just double the filling and use 2 recipes double-crust All-Butter Pie Dough. Rolling out the pie dough to those dimensions may seem ambitious and slightly scary, but you got this! Remain cool, calm, and collected. And definitely roll the dough between two large pieces of parchment paper to keep it from sticking and make it easier transport to the pan. Alternatively, for the bottom crust, roll out two medium pieces and press them together in the pan.

HOW TO

Crimp a Pie

Make a Classic Crimped Edge

* * *

1 Fold the overhanging dough from the bottom crust up and over the ends of the lattice strips or solid top crust. Press to seal.

2 Use the thumb of your dominant hand to press the inside of the edge outward. Simultaneously, use the thumb and index finger of your opposite hand to press the edge of the pie dough inward on either side of your dominant thumb. Continue around the whole pie.

FOR A SMALLER CRIMP, use the tip of your index finger instead of your thumb.

FOR A MORE DEFINED FLUTED EDGE, go back around the edge of the pie and secure the edges to the rim of the pie pan. Gently hook the index finger of your dominant hand in the inward-facing crimp. Place the thumb and index finger of your opposite hand on the crimped edges on either side of your dominant index finger. Gently pull your hands away from each other, pressing down on the outward-facing crimps to secure them to the pie pan. Continue around the whole pie.

IF AT ANY POINT THE DOUGH BECOMES TOO SOFT TO CRIMP, chill the pie in the refrigerator for about 20 minutes before continuing.

Chai Walnut Cake

One of the more impactful ways to add flavor to frosting is to infuse the butter with tea. The London Fog Cake in my first cookbook, Layered, *was frosted in Earl Grey buttercream and ended up being the biggest fan favorite of the entire book. I was a bit surprised by how much everyone shares my affinity for tea-flavored cakes, but not* that *surprised—that cake is delicious!*

For this recipe, I've used the same technique with chai tea. The sweet and tangy apricot filling pairs perfectly with the warm, spicy flavors. I've given the cake a rustic, seminaked finish to make sure the buttercream doesn't outshine the nutty, earthy walnut cake. MAKES ONE THREE-LAYER 8-INCH (20-CM) CAKE; SERVES 12 TO 16

FOR THE WALNUT CAKE:

1¾ cups (220 g) whole wheat pastry flour

1 cup (125 g) all-purpose flour

1 tablespoon baking powder

1½ teaspoons ground cinnamon

½ teaspoon ground cardamom

½ teaspoon salt

½ cup (40 g) ground walnuts (see Notes)

1 cup (240 ml) whole milk

⅓ cup (80 ml) sour cream or plain Greek yogurt

1 cup (2 sticks/225 g) unsalted butter, at room temperature

1 cup (200 g) granulated sugar

¾ cup (165 g) packed brown sugar

2 teaspoons pure vanilla extract

4 large eggs

¾ cup (90 g) toasted walnuts, finely chopped (see Notes)

FOR THE CHAI BUTTERCREAM:

2 cups (4 sticks/450 g) unsalted butter

4 tablespoons (25 g) loose-leaf chai tea (see Notes)

4 large egg whites

1⅓ cups (265 g) granulated sugar

2 teaspoons pure vanilla extract

TO ASSEMBLE AND DECORATE:

½ cup (120 ml) apricot jam

Fresh flowers (optional; see page 209)

MAKE THE WALNUT CAKE

Preheat the oven to 350°F (175°C). Grease and flour three 8-inch (20-cm) cake pans.

Sift together the flours, baking powder, cinnamon, cardamom, and salt into a large bowl. Stir in the ground walnuts. In a small bowl or liquid measuring cup, stir together the milk and sour cream.

In the bowl of a stand mixer fitted with the paddle attachment, beat the butter on medium speed for 2 minutes. Add the sugars and mix on medium-high until light and fluffy, 3 to 5 minutes. Stop the mixer and scrape down the bowl.

Turn the mixer to medium-low and add the vanilla. Add the eggs one at a time, mixing until each is incorporated before adding the next. Mix until combined. Stop the mixer and scrape down the bowl.

Turn the mixer to low and add the flour mixture in three batches, alternating with the milk mixture, starting and ending with the flour mixture. After the last streaks of the flour mixture are combined, mix on medium for no more than 30 seconds. Stop the mixer and fold in the chopped walnuts by hand.

Evenly divide the batter among the prepared pans. Bake for 24 to 28 minutes, until a toothpick inserted into the center of each cake comes out clean. Let the cakes cool on a wire rack for 10 to 15 minutes before removing from the pans. Allow the cakes to cool completely, right-side up, on the wire rack. Level the tops of the cakes with a long serrated knife as needed.

MAKE THE CHAI BUTTERCREAM

While the cakes are cooling, make the chai buttercream. In a small saucepan, combine 1 cup (2 sticks/225 g) of the butter and the loose tea. Melt the butter over medium heat, then reduce the heat to low and simmer for 5 minutes. Remove from the heat and let steep for 5 minutes. Strain the butter through a fine-mesh sieve set over a bowl (small bits of tea may remain in the butter—this is okay); discard the tea. Refrigerate the butter until it has the same consistency as room-temperature butter, 45 to 60 minutes. Bring the remaining 1 cup (2 sticks/225 g) butter to room temperature.

Put the egg whites and sugar in the bowl of a stand mixer. Gently whisk them by hand until just combined. In a medium saucepan, bring an inch or two (2.5 to 5 cm) of water to a simmer over medium-low heat. Place the mixer bowl on top of the saucepan to create a double boiler (be sure the bottom of the bowl does not touch the water). Heat the egg mixture, whisking intermittently, until it reaches 160°F (70°C) on a candy thermometer.

Carefully affix the mixer bowl to the stand mixer (it may be hot) and fit the mixer with the whisk attachment. Beat the egg white mixture on high speed for 8 to 10 minutes, until the mixture holds medium-stiff peaks and the outside of the bowl has cooled to room temperature.

Turn the mixer down to low and add the vanilla, tea-infused butter, and remaining 1 cup (2 sticks/ 225 g) room-temperature butter, a couple tablespoons at a time. Stop the mixer and swap out the whisk for the paddle attachment.

Turn the mixer to medium-high and beat until the buttercream is silky smooth, 3 to 5 minutes.

ASSEMBLE AND DECORATE THE CAKE

To assemble the naked cake, place one cake layer on a cake board or serving plate. Fill a piping bag fitted with a large round tip with buttercream. Pipe a ring around the top edge of the cake and fill with about 1 cup (240 ml) of the buttercream. Smooth the buttercream with an offset spatula or the back of a spoon. Dollop half of the apricot jam on top of the buttercream and smooth. Top with a second cake layer and repeat; place the final cake layer on top. Use the remaining buttercream to frost the top of the cake and give the sides a semi-naked look. Top with fresh flowers, if desired (see page 209).

If eating the cake the same day as assembled, store it at room temperature until ready to serve. If assembled in advance, wrap the sides of the cake in plastic and store in the refrigerator overnight. Bring to room temperature for 30 minutes before serving. Store leftovers loosely covered with plastic wrap in the refrigerator for up to 3 days.

NOTES: Grind the walnuts in a spice grinder or small food processor. Grind 1 tablespoon uncooked white rice in the spice grinder to clean it before and after grinding the walnuts. You can also substitute store-bought almond flour for the ground walnuts.

Be sure to chop walnuts fine enough, or the cake will be difficult to slice.

For a fully iced cake, follow the instructions for the chai buttercream but use the quantities given for a large batch of Swiss meringue buttercream (page 262), and increase the chai tea to 6 tablespoons.

You may use chai tea from a tea bag, but it may be more finely ground than loose tea.

If you haven't tried the London Fog Cake yet, you must! Simply swap out the chai tea for Earl Grey and pair it with the Classic Chocolate Cake (page 66), then drizzle the whole thing with homemade Caramel Sauce (page 263).

Mix-and-Match Fruit Tarts

There is nothing more naturally beautiful than a fresh fruit tart. Imagine feeling the weight of your spoon dive deep into the velvety pastry cream before hitting the crisp, buttery crust and breaking through with a "snap!" The contrasting textures create the perfect bite—all topped off with blushing apricots, juicy cherries, tart raspberries, sweet mango, or succulent figs. Here are four of my favorite summer fruit combinations, but feel free to mix and match the vanilla, chocolate, and nutty whole wheat shells with any of the pastry creams or fruit that is in season. MAKES ONE 9- OR 10-INCH (23- OR 25-CM) TART OR 6 TO 8 INDIVIDUAL TARTS; SERVES 6 TO 8

Square Summer Berry Tart

At the peak of summer, when wild strawberries are red to the core and tree limbs bow heavy with fresh cherries, enjoy a slice of this scarlet and marigold tart. Sticking to my two-toned color palette, I've topped this tart with apricots, ruby and yellow cherries, red and golden raspberries, fresh strawberries, and jewel-like currants in an organic motif of halved and whole fruit.

FOR THE PÂTE SUCRÉE (SWEET PASTRY DOUGH; SEE NOTE):

1½ cups (190 g) all-purpose flour

½ cup (65 g) confectioners' sugar

½ teaspoon salt

Pinch of freshly grated nutmeg

Finely grated zest of ½ lemon

9 tablespoons (130 g) unsalted butter, diced and chilled

1 large egg yolk, stirred

1 to 2 teaspoons ice water

TO ASSEMBLE:

1 large recipe Vanilla Pastry Cream (page 264)

2 to 3 apricots, halved and sliced

A few sprigs fresh currants

1 cup (145 g) strawberries

1 to 1½ cups (125 to 185 g) raspberries

5 to 10 cherries, halved

* * *

NOTE: The pâte sucrée recipe makes enough for one 9- or 10-inch (23- or 25-cm) round or 9-inch (23-cm) square tart.

MAKE THE PÂTE SUCRÉE

In a large bowl, combine the flour, confectioners' sugar, salt, nutmeg, and lemon zest. Using a pastry cutter or your fingertips, cut the butter into the flour mixture until the bits of butter are about the size of peas. Stir in the egg yolk.

Gradually add just enough ice water, a teaspoon or two at a time, so that when you press the dough together it stays intact. Do not add too much water; the dough should still be shaggy and crumbly.

Press the dough into a 9-inch (23-cm) square tart pan with a removable bottom. Start by pressing the dough up the sides as evenly as possible, then fill in the bottom. Reserve a bit of the dough to repair any cracks that may occur during baking. Chill in the refrigerator for 30 minutes.

Preheat the oven to 375°F (190°C).

Line the tart dough with foil, shiny-side down. Fill with pie weights or dried beans and bake for 20 minutes. Remove from the oven and very carefully take out the weights and foil (keep the oven on). Patch any minor cracks with the reserved dough. Return the tart to the oven and bake for 5 to 10 minutes, until the crust is light golden brown. If the center puffs up during baking, gently press it back down with a piece of foil or parchment paper. Let the shell cool completely on a wire rack before filling.

ASSEMBLE THE TART

Gently whisk the pastry to cream to loosen. Fill a piping bag fitted with a large round tip with the pastry cream and pipe it into the baked tart shell (or spread it in with a small offset spatula). Pick a corner to start from and work your way around, fitting in the fruit like a puzzle. Keep the apricot slices together, then fan them out on top of the pastry cream. Use the smaller berries, currants, and cherry halves to fill in the gaps.

Chocolate Raspberry Tart

I love the shape of this skinny rectangular tart, but the luscious chocolate pastry cream and raspberries would be equally tasty as a circle, heart, diamond, or any other geometrical shape. I started by meticulously placing each raspberry in a straight line, but then threw caution to the wind and tossed on a few stray cherries and sprigs of currants for a touch of movement and whimsy.

FOR THE CHOCOLATE SPICE TART DOUGH:

1¼ cups (155 g) all-purpose flour

¼ cup (25 g) unsweetened cocoa powder

¼ cup (50 g) granulated sugar

1 teaspoon ground cinnamon

½ teaspoon ground cardamom

¼ teaspoon salt

9 tablespoons (130 g) unsalted butter, diced and chilled

1 large egg yolk, stirred

1 to 2 teaspoons ice water

FOR THE CHOCOLATE PASTRY CREAM:

2 tablespoons unsalted butter, diced

2 cups (480 ml) whole milk

8 tablespoons (100 g) granulated sugar

3 tablespoons cornstarch

4 teaspoons all-purpose flour

4 teaspoons unsweetened cocoa powder

4 large egg yolks

½ teaspoon espresso powder (optional)

1 ounce (28 g) dark chocolate, melted and cooled

1 teaspoon pure vanilla extract

Pinch of salt

TO ASSEMBLE:

2 to 3 cups (250 to 375 g) fresh raspberries

6 to 8 fresh cherries

3 or 4 sprigs fresh red currants

MAKE THE CHOCOLATE SPICE TART DOUGH

In a large bowl, combine the flour, cocoa powder, sugar, cinnamon, cardamom, and salt. Using a pastry cutter or your fingertips, cut the butter into the flour mixture until the bits of butter are about the size of peas. Stir in the egg yolk.

Gradually add just enough ice water, a teaspoon or two at a time, so that when you press the dough together it stays intact. Do not add too much water; the dough should still be shaggy and crumbly.

Press half of the dough into a 4 by 14-inch (10 by 35-cm) rectangular tart pan with a removable bottom. Start by pressing the dough up the sides as evenly as possible, then fill in the bottom. Divide the remaining dough and press into 3 or 4 mini-tart pans. Reserve a bit of the dough to repair any cracks that may occur during baking. Chill in the refrigerator for 30 minutes.

Preheat the oven to 375°F (190°C).

Line all of the tart pans with foil, shiny-side down. Fill the pans with pie weights or dried beans and bake for 20 minutes. Remove from the oven and very carefully take out the weights and foil (keep the oven on). Patch up any minor cracks with the reserved dough. Return the tarts pans to the oven. Bake for 5 to 10 minutes. If the centers puff up during baking, carefully press them back down using a piece of foil or parchment paper. Let the shells cool completely on a wire rack before filling.

MAKE THE CHOCOLATE PASTRY CREAM

Use the same method as for the Vanilla Pastry Cream (page 264), omitting the vanilla bean and adding the cocoa powder with the flour. Once the custard thickens but before it is strained over the butter, remove it from the heat and stir in the espresso powder (if using) and melted chocolate. Stir in the salt at the end.

ASSEMBLE THE TART

Fill a piping bag fitted with a large round tip with the pastry cream and pipe it into the tart shells (or spread it in with a small offset spatula). Place the raspberries in neat rows or concentric circles (if using a round tart pan—see Note). Interrupt the pattern by replacing a few of the raspberries with cherries or currants wherever you see fit.

NOTE: If you don't have a rectangular tart pan, the chocolate tart dough and pastry cream can also be used to make one 9-inch (23-cm) round tart.

Tropical Tart

Chocolate Raspberry Tart

Square Summer Berry Tart

Fig Blueberry Tart

Fig and Blueberry Tart

This might be my favorite combination: velvety sweet figs, plump berries, pistachio pastry cream, and a nutty, slightly spiced shell. The contrasting colors of the dark blue and blackberries with the rosy flesh of the figs are absolutely stunning.

FOR THE NUTTY WHOLE WHEAT TART DOUGH:

½ cup (60 g) almond flour

½ cup (65 g) all-purpose flour

½ cup (65 g) whole wheat pastry flour

¼ cup (50 g) granulated sugar

2 teaspoons unsweetened cocoa powder

½ teaspoon ground cinnamon

Pinch of freshly grated nutmeg

Pinch of salt

9 tablespoons (130 g) unsalted butter, diced and chilled

1 large egg yolk, stirred

1 to 2 teaspoons ice water

FOR THE PISTACHIO PASTRY CREAM:

2 cups (480 ml) whole milk

8 tablespoons (100 g) granulated sugar

4 large egg yolks

3 tablespoons cornstarch

2 tablespoons all-purpose flour

1 teaspoon pure vanilla extract

⅓ cup (80 ml) pistachio paste, stirred well

TO ASSEMBLE:

2 cups (280 g) blackberries

2 cups (145 g) blueberries

3 or 4 fresh figs, cut in half

¼ cup (30 g) golden raspberries

1 tablespoon honey

NOTES: All the tart shells can be made in advance, wrapped in plastic wrap, and stored at room temperature for a few days or in the freezer for a couple of months.

All the pastry creams can be made in advance, covered with plastic wrap pressed directly against the surface to prevent a skin from forming, and stored in the refrigerator for up to 3 days.

Assemble the tarts the same day they are to be served. Leftovers can be wrapped in plastic wrap and stored in the refrigerator for about 2 days.

MAKE THE NUTTY WHOLE WHEAT TART DOUGH

In a large bowl, combine the flours, sugar, cocoa powder, cinnamon, nutmeg, and salt. Using a pastry cutter or your fingertips, cut the butter into the flour mixture until the bits of butter are about the size of peas. Stir in the egg yolk.

Gradually add just enough ice water, a teaspoon or two at a time, so that when you press the dough together it stays intact. Do not add too much water; the dough should still be shaggy and crumbly.

Press the dough into a 9-inch (23-cm) round tart pan with a removable bottom. Start by pressing the dough up the sides as evenly as possible, then fill in the bottom. Reserve a bit of the dough to repair any cracks that may occur during baking. Chill in the refrigerator for 30 minutes.

Preheat the oven to 375°F (190°C).

Line the tart dough with foil, shiny-side down. Fill with pie weights or dried beans and bake for 20 minutes. Remove from the oven and very carefully take out the weights and foil (keep the oven on). Patch up any minor cracks with the reserved dough. Return the tart to the oven and bake for 5 to 10 minutes. If the center puffs up during baking, carefully press it back down using a piece of foil or parchment paper. Let the shell cool completely on a wire rack before filling.

MAKE THE PISTACHIO PASTRY CREAM

Use the same method as for the Vanilla Pastry Cream (page 264), omitting the butter and vanilla bean (strain the custard into an empty bowl) and stirring in the pistachio paste with the vanilla extract at the end.

ASSEMBLE THE TART

Fill a piping bag fitted with a large round tip with the pastry cream and pipe it into the tart shell (or spread it in with a small offset spatula). Create patches of blackberries and blueberries on top of the pastry cream, then fill in the gaps with halved figs and golden raspberries. Mix the honey with a splash of water and brush it onto the cut side of the figs to keep them moist and glistening.

Tropical Tart

Ripe mango and coconut pastry cream give this tart a delightful tropical twist. I've kept the design quite random, but feel free to arrange the fruit in a circular pattern for a more traditional feel.

FOR THE PÂTE SABLÉE:

½ cup (1 stick/115 g) unsalted butter, at room temperature

⅓ cup (40 g) confectioners' sugar

1 large egg yolk

½ vanilla bean, split lengthwise and seeds scraped out

Finely grated zest of ½ lemon

1¼ cups (155 g) all-purpose flour

Pinch of salt

1 to 2 teaspoons whole milk or heavy cream, if needed

FOR THE COCONUT PASTRY CREAM:

2 tablespoons unsalted butter, diced

1 cup (240 ml) whole milk

1 cup (240 ml) full-fat coconut milk

8 tablespoons (100 g) granulated sugar

4 large egg yolks

3 tablespoons cornstarch

2 tablespoons all-purpose flour

1 teaspoon pure vanilla extract

1 teaspoon rum or bourbon (optional)

TO ASSEMBLE:

1 or 2 kiwis, peeled

1 mango, peeled and sliced

½ cup (75 g) blueberries

⅓ cup (45 g) blackberries

5 to 8 cherries

½ to 1 cup (75 to 145 g) strawberries

Fresh mint sprigs (optional)

MAKE THE PÂTE SABLÉE

In the bowl of a stand mixer, beat the butter until smooth. Add the confectioners' sugar and mix until creamy. Beat in the egg yolk until combined. Stop the mixer and scrape down the sides and bottom of the bowl.

With the mixer running on low speed, add the vanilla seeds and lemon zest. Add the flour and salt and mix just until the last streaks of flour disappear. Do not overmix. When done, the dough should hold together when pressed. If it is too dry, add the milk as needed, a tablespoon at a time.

Turn out the dough on top of a piece of plastic wrap. Gather the dough and press it into a disc. Wrap in the plastic and chill in the refrigerator for at least 1 hour.

Remove the chilled dough from the refrigerator and let rest at room temperature until pliable, about 10 minutes. Between two pieces of parchment paper, roll out the dough to an 11- to 12-inch (28- to 30-cm) round.

Remove the top layer of parchment and carefully invert the dough into a 9-inch (23-cm) round tart pan with a removable bottom. Remove the top piece of parchment, then fit the dough into the corners of the pan. Run a paring knife around the top edge of the pan to trim excess dough. Fill in any holes with the scraps as needed. Wrap loosely with plastic wrap and chill in the refrigerator for 30 minutes.

Preheat the oven to 350°F (175°C).

Line the tart dough with a piece of foil and fill with pie weights or dried beans. Place the tart shell on a baking sheet and bake for 20 minutes. Remove the tart and baking sheet from the oven and very carefully take out the foil and pie weights (keep the oven on). Return the tart shell to the oven and bake for 5 to 10 more minutes, until lightly golden. Let the shell cool completely on a wire rack before filling.

MAKE THE COCONUT PASTRY CREAM

Use the same method as for the Vanilla Pastry Cream (page 264), substituting coconut milk for half of the whole milk and omitting the vanilla bean. Stir in the rum (if using) with the vanilla extract at the end.

ASSEMBLE THE TART

Fill a piping bag fitted with a large round tip with the pastry cream and pipe it into the tart shell (or spread it in with a small offset spatula). To create the kiwi flowers, use a small paring knife to cut a zigzag pattern around the belly of the fruit, making sure each slice goes all the way to the center of the fruit. When done, gently pull the layers apart. Start adding fruit around the edges, mirroring patterns across the tart (like placing the sliced mango at 5 o'clock and 11 o'clock as shown). Fill in the center with the remaining fruit and kiwi flowers. Add sprigs of fresh mint, if desired.

✳   ✳   ✳

NOTES: Pâte Sucrée is a sweet, short crust dough. It is straightforward and versatile, and may be pressed in the pan or rolled out (see recipe, page 200).

Pâte Sablée is more similar to a sablée cookie: sandy, buttery, and tender (see recipe, this page).

Try both recipes and use your favorite interchangeably.

Victoria Sponge Cake

FEATURED DECORATING TECHNIQUES: STACKING A CAKE, NAKED CAKE,
VARIOUS PIPING, WORKING WITH FRESH FLOWERS

*Named after Queen Victoria, the traditional version of this cake was not much more than a basic
sponge cake sandwiched with raspberry jam. Adorned only with a dusting of confectioners' sugar, it
was (and still is) the perfect, simple bite to serve along with afternoon tea. The whipped cream was
introduced later, but I've opted for buttercream to help stabilize this two-tiered "naked" cake, which,
when stacked and covered in berries, makes quite the impression.*

*The buttermilk cake is extremely versatile and acts as a terrific base recipe for any cakes that you
may want to invent. I find that a combination of all-purpose and cake flours creates a tender yet stable
cake crumb that is perfect for stacking. Top the cake with any fruit that is in season and feel free to use
the jam of your choice.* MAKES ONE TWO-TIERED CAKE; SERVES 22 TO 28

**FOR THE 6-INCH
(15-CM) CAKE:**

1 cup plus 2 tablespoons
(140 g) all-purpose flour

1¼ cups (165 g) cake
flour

2½ teaspoons baking
powder

¾ teaspoon salt

¾ cup (1½ sticks/170 g)
unsalted butter, at room
temperature

1½ cups (300 g)
granulated sugar

2 teaspoons vanilla bean
paste or pure vanilla
extract

3 large eggs

1 cup plus 1 tablespoon
(255 ml) buttermilk

**FOR THE 8-INCH
(20-CM) CAKE:**

1½ cups plus
2 tablespoons (200 g)
all-purpose flour

1½ cups (195 g) cake flour

1 tablespoon plus
½ teaspoon baking
powder

1 teaspoon salt

1 cup (2 sticks/225 g)
unsalted butter, at room
temperature

2 cups (400 g)
granulated sugar

1 tablespoon vanilla bean
paste or pure vanilla
extract

4 large eggs

1⅓ cups (320 ml)
buttermilk

**FOR THE WHIPPED
MASCARPONE
BUTTERCREAM:**

1 cup (2 sticks/225 g)
unsalted butter, at
room temperature

½ cup (115 g)
mascarpone, at room
temperature

4½ to 5½ cups (560 to
690 g) confectioners'
sugar, sifted if needed

2 tablespoons whole milk

1 tablespoon pure vanilla
extract

**TO ASSEMBLE AND
DECORATE:**

1¼ cups (300 ml)
strawberry jam

4 wooden cake dowels or
thick plastic straws

2 cups (145 g)
strawberries

Fresh flowers (optional;
see page 209)

MAKE THE 6-INCH (15-CM) CAKE

Preheat the oven to 350°F (175°C). Grease and flour
three 6-inch (15-cm) cake pans and line the bottoms
with parchment paper.

Sift together the flours, baking powder, and salt into
a large bowl.

In the bowl of a stand mixer fitted with the paddle
attachment, beat the butter on medium speed for
2 minutes. Add the sugar and mix on medium-high
until light and fluffy, 3 to 5 minutes. Stop the mixer
and scrape down the bowl.

Turn the mixer to medium-low and add the
vanilla. Add the eggs one at a time, mixing until
each is incorporated before adding the next. Mix
until combined. Stop the mixer and scrape down
the bowl.

Turn the mixer to low and add the flour mixture in three batches, alternating with the buttermilk, beginning and ending with the flour mixture. After the last streaks of the flour mixture are combined, mix on medium for no more than 30 seconds.

Evenly divide the batter among the prepared pans. Bake for 26 to 30 minutes, until a toothpick inserted into the center of each cake comes out clean. Remove the cakes from the oven but keep the oven on. Let the cakes cool on a wire rack for 10 to 15 minutes before removing from the pans. Allow the cakes to cool completely, right-side up, on the wire rack before removing the parchment. Level the tops of the cakes with a long serrated knife as needed.

MAKE THE 8-INCH (20-CM) CAKE

Grease and flour three 8-inch (20-cm) cake pans and line the bottoms with parchment paper.

Make the batter using the same method as above. Evenly divide the batter among the prepared pans. Bake for 25 to 28 minutes, until a toothpick inserted into the center of each cake comes out clean. Let the cakes cool on a wire rack for 10 to 15 minutes before removing from the pans. Allow the cakes to cool completely, right-side up, on a wire rack before removing the parchment. Level the tops of the cakes with a long serrated knife as needed.

MAKE THE WHIPPED MASCARPONE BUTTERCREAM

In the bowl of a stand mixer fitted with the paddle attachment (or in a large bowl using a handheld mixer), beat the butter and mascarpone on medium speed until smooth and creamy. With the mixer running on low, slowly add 4½ cups (560 g) of the confectioners' sugar, the milk, and vanilla. Once incorporated, turn the mixer up to medium-high and mix for 4 to 6 minutes, until the buttercream is white, fluffy, and smooth. Add the remaining 1 cup (125 g) confectioners' sugar ¼ cup (30 g) at a time and mix until the desired consistency is reached; the buttercream should be soft and spreadable, but not runny.

ASSEMBLE AND STACK THE CAKES

Place one 8-inch (20-cm) cake layer on a large cake board or serving plate. Fill a piping bag fitted with a large round tip with buttercream. Pipe kisses around the top edge of the cake. Spoon in ⅓ to ½ cup (80 to 120 ml) of the jam and smooth with the back of a spoon. Top with a second cake layer and gently press down to secure. Repeat with the buttercream and jam; place the final cake layer on top.

Place one 6-inch (15-cm) cake layer on a 6-inch (15-cm) cake board. Refill the piping bag with the large round tip with buttercream, if necessary. Pipe kisses around the top edge of the cake. Spoon in ¼ cup (60 ml) of the jam and smooth with the back of a spoon. Top with a second cake layer and gently press down to secure. Repeat with the buttercream and jam; place the final cake layer on top.

To support the top tier, cut and insert the dowels or straws in the 8-inch (20-cm) cake as described on page 279. Using a large offset spatula, carefully lift and place the 6-inch (15-cm) cake in the center of the bottom tier.

DECORATE THE CAKE

To decorate the naked cake, fill a piping bag fitted with a large round tip with buttercream. Pipe kisses around the top edge of the top tier of cake. Fill a piping bag fitted with a small round tip with buttercream and pipe a pearl border where the two tiers meet (see page 275). Decorate with fresh strawberries and flowers, if desired.

If eating the cake the same day as assembled, store it at room temperature until ready to serve. If assembled in advance, wrap the sides in plastic wrap and store in the refrigerator overnight. Bring to room temperature for 30 minutes before serving. Store leftovers loosely covered with plastic wrap in the refrigerator for up to 3 days.

Working with Fresh Flowers

* * *

Using fresh flowers and herbs is an easy way to add a touch of flair to your cakes and bakes, but there are A FEW RULES TO ABIDE BY:

1   Be sure that any flower used on or near food is nontoxic. They should be organic when possible and unsprayed.

2   Do not poke the stems of the flowers directly into the cake. If needed, wrap the stems in floral tape or plastic wrap before anchoring the flowers in the cake.

3   Alternatively, insert a plastic or paper straw into the cake and place the wrapped stem of the flower inside.

SOME SAFE FLOWERS AND HERBS: Roses, Marigolds, Violets, Sunflowers, Hibiscus, Carnations, Chamomile, Gardenias, Lilacs, Pansies, Baby's breath, Jasmine, Lavender, Rosemary, Thyme, Mint

Angel Food Cupcakes

FEATURED DECORATING TECHNIQUE:
CLOUD CUPCAKE FROSTING

These cupcakes are like little fluffy clouds of deliciousness. The cake is so springy, light, and not at all weighed down by the equally heavenly whipped cream. The pillow-soft cupcakes with refreshing mint cream may be understated, but, trust me, they are also unexpectedly delightful. My dad says these are the best cupcakes he's ever tasted; I hope you agree.

I've steeped fresh mint in the cream overnight, but you could also do the same with fresh basil, lavender, or crushed coffee beans—the longer the infusion, the stronger the flavor will be.

MAKES 10 TO 12 EXTRA-LARGE OR 16 REGULAR CUPCAKES

FOR THE FRESH MINT WHIPPED CREAM:

1½ cups (360 ml) heavy cream

½ cup (25 g) lightly packed chopped fresh mint

3 tablespoons confectioners' sugar

1 or 2 drops pure peppermint extract (optional)

FOR THE CUPCAKES:

6 large egg whites

¾ teaspoon cream of tartar

¾ cup plus 1 tablespoon (160 g) granulated sugar

Pinch of salt

½ teaspoon vanilla bean paste or pure vanilla extract

½ cup (65 g) cake flour

TO ASSEMBLE:

Fresh raspberries

Fresh mint leaves

MAKE THE FRESH MINT WHIPPED CREAM

Put the cream and mint in a container and stir together. Cover and chill in the refrigerator for 8 hours or up to overnight.

When ready to assemble, strain the cream through a fine-mesh sieve into a large bowl or the bowl of a stand mixer, pressing gently on the mint with a rubber spatula to extract all of the cream. Discard the mint.

Using a handheld mixer or the stand mixer fitted with the whisk attachment, whip the infused cream with the confectioners' sugar on high speed until it holds medium-soft peaks. For a more intense mint flavor, add a drop or two of peppermint extract. Whisk to combine.

MAKE THE CUPCAKES

Preheat the oven to 350°F (175°C). Line two regular cupcake pans with regular or extra-large paper liners.

Put the egg whites in the bowl of a stand mixer fitted with the whisk attachment. Sprinkle in the cream of tartar. Mix on low speed until the egg whites begin to form small, tight bubbles. Over the course of a couple of minutes, gradually increase the speed to medium-high while slowly adding the sugar, followed by the salt. Mix on medium-high until medium-stiff peaks form. The whites should still be pillowy, but not dry or clumpy. (Unlike a true meringue, which contains twice the amount of sugar, they will not be particularly glossy.) Add the vanilla and whip again just until combined.

Stop the mixer. Using a rubber spatula, carefully fold in the flour in two or three batches; be thorough, but do your best not to deflate the batter.

Use a small disher or mechanical ice cream scoop or two spoons to plop the batter into the cupcake liners, filling them nearly to the top. With the back of a spoon or a small offset spatula, smooth the tops into small domes.

Bake until the tops are browned and a toothpick inserted into the center of a cupcake comes out clean, 14 to 16 minutes for regular cupcakes or 20 to 23 minutes for extra-large ones. Let the cupcakes cool in the pans for about 5 minutes before moving them to a wire rack to cool completely. The cupcakes may contract/shrink slightly as they cool.

ASSEMBLE THE CUPCAKES

Fill a piping bag fitted with a large round tip with the mint whipped cream. Pipe the whipped cream on top of the cooled cupcakes. To decorate with the cloud cupcake frosting technique, hover the tip ½ inch (1.5 cm) over the top of the cupcake and apply continuous pressure to the piping bag, keeping the bag perpendicular to the top of the cupcake, until a large mound of icing covers the top of the cupcake (see page 273). Garnish with raspberries and mint.

Serve the cupcakes within 30 minutes of assembling. Store leftovers loosely covered with plastic wrap or in a cake box in the refrigerator for 2 to 3 days.

Mini Mocha Cakes

FEATURED DECORATING TECHNIQUE: ROSETTE FROSTING

These mini-cakes are extremely versatile and should find their way into your party recipe rotation. Guests will be so thrilled to have their own, individual cakes that they will never guess that these minis were easier to assemble than a full-size layer cake. MAKES ABOUT 9 MINI-CAKES

FOR THE BROWN BUTTER BUTTERCREAM:

¾ cup (1½ sticks/170 g) unsalted butter

2½ cups (315 g) confectioners' sugar, sifted if needed

1 teaspoon pure vanilla extract

Pinch of salt

1 to 2 tablespoons whole milk, if needed

FOR THE CHOCOLATE SHEET CAKE:

1½ cups (190 g) all-purpose flour

½ teaspoon baking soda

½ teaspoon baking powder

½ teaspoon salt

⅓ cup (80 ml) sour cream or full-fat plain yogurt

1 large egg

1 large egg yolk

1½ teaspoons pure vanilla extract

¼ teaspoon pure almond extract (optional)

¾ cup (180 ml) brewed coffee or water

¾ cup (1½ sticks/170 g) unsalted butter

1½ cups (300 g) granulated sugar

¼ cup (25 g) unsweetened cocoa powder

TO ASSEMBLE:

1 recipe Coffee Simple Syrup (page 168)

Unsweetened cocoa powder, for dusting

MAKE THE BROWN BUTTER BUTTERCREAM

In a light-colored medium saucepan, melt the butter over medium-low heat. Increase the heat to medium-high and cook, stirring to keep the milk solids from sticking and burning at the bottom of the pan, for about 8 minutes, until the butter is very fragrant and nutty, and light-medium amber in color; there will be dark brown bits at the bottom of the pan.

Strain the browned butter through a fine-mesh sieve into a heatproof container and discard any burnt milk solids. Chill the browned butter in the refrigerator until it has the consistency of room-temperature butter, about 1 hour.

In the bowl of a stand mixer fitted with the paddle attachment (or in a large bowl using a handheld mixer), mix the browned butter on low until smooth. Slowly add the confectioners' sugar, vanilla, and salt. Once incorporated, turn the mixer up to medium speed and mix for a couple of minutes, or until smooth and creamy. If the filling is too thick, add the milk 1 tablespoon at a time until the desired consistency is reached.

MAKE THE CHOCOLATE SHEET CAKE

Preheat the oven to 350°F (175°C). Grease a 9 by 13-inch (23 by 33-cm) cake pan and line the bottom with parchment paper.

Sift together the flour, baking soda, baking powder, and salt into a medium bowl.

In a separate medium bowl, whisk together the sour cream, egg, egg yolk, vanilla, and almond extract (if using).

In a medium-large saucepan, combine the coffee and butter and heat over medium heat until the butter has melted. Whisk the sugar and cocoa powder into the coffee mixture until well combined. Remove the saucepan from the heat and stir in the sour cream mixture. Whisk in the flour mixture until smooth.

Tip the batter into the prepared pan. Bake for 20 to 22 minutes, until a toothpick inserted into the center of the cake comes out clean. Let the cake cool for at least 15 to 20 minutes on a wire rack before removing the cake from the pan. Let the cake cool completely before assembling.

ASSEMBLE THE CAKES

Generously brush the top of the cooled sheet cake with the coffee simple syrup. Using a 2- to 2½-inch (5- to 6-cm) round cutter, punch out rounds of cake and transfer them to a clean baking sheet or cutting board.

Fill a piping bag fitted with a star tip with the buttercream. Pipe rosettes (page 275) on half of the cake rounds. Place the plain cake rounds on top to create miniature two-layer cakes. Pipe rosettes on the top of each cake and dust with cocoa powder.

Place the mini-cakes in a cake pan and loosely wrap with plastic if you're not serving them immediately. Store, covered, at room temperature for up to 2 days.

Hand Pies and Pie Pops

FEATURED DECORATING TECHNIQUES: PIE DOUGH CUT-OUTS AND APPLIQUÉS

These individual treats make pie baking so easy. Whether on a stick or of the handheld variety, these single-serving pies are quick and simple. The mix-and-match fillings are perfect for making by yourself or with the family—plus, you can use whatever you already have in your pantry! Everett loves to help by sprinkling on bits of chocolate and berries, when he is not trying to sneak handfuls of blueberries into his mouth, that is. My personal favorites are apricot jam with tart raspberries, and dark chocolate with fresh cherry halves, but please get creative with whatever combinations you'd like! Serving a crowd? Feel free to double the recipe! MAKES 10 TO 14 PIE POPS OR 8 TO 12 HAND PIES

Hand Pies

1 recipe single-crust All-Butter Pie Dough (page 183), chilled

½ cup (120 ml) assorted jams, apple butter, or Nutella

Berries or halved cherries

Chopped nuts (pistachio, almonds, or walnuts)

Chopped chocolate

TO ASSEMBLE:

1 large egg

1 tablespoon whole milk

Granulated or turbinado sugar, for sprinkling

Line a baking sheet with parchment paper. Let the chilled pie dough soften at room temperature for about 10 minutes.

Roll out the pie dough to ⅛ to ¼ inch (3 to 6 mm) thick. Cut out rounds of pie dough using a 3- to 4-inch (8- to 10-cm) round cookie or biscuit cutter. Gently stack the pie dough scraps, reroll, and cut out as many rounds as you can.

Fill the center of each dough round with a tablespoon of jam, a fresh berry or two, a sprinkle of chopped nuts, a few pieces of chopped chocolate, or a combination of any of the ingredients, leaving the edges of the pie dough exposed. Do not overfill. Brush the edges with a small amount of water and fold the dough over on itself to form half-moons. Press the edges together and crimp with the tines of a fork to seal. Vent the hand pies by carefully cutting small slits in the tops with a paring knife. Place them on the prepared baking sheet and chill in the refrigerator for 15 to 20 minutes.

Preheat the oven to 375°F (190°C).

FINISH THE HAND PIES

When ready to bake, whisk together the egg and milk to make an egg wash. Brush the egg wash over the chilled hand pies and sprinkle them with sugar. Bake for 16 to 20 minutes, until the crusts are golden brown. Let cool on the baking sheet on a wire rack before serving.

Hand pies are best eaten the day that they are made. Store leftovers wrapped with plastic or foil at room temperature for 2 to 3 days.

Pie Pops

1 recipe single-crust All-Butter Pie Dough (page 183), chilled

½ cup (120 ml) assorted jams, apple butter, or Nutella

Berries or halved cherries

Chopped nuts (pistachios, almonds, or walnuts)

Chopped chocolate

TO ASSEMBLE:

1 large egg

1 tablespoon whole milk or water

Granulated or turbinado sugar, for sprinkling

Line a baking sheet with parchment paper. Let the chilled pie dough soften at room temperature for about 10 minutes.

Roll out the dough to ⅛ to ¼ inch (3 to 6 mm) thick. Cut out rounds of dough using a 2- to 2½-inch (5- to 6-cm) round cookie or biscuit cutter. Gently stack the dough scraps, reroll, and cut as many rounds as you can.

HOW TO MAKE

Pie Dough Cut-Outs

Place half of the pie dough rounds on the prepared baking sheet. Fill the center of each with a couple teaspoons of jam, a fresh berry or two, a sprinkle of chopped nuts, a few pieces of chopped chocolate, or a combination of any of the fillings, leaving the edges of the pie dough exposed. Do not overfill.

To decorate the pie pops with pie dough cut-outs and appliqués, use a small cookie cutter (like mini hearts or stars) to cut out small shapes from the centers of the remaining pie dough rounds or make appliqués from the pie dough scraps. Attach appliqués to the tops of the rounds with a dab of water.

Place a lollipop stick on top of the filling, halfway up from the bottom of the pie dough rounds, and gently press down. Brush the edges of the bottom rounds with a small amount of water and place a second dough round (decorated or not) on top. Use a spare lollipop stick or the tines of a fork to crimp the edges and seal together the top and bottom pieces, concentrating on either side of the stick to make sure it is secure. Place the baking sheet with the pie pops in the refrigerator for 15 to 20 minutes.

Preheat the oven to 375°F (190°C).

FINISH THE PIE POPS

When ready to bake, whisk together the egg and milk to make an egg wash. Brush the egg wash over the chilled pie pops and sprinkle them with sugar. Bake for 14 to 18 minutes, until the crusts are golden brown. Let the pie pops cool completely on the baking sheet on a wire rack before serving. The lollipop stick will feel much more secure once the pops cool.

Pie pops are best eaten the day they are made. Store leftovers wrapped with plastic or foil at room temperature for 2 to 3 days.

Celebration Cakes and Seasonal Sweets

Decorative desserts and creative cakes are meant for sharing, and there is no better time to gather 'round and eat delicious treats together than the holidays. Ring in the new year with a Sparkling Raspberry Cake, enjoy a picnic of summer pies, and embrace fall's bounty with Maple Applesauce and Molasses Pumpkin Spice Cakes. Of course, you don't always need a reason to celebrate, but I definitely encourage you to make your special occasions even sweeter with these sensational creations all year long.

Sparkling Raspberry Cake

FEATURED DECORATING TECHNIQUES: SMOOTH FROSTING, FONDANT POLKA DOTS

Kick off the new year with this sparkling beauty! The raspberry curd is bright and bold, and pairs perfectly with the velvety butter cake and Champagne buttercream. My favorite part? The glistening polka dots that mirror the bubbles in a glass of Champagne! Using the wide end of a small piping tip, the polka dots are a breeze to make and are the perfect decoration for nearly any cake. Life is short; eat the cake and save your resolutions for January 2nd. MAKES ONE FOUR-LAYER 6-INCH (15-CM) CAKE; SERVES 10 TO 12

FOR THE RASPBERRY CURD:

1¼ cups (155 g) fresh or frozen raspberries

6 tablespoons (85 g) unsalted butter, diced

2 tablespoons fresh lemon juice

3 large egg yolks

1 large egg

⅔ cup (135 g) granulated sugar

FOR THE VANILLA BUTTER CAKE:

2⅓ cups (305 g) cake flour

1 tablespoon plus ½ teaspoon baking powder

½ teaspoon salt

¾ cup (1½ sticks/ 170 g) unsalted butter, at room temperature

1½ cups (300 g) granulated sugar

2 teaspoons vanilla bean paste

3 egg yolks

1 large egg

1 cup (240 ml) whole milk

FOR THE CHAMPAGNE BUTTERCREAM:

1 small recipe Swiss Meringue Buttercream (page 262)

¼ cup to ⅓ cup (60 to 80 ml) Champagne or other sparkling wine

TO ASSEMBLE AND DECORATE:

Gel food coloring

1 to 2 ounces (30 to 55 g) fondant or marzipan

Cornstarch, for rolling

Gold and silver luster dust

Wire sparklers (see Note)

MAKE THE RASPBERRY CURD

In a small saucepan, heat the raspberries over medium-high heat until they start to break down, about 10 minutes. Strain the raspberries through a fine-mesh sieve into a bowl, pressing the fruit solids against the sieve with a spoon or rubber spatula to extract as much liquid as possible. Discard the solids in the sieve. Measure out ¼ cup (60 ml) of the raspberry juice.

Put the butter in a heatproof bowl and set a fine-mesh sieve over the top.

In a medium saucepan, combine the ¼ cup (60 ml) raspberry juice, the lemon juice, egg yolks, egg, and sugar and whisk to combine. Cook over medium heat, stirring continuously, until the mixture is thick enough to coat the back of a spoon and registers 160°F (70°C) on a candy thermometer, 6 to 8 minutes. If the sides of the saucepan become hot to the touch, reduce the heat to low to keep the eggs from curdling.

Strain the mixture through the sieve over the bowl of butter. Stir until the butter has melted and the mixture is thoroughly combined. Cover with plastic wrap, pressing it directly against the surface of the curd to prevent a skin from forming. Refrigerate until set, at least 4 hours or overnight. (The raspberry curd may be made 1 to 2 weeks in advance and stored in the refrigerator.)

MAKE THE VANILLA BUTTER CAKE

Preheat the oven to 350°F (175°C). Grease and flour four 6-inch (15-cm) cake pans and line the bottoms with parchment paper (see Notes).

Sift together the flour, baking powder, and salt in a large bowl.

In the bowl of a stand mixer fitted with the paddle attachment, beat the butter on medium speed for 2 minutes. Add the sugar and mix on medium-high until light and fluffy, 3 to 5 minutes. Stop the mixer and scrape down the bowl.

Turn the mixer to medium-low and add the vanilla. Add the egg yolks and egg one at a time, mixing until each is incorporated before adding the next. Mix until combined. Stop the mixer and scrape down the bowl.

Turn the mixer to low and add the flour mixture in three batches, alternating with the milk, beginning and ending with the flour mixture. After the last streaks of the flour mixture are combined, mix on medium for no more than 30 seconds.

Evenly divide the batter among the prepared pans. Bake for 24 to 28 minutes, until a toothpick inserted into the center of each cake comes out clean. Let the cakes cool on a wire rack for 10 to 15 minutes before removing from the pans. Allow the cakes to cool completely, right-side up, on the wire rack before removing the parchment. Level the tops of the cakes with a long serrated knife as needed.

MAKE THE CHAMPAGNE BUTTERCREAM

In the bowl of a stand mixer fitted with the paddle attachment, mix the buttercream until silky smooth. Slowly add the ¼ cup (60 ml) of Champagne and mix until combined. Add more to taste, 1 tablespoon at a time, making sure not to "break" the buttercream.

ASSEMBLE THE CAKE

Place one cake layer on a cake board or serving dish. Fill a piping bag fitted with a large round tip with the buttercream. Pipe a ring of buttercream around the top edge of the cake to create a "dam." Fill the ring with one-third of the raspberry curd. Top with a second cake layer and repeat. Repeat with a third cake layer, then place the final cake layer on top.

Crumb coat the cake with the buttercream and chill in the refrigerator for 15 minutes.

DECORATE THE CAKE

Smoothly frost the cake with the remaining buttercream.

To decorate the cake with fondant polka dots, knead the gel food coloring into the fondant to create your desired colors. On a surface lightly dusted with cornstarch, roll out the fondant to ⅛ to ¼ inch (3 to 6 mm) thick. Using the wide end of a small piping tip, cut out polka dots of fondant. Dust them with the luster dust as desired. Place the polka dots on the top and sides of the frosted cake, gently pressing them into the buttercream to adhere.

Loosely cover the cake with plastic wrap or store in a cake box in the refrigerator until 30 minutes before serving. Let the cake sit at room temperature for 30 minutes before serving. Store leftovers loosely covered with plastic wrap or in a cake box in the refrigerator for 3 to 4 days.

*　　*　　*

NOTES: Wrap the sparkler stems in floral tape before inserting them into cake, or use regular candles.

If you don't have four 6-inch (15 cm) pans, the cake may be baked in three 6-inch (15 cm) cake pans for 28 to 32 minutes. Be careful not to fill the pans more than three-quarters of the way full. Extra batter may be baked off as cupcakes for 22 to 25 minutes.

Meringue Gems

FEATURED DECORATING TECHNIQUE:
ROSETTE PIPING

I typically think of Valentine's Day treats as being insanely decadent and chocolaty. However, if you find yourself and your sweetheart dining out on rich foods for dinner, then sometimes a light bite for dessert might be the perfect ending to a romantic date. Like a mini-pavlova, these Meringue Gems are light, crisp, creamy, and fresh—all in a cute, two-bite package!

MAKES ABOUT 36 MERINGUES

FOR THE MERINGUES:

3 large egg whites

¾ cup (150 g) granulated sugar

¼ teaspoon cream of tartar

½ teaspoon vanilla bean paste or pure vanilla extract

Pink gel food coloring

TO ASSEMBLE:

¼ teaspoon rose water (optional)

½ recipe Whipped Cream (page 263)

36 fresh raspberries

MAKE THE MERINGUES

Preheat the oven to 225°F (110°C). Line two baking sheets with parchment paper.

In the bowl of a stand mixer fitted with the whisk attachment, begin beating the egg whites on low speed until they foam, form small, tight bubbles, and turn opaque. Over the course of 2 to 3 minutes, gradually increase the speed to medium while slowly adding the sugar and cream of tartar. Mix on medium-high speed until the egg whites hold glossy, stiff peaks. Add the vanilla and gel food coloring. Mix until incorporated.

Fill a piping bag fitted with a medium-large star tip (Wilton #1M) with the meringue. Pipe rosettes onto the prepared baking sheets (see page 275). Bake for 1 hour to 1 hour 15 minutes, until the meringues are crisp on the outside and easily peel off the parchment paper. The baked meringues can be stored in an airtight container at room temperature for up to 5 days.

Gently whisk the rose water (if using) into the whipped cream. Fill a piping bag fitted with a large round tip with the whipped cream. Pipe a small dollop of cream in the center of each meringue rosette. Top with a fresh raspberry.

Serve immediately. Store leftovers in an airtight container in the refrigerator for up to 1 day. If making in advance, store the meringues and whipped cream separately and assemble just before serving.

Chocolate Malt Easter Egg Macarons

FEATURED DECORATING TECHNIQUE: CHOCOLATE SPLATTER

The chocolate malted milk powder added to this fudgy filling is everything you didn't know you needed from these cute, whimsical macarons. It adds depth and creaminess to the otherwise sweet and sugary filling. From their curvy shapes to their robin's egg blue color and realistic speckle finish, these are the perfect Easter or spring celebration treat! MAKES 24 TO 36 MACARONS

FOR THE EGG-SHAPED MACARON SHELLS:

Batter for 1 recipe French- or Italian-Method Macaron Shells (page 99), tinted blue (I recommend a few drops of AmeriColor Electric Blue)

TO DECORATE:

1 tablespoon unsweetened cocoa powder

A few drops of vodka or other clear alcohol

FOR THE CHOCOLATE MALT FILLING:

1 cup (2 sticks/225 g) unsalted butter, at room temperature

2 to 3 cups (250 to 375 g) confectioners' sugar, sifted if needed

½ cup (50 g) chocolate malted milk powder, such as Ovaltine

2 tablespoons whole milk

1 teaspoon pure vanilla extract

MAKE THE EGG-SHAPED MACARON SHELLS

Line two or three baking sheets with parchment paper or silicone baking mats. Fit a large piping bag with a plain round tip and fill with the macaron batter.

Pipe the egg-shaped macarons by holding the piping bag perpendicular to the prepared baking sheet. Keeping continuous pressure, count "1, 2" then pull down slightly for "3." Release the pressure before pulling the piping bag completely away. The egg shape is subtle; there is no need to exaggerate it.

Once one baking sheet is full, tap the bottom of the sheet a few times in each corner with the palm of your hand. Set aside and repeat with the remaining prepared baking sheet(s). Set the piped macaron shells aside to rest for 20 to 40 minutes, until a skin forms over the shells and the tops feel dry to the touch.

Follow the baking and cooling instructions for macarons (page 99).

DECORATE THE MACARONS

To decorate the macarons with the chocolate spatter technique, stir together the cocoa powder and vodka in a small bowl to create a thick paint.

Place the macaron shells on a piece of parchment paper or baking sheet. Dip a pastry brush or clean paintbrush into the cocoa mixture. Using your finger, flick the brush over the macaron shells to create the speckled/spatter effect. Let dry before filling, about 1 hour.

MAKE THE CHOCOLATE MALT FILLING

In the bowl of a stand mixer fitted with the paddle attachment (or in a large bowl using a handheld mixer), beat the butter on medium speed until smooth and creamy. With the mixer running on low, slowly add 2½ cups (250 g) of the confectioners' sugar, the chocolate malt powder, milk, and vanilla. Once incorporated, turn the mixer up to medium-high and mix for 3 to 5 minutes, until the buttercream is fluffy and smooth and the malt powder has dissolved. Add the remaining ½ cup (65 g) confectioners' sugar as needed ¼ cup (30 g) at a time, until the desired consistency is reached; the buttercream should be soft and spreadable, but not runny.

ASSEMBLE THE MACARONS

Match the macaron shells by size. Fill a piping bag fitted with a plain round tip with the filling and pipe it onto the bottom (flat side) of half of the macaron shells, staying within the edges of the shells. Top with a matching-size shell, flat-side down, and gently press together until the filling is pushed to the edges of the feet. Do not overfill.

Serve at room temperature. Store leftovers in an airtight container in the refrigerator for 3 to 4 days.

Hibiscus Lemon Marbled Macarons

FEATURED DECORATING TECHNIQUE: MARBLE ICING

There are not many people in this world whom I respect as much as I do my mother. As a stay-at-home mom when we were kids, she was one of the hardest-working people I know. And still is. I've never known someone so dependable and generous with her time and love. We've butted heads more times than I am able to keep track of, but now I can easily call her my best friend.

These marbled macarons are as beautiful as my mother's soul. The bright and punchy hibiscus-lemon filling makes these the perfect Mother's Day treat. I love the soft colors and how each macaron swirl is as unique as all our mothers. MAKES 24 TO 36 MACARONS

FOR THE ROYAL ICING:

1 cup (125 g) confectioners' sugar

2¼ teaspoons meringue powder

½ teaspoon fresh lemon juice

Gel food coloring

FOR THE HIBISCUS-LEMON BUTTERCREAM:

¼ cup (50 g) granulated sugar

5 hibiscus tea bags

3 cups (720 ml) Whipped Vanilla Buttercream (page 261; see Notes)

½ teaspoon finely grated lemon zest

1 teaspoon fresh lemon juice

TO ASSEMBLE:

1 recipe French- or Italian-Method Macaron Shells (page 99), tinted the color of your choice, baked

MAKE THE ROYAL ICING

In a medium bowl or the bowl of a stand mixer, whisk together the confectioners' sugar and meringue powder until combined. Add the lemon juice and 2 tablespoons water. Using a handheld mixer or the stand mixer fitted with the whisk attachment, beat the sugar mixture on high until glossy, stiff peaks form. Add 1 to 2 tablespoons more water and stir until the icing has the consistency of Elmer's glue. Transfer to a clean bowl and use immediately.

ASSEMBLE AND DECORATE THE MACARONS

Match the macaron shells by size and set them on a baking sheet.

Use a toothpick to drag gel food coloring in the colors of your choice over the surface of the royal icing. Swirl the colors gently with the toothpick, being careful not to overblend them and lose the marbled detail (see Notes).

To decorate the macarons with the marble icing technique, hold the edges of a macaron shell and carefully dip the top into the marbled royal icing. Swirl, lift, and shake the shell, allowing any excess icing to fall back into the bowl. Flip the shell icing-side up and set it on a baking sheet. Gently rap the shell on the sheet to help the icing settle and get rid of any air bubbles. Wipe the edges with your clean finger or a paintbrush, as needed. Repeat to coat half of the macaron shells. Add more food coloring to the royal icing as you go. As you dip, the colors may become more muted and blended. Let the icing dry completely, at least 2 hours, before filling the macarons.

MAKE THE HIBISCUS-LEMON BUTTERCREAM

Place 1 cup (240 ml) water in a saucepan and bring to a boil. Reduce the heat and stir in the sugar. Add the tea bags and simmer for about 10 minutes. Carefully remove the tea bags, squeezing out any liquid, and cook until the mixture reduces to ¼ cup (60 ml), an additional 10 minutes. Let the syrup cool.

In the bowl of a stand mixer fitted with the paddle attachment, whip the buttercream until soft and fluffy. Add 3 tablespoons of the hibiscus tea syrup, the lemon zest, and the lemon juice and mix until combined. Taste and add more syrup to your liking.

Put the buttercream in a piping bag fitted with a small star tip (Wilton #18). Pipe the filling onto the bottom (flat side) of the undipped macaron shells, staying within the edges of the shells. Top with a matching-size shell with a dipped top, flat-side down, and gently press together until the filling is pushed to the edges of the feet. Do not overfill.

Serve at room temperature. Store leftovers in an airtight container at room temperature for up to 1 day or in the refrigerator for 3 to 4 days.

*   *   *

NOTES: Use the small Whipped Vanilla Buttercream recipe, which yields 3½ cups (840 ml). You'll have a bit left over, but you can store it in the refrigerator for 1 to 2 weeks or in the freezer for up to 3 months. Thaw leftover buttercream in the refrigerator, then bring to room temperature before using.

If you find that the color from your gel food coloring is too saturated, blend with a little of the royal icing in a separate bowl, then return it to the bowl of icing to swirl.

If the royal icing is too thick and won't settle on the macarons, try adding a bit more water.

Apple Blackberry Pie

FEATURED DECORATING TECHNIQUES:
CRIMPED EDGES, PIE DOUGH ROSES

You might think the rosette crust is the star here, but the vanilla-specked and cinnamon-spiced filling is so delicious it practically steals the show. The blackberries tint everything pink, and the vanilla bean paste pairs beautifully with the apples for a delightful, year-round flavor palette. Feel free to skip the roses, if you'd like, and decorate the top as desired. MAKES ONE 9-INCH (23-CM) PIE; SERVES 10 TO 12

3 recipes single-crust All-Butter Pie Dough (page 183)

2 to 2 ½ pounds (900 g to 1 kg) (approximately 5) apples, peeled, cored, and cut into ¼-inch-thick (6-mm) slices

½ cup plus 2 tablespoons (125 g) granulated sugar

2 tablespoons fresh lemon juice

2 cups (280 g) blackberries, large ones cut in half

3 tablespoons all-purpose flour

2 tablespoons cornstarch

2 teaspoons vanilla bean paste

1 teaspoon ground cinnamon

Pinch of salt

TO ASSEMBLE:

1 large egg

1 tablespoon whole milk

Granulated or turbinado sugar, for sprinkling

To make the pie dough roses, let two discs of the chilled pie dough soften at room temperature for 10 minutes, or until it can be easily rolled out.

On a lightly floured surface, roll out each disc of dough until it is ⅛ to ¼ inch (3 to 6 mm) thick. Using 2- and 3½-inch (5- and 8-cm) round cookie or biscuit cutters, cut out as many rounds of pie dough as possible. Stack the scraps, reroll, and cut out as many more rounds as you can.

Line up 4 rounds of the same size in a row with the edges slightly overlapping. Press the overlapping edges to seal. Starting from one short side, carefully roll up the rounds. Using a paring knife, cut off both ends of the rolled-up rounds. Pinch the cut ends of each rose so the rounded "petals" open. Use your fingers to pull and shape the flowers as needed. Trim the base of each flower, as excess dough will keep the crust from baking all the way through. Place the pie dough roses on a baking sheet and chill in the refrigerator. Continue and repeat until all the roses are made. You will need 30 to 40 roses of various sizes to cover a 9-inch (23-cm) pie.

In a large skillet, combine the apple slices, ¼ cup (50 g) of the sugar, and 1 tablespoon of the lemon juice. Cook over medium heat until the apples just begin to soften, about 10 minutes. Remove from the heat and place in a large bowl to cool.

In a small bowl, toss the blackberries with 2 tablespoons of the remaining sugar and the remaining 1 tablespoon lemon juice. Set aside to macerate for 20 minutes.

Remove the remaining chilled pie dough from the refrigerator and let soften at room temperature for 10 minutes.

On a lightly floured surface, roll out the pie dough until it is ⅛ to ¼ inch (3 to 6 mm) thick and 12 inches (30 cm) in diameter. Fit the pie dough into a 9-inch (23-cm) pie pan. Trim the excess dough, leaving a 1-inch (2.5-cm) overhang all around. Tuck the overhanging pie dough under itself and crimp (see page 195). Place in the refrigerator.

HOW TO MAKE
Pie Dough Roses

Stack the dough scraps and reroll. Using a paring knife, cut out leaves. Using the back of the knife, gently score the leaves down the center and pinch one end to shape. Place the leaves on the baking sheet with the roses and chill as you finish the filling.

Drain the berries in a fine-mesh sieve and add them to the bowl with the apples. Add the remaining ¼ cup (50 g) sugar, the flour, cornstarch, vanilla, cinnamon, and salt. Toss to combine.

Remove the prepared bottom crust from the refrigerator. Arrange the apples slices in tight layers in the pie pan, with the blackberries evenly scattered throughout. Place the pie dough roses and leaves over the filling. Gently tug on the petals for full coverage. Leaving a few spaces between roses is okay. Refrigerate the filled pie for 30 minutes.

Preheat the oven to 425°F (220°C) with a rack in the lowest position.

FINISH THE PIE

When ready to bake, gently whisk together the egg and milk to make an egg wash. Brush the egg wash over the pie with a pastry brush and sprinkle the pie with sugar. Place the pie on a rimmed baking sheet and bake for 25 minutes. Lower the oven temperature to 375°F (190°C) and bake for 30 to 40 minutes more, until the crust is golden brown, the juices are bubbling, and the tip of a pairing knife easily pierces through the fruit (in between the roses).

Let the pie cool completely before slicing, at least 4 hours. Store leftovers covered with foil or plastic wrap at room temperature for up to 2 days or in the refrigerator for up to 3 days.

Cinnamon Peach Apricot Pie

FEATURED DECORATING TECHNIQUES: PIE DOUGH BRAIDS, CRIMPED EDGES

I prefer an even mix of peaches and apricots in this sweet summer pie. I've also added a layer of crushed cookies at the bottom of the pie to make sure the piecrust doesn't become soggy. MAKES ONE 9-INCH (23-CM) PIE; SERVES 10 TO 12

1 recipe double-crust All-Butter Pie Dough (page 183), chilled

1 pound (455 g) ripe but firm peaches, pitted and sliced about ½ inch (1.5 cm) thick

1 pound (455 g) ripe but firm apricots, pitted and sliced about ½ inch (1.5 cm) thick

½ cup (100 g) granulated sugar

2 tablespoons fresh lemon juice

1 apple, peeled, cored, and grated

2 tablespoons tapioca starch

2 tablespoons all-purpose flour

1½ teaspoons ground cinnamon

¼ teaspoon freshly grated nutmeg

1 teaspoon pure vanilla extract

½ teaspoon pure almond extract

⅓ cup (40 g) amaretti or graham cracker crumbs, from 8 to 10 cookies

TO ASSEMBLE:

1 large egg

1 tablespoon whole milk

Granulated or turbinado sugar, for sprinkling

To make the pie dough braids, let one disc of the chilled pie dough soften at room temperature for 10 minutes. On a lightly floured surface, roll out the pie dough into a large oval, ⅛ to ¼ inch (3 to 6 mm) thick. Using a paring knife or pastry cutter, cut the oval lengthwise into ½- to 1-inch-wide (1.5- to 2.5-cm) strips. Working with 3 strips at a time, pinch the strips together at the top and gently braid them. The thinner the strips are, the more braids you'll need. The longest braid will need to be about 10 inches (25 cm) long. Place the braids on a baking sheet and chill in the refrigerator.

Remove the remaining dough from the refrigerator and let soften at room temperature for 10 minutes.

Put the peach and apricot slices in a large bowl and toss with ¼ cup (50 g) of the sugar and the lemon juice. Let stand for 20 to 30 minutes.

On a lightly floured surface, roll out the pie dough until it is ⅛ to ¼ inch (3 to 6 mm) thick and 12 to 13 inches (30 to 33 cm) in diameter. Fit the dough round into a 9-inch (23cm) pie pan. Trim the excess dough, leaving a 1-inch (2.5-cm) overhang all around. Chill in the refrigerator.

Drain the juices from the peach mixture, being careful not to crush the fruit. Add the remaining ¼ cup (50 g) sugar and the apple and toss to combine. Add the tapioca starch, flour, cinnamon, nutmeg, vanilla, and almond extract and toss to combine.

Remove the prepared bottom crust from the refrigerator. Sprinkle the cookie crumbs over the bottom of the crust and lightly press them into the dough. Tip the fruit filling into the pan, leaving the juices behind. Lay the chilled braids on top of the filling in parallel rows and trim the ends, leaving a ½ inch (1.5-cm) overhang all around. Fold the overhanging dough of the bottom crust up and over the ends of the braids. Crimp the edges (see page 195) and press them to the pie pan to secure. Refrigerate the filled pie for 30 minutes.

Preheat the oven to 425°F (220°C) with a rack in the lowest position.

FINISH THE PIE

When ready to bake, gently whisk together the egg and milk to make an egg wash. Brush the egg wash over the pie with a pastry brush and sprinkle the pie with sugar. Place the pie on a rimmed baking sheet and bake for 25 minutes. Lower the oven temperature to 375°F (190°C) and bake for 30 to 40 minutes more, until the crust is golden brown and the juices are bubbling.

Let the pie cool completely before slicing, at least 4 hours. Store leftovers covered at room temperature for up to 2 days or in the refrigerator for up to 3 days.

Blueberry Plum Nectarine Pie

FEATURED DECORATING TECHNIQUES: CLASSIC LATTICE, FIVE-STRAND BRAID EDGE, PIE DOUGH CUT-OUTS

The lavender sugar adds subtle floral notes to this late-summer combination. If using frozen blueberries, do not thaw them before mixing with the other fruits. Macerating the stone fruit ahead of time will draw out any excess liquid, and the pectin in the shredded apple will help thicken everything up. Be sure to bake until the filling is really bubbling to ensure that the tapioca flour does its job. MAKES ONE 9-INCH (23-CM) PIE; SERVES 10 TO 12

3 recipes single-crust All-Butter Pie Dough (page 183)

¾ pound (340 g) plums, pitted and sliced about ½ inch (1.5 cm) thick

¾ pound (340 g) nectarines, pitted and sliced about ½ inch (1.5 cm) thick

⅔ cup plus 2 tablespoons (160 g) granulated sugar

2 tablespoons fresh lemon juice

2 teaspoons dried culinary lavender

1½ cups (220 g) fresh or frozen blueberries

1 apple, peeled, cored, and grated

¼ cup (35 g) tapioca starch (see Notes)

1 tablespoon all-purpose flour

Pinch of salt

TO ASSEMBLE:

1 large egg

1 tablespoon whole milk

Granulated or turbinado sugar, for sprinkling

To make the five-strand braid edge, let one disc of the chilled pie dough soften at room temperature for 10 minutes, or until it can be easily rolled out.

On a lightly floured surface, roll out the pie dough into a large oval, ⅛ to ¼ inch (3 to 6 mm) thick. Using a paring knife or pastry cutter, cut the oval crosswise into ¼-inch-wide (6-mm) strips. Working with 5 strips at a time, pinch the strips together at the top and gently braid them (see Notes). You will need 3 braids, each about 9 inches (23 cm) long. Place the braids on a baking sheet and chill in the refrigerator. Wrap any leftover dough in plastic wrap and refrigerate.

Put the plum and nectarine slices in a large bowl and toss with ⅓ cup (65 g) of the sugar and the lemon juice. Let stand for 20 to 30 minutes.

Remove a second disc of chilled pie dough from the refrigerator and let soften at room temperature for 10 minutes, or until it can be easily rolled out.

On a lightly floured surface, roll out the pie dough until it is ⅛ to ¼ inch (3 to 6 mm) thick and 12 inches (30 cm) in diameter. Fit the pie dough into a 9-inch (23-cm) pie pan. Trim the excess dough, leaving a 1-inch (2.5-cm) overhang all around. Place in the refrigerator.

Meanwhile, using a mortar and pestle, crush 2 tablespoons of the remaining sugar and the lavender until finely ground. Sift the mixture through a fine-mesh sieve into a bowl to remove any large pieces of lavender from the sugar.

Remove the remaining disc of chilled pie dough from the refrigerator and let soften at room temperature for 10 minutes, or until it can be easily rolled out.

Roll out the remaining pie dough into an oval ⅛ to ¼ inch (3 to 6 mm) thick. Using a paring knife or pastry cutter, cut the oval crosswise into 7 or 8 long strips, about 1½ inches (4 cm) wide. The longest strips should be 10 to 11 inches (25 to 28 cm) long. Place them on a baking sheet and chill in the refrigerator while you finish the filling.

Drain the juices from the plum mixture, being careful not to crush the fruit. Add the blueberries, shredded apple, the remaining ⅓ cup (65 g) granulated sugar, and the lavender sugar and toss to combine. Add the tapioca starch, flour, and salt. Toss to combine.

Remove the prepared bottom crust from the refrigerator. Tip the filling into the pan, leaving the juices behind. Using the chilled strips of dough, create a lattice top (see page 190). Trim the ends of the strips with a paring knife or kitchen shears, leaving about ½ inch (1.5 cm) overhanging all around. Tuck the overhanging ends of the strips over the overhanging dough from the bottom crust. Press the edges to the rim of the pie pan to secure. Using a touch of water as "glue," attach the braids around the outer edge of the pie, trimming their ends as needed.

To finish with pie dough cut-outs, roll out any remaining dough. Using a paring knife, cut out free-form leaves. Using the back of the knife, gently score the leaves down the center and pinch the ends. Place them on top of the pie where the braids meet, or as desired. Attach with a dab of water, as needed. Refrigerate the filled pie for 30 minutes.

Preheat the oven to 425°F (220°C) with a rack in the lowest position.

FINISH THE PIE

When ready to bake, gently whisk together the egg and milk to make an egg wash. Brush the egg wash over the pie with a pastry brush and sprinkle the pie with sugar. Place the pie on a rimmed baking sheet and bake for 25 minutes. Lower the oven temperature to 375°F (190°C) and bake for 30 to 45 minutes more, until the crust is golden brown and the juices are bubbling.

Let the pie cool completely before slicing, at least 4 hours. Store leftovers covered with foil or plastic wrap at room temperature for up to 2 days or in the refrigerator for up to 3 days.

HOW TO MAKE A
Five-Strand Braided Edge Pie

NOTES: For tapioca starch, look for brands like Bob's Red Mill. Cornstarch can be used instead of tapioca starch if you can't find it or prefer not to use it.

For a braid, take the outer strip and bring it up and over to the center, dividing the other four strands in half. Repeat with the outermost strip from the opposite side, crossing it over the strip in the center, and continue down the length of the braid.

Maple Applesauce Cake

FEATURED DECORATING TECHNIQUES: SMOOTH FROSTING, STAR PIPING, ROSETTE PIPING

The maple brown butter buttercream that smothers this easy applesauce cake is like a giant cuddle. So warm and comforting! The method for the buttercream might appear long, but it is simply a Swiss meringue buttercream with a couple of modifications. A portion of the butter is browned and part of the sugar is replaced with maple syrup. Homemade applesauce made with apples straight from the orchard would be a lovely addition to this cake, but a store-bought variety is more than acceptable. MAKES ONE THREE-LAYER 8-INCH (20-CM) CAKE; SERVES 12 TO 16

FOR THE MAPLE BROWN BUTTER BUTTERCREAM:

3 cups (6 sticks/675 g) unsalted butter

6 large egg whites

1 cup (200 g) granulated sugar

1 cup (240 ml) pure maple syrup

2 teaspoons pure vanilla extract

FOR THE APPLESAUCE CAKE:

3 cups (375 g) all-purpose flour

1 tablespoon baking powder

½ teaspoon baking soda

2 teaspoons ground cinnamon

1 teaspoon ground cardamom

1 teaspoon salt

¼ teaspoon freshly grated nutmeg

1 cup (2 sticks/225 g) unsalted butter, at room temperature

1½ cups (330 g) packed light brown sugar

2 tablespoons grapeseed or canola oil

2 teaspoons pure vanilla extract

4 large eggs

2 cups (480 ml) unsweetened applesauce

¾ cup (90 g) walnuts, toasted and finely chopped

TO DECORATE:

Gel food coloring

Sugar pearls (optional)

MAKE THE MAPLE BROWN BUTTER BUTTERCREAM

In a light-colored medium saucepan, melt 1½ cups (3 sticks/340 g) of the butter over medium-low heat. Increase the heat to medium-high and cook, stirring to keep the milk solids from sticking and burning at the bottom of the pan, for about 8 minutes, until the butter is very fragrant and nutty, and light-medium amber in color; there will be dark brown bits at the bottom of the pan. Strain the browned butter through a fine-mesh sieve into a heatproof container and discard any burnt milk solids. Chill the browned butter in the refrigerator until it has the consistency of room-temperature butter, 45 minutes to 1 hour. Bring the remaining 1½ cups (3 sticks/340 g) butter to room temperature.

Put the egg whites, sugar, and maple syrup in the bowl of a stand mixer. Gently whisk them by hand until just combined. In a medium saucepan, bring an inch or two (2.5 to 5 cm) of water to a simmer over medium-low heat. Place the mixer bowl on top of the saucepan to create a double boiler (be sure the bottom of the bowl does not touch the water). Heat the egg mixture, whisking intermittently, until it reaches 160°F (70°C) on a candy thermometer.

Carefully affix the mixer bowl to the stand mixer (it may be hot) and fit the mixer with the whisk attachment. Beat the egg white mixture on high speed for 8 to 10 minutes, until the mixture holds medium-stiff peaks and the outside of the bowl has cooled to room temperature.

Turn the mixer down to low and add the vanilla. Add the softened butter and browned butter a couple of tablespoons at a time, mixing until each is incorporated before adding the next. Stop the mixer and swap out the whisk for the paddle attachment.

Turn the mixer to medium-high and beat until the buttercream is silky smooth, 3 to 5 minutes.

MAKE THE APPLESAUCE CAKE

Preheat the oven to 350°F (175°C). Grease and flour three 8-inch (20-cm) cake pans.

Sift together the flour, baking powder, baking soda, cinnamon, cardamom, salt, and nutmeg into a large bowl.

In the bowl of a stand mixer fitted with the paddle attachment, beat the butter on medium speed for 2 minutes. Add the brown sugar and mix on medium-high until light and fluffy, 3 to 5 minutes. Add the oil and mix until combined. Stop the mixer and scrape down the bowl.

Turn the mixer to medium-low and add the vanilla. Add the eggs one at a time, mixing until each is incorporated before adding the next. Mix until combined. Stop the mixer and scrape down the bowl.

Turn the mixer to low and add the flour mixture in three batches, alternating with the applesauce, starting and ending with the flour mixture. After the last streaks of the flour mixture are combined, mix on medium for no more than 30 seconds. Stop the mixer and fold in the walnuts by hand.

Evenly divide the batter among the prepared pans. Bake for 22 to 25 minutes, until a toothpick inserted into the center of each cake comes out clean. Let the cakes cool on a wire rack for 10 to 15 minutes before removing from the pans. Allow the cakes to cool completely, right-side up, on the wire rack. Level the tops of the cakes with a long serrated knife as needed.

ASSEMBLE THE CAKE

Place one cake layer on a cake board or serving plate. Place about 1 cup (240 ml) of buttercream on top and spread it out with an offset spatula. Top with a second cake layer and repeat; place the final cake layer on top.

Crumb coat the cake with the buttercream and chill in the refrigerator for 15 minutes.

DECORATE THE CAKE

Divide 1 to 1½ cups (240 to 360 ml) of the buttercream among three or four bowls. Tint each bowl with your choice of gel food coloring.

Smoothly frost the cake with the remaining untinted buttercream. Fill a piping bag fitted with a large star tip (Wilton #1B) with one shade of buttercream. Pipe rosettes in a crescent shape on top of the cake (see page 275). Slightly overlap the rosettes to add dimension. Repeat with a second color of buttercream, making more rosettes and slightly overlapping them. Using the same piping tip, pipe stars to fill in any gaps in the rosette crescent. Fill piping bags fitted with small star tips with the remaining shades of buttercream and pipe small stars on top and near the edges to extend the crescent shape. Sprinkle with sugar pearls, if desired.

If eating the cake the same day as assembled, store it at room temperature until ready to serve. If assembled in advance, store in a cake box in the refrigerator overnight. Bring to room temperature for 30 minutes before serving. Store leftovers loosely covered with plastic wrap in the refrigerator for 3 to 4 days.

Molasses Pumpkin Spice Cake

FEATURED DECORATING TECHNIQUES: SMOOTH FROSTING, WEAVE PIPING

I tested this cake with both roasted and canned pumpkin. By the time it gets baked into the fragrant spice cake, you can't even taste the difference, so choose a canned pumpkin that is indeed 100% pumpkin and save your energy for the molasses buttercream. Using egg yolks instead of whites, this French meringue buttercream is rich, creamy, and utterly luxurious. A splash of molasses and a pinch of cinnamon really complement the warm spices of the pumpkin cake. MAKES ONE THREE-LAYER 8-INCH (20-CM) CAKE; SERVES 12 TO 16

FOR THE PUMPKIN SPICE CAKE:

- 3 cups (375 g) all-purpose flour
- 2 teaspoons baking powder
- 1 teaspoon baking soda
- 1 teaspoon salt
- 2½ teaspoons ground cinnamon
- 1½ teaspoons ground cardamom
- 1½ teaspoons ground ginger
- ¼ teaspoon ground cloves
- ¾ cup (1½ sticks/175 g) unsalted butter, at room temperature
- 2 cups (440 g) packed brown sugar
- 3 tablespoons grapeseed oil
- 2 teaspoons pure vanilla extract
- 4 large eggs
- ½ cup (120 ml) sour cream
- 1½ cups (360 ml) pure pumpkin puree

FOR THE MOLASSES BUTTERCREAM:

- 5 large egg yolks
- 1 whole egg
- 1 cup (200 g) granulated sugar
- 2 cups (4 sticks/450 g) unsalted butter, slightly softened
- 2 tablespoons molasses
- 1 teaspoon pure vanilla extract
- ½ teaspoon ground cinnamon

MAKE THE PUMPKIN SPICE CAKE

Preheat the oven to 350°F (175°C). Grease and flour three 8-inch (20-cm) cake pans.

Sift together the flour, baking powder, baking soda, salt, cinnamon, cardamom, ginger, and cloves into a large bowl.

In the bowl of a stand mixer fitted with the paddle attachment, beat the butter on medium speed for 2 minutes. Add the brown sugar and mix on medium-high until light and fluffy, 3 to 5 minutes. Add the oil and mix until combined. Stop the mixer and scrape down the bowl.

Turn the mixer to medium-low and add the vanilla. Add the eggs one at a time, mixing until each is incorporated before adding the next. Mix until combined. Stop the mixer and scrape down the bowl.

Turn the mixer to low and add the flour mixture in two batches, alternating with the sour cream, starting and ending with the flour mixture. After the last streaks of the flour mixture are combined, mix on medium for no more than 30 seconds. Add the pumpkin puree and mix until smooth.

Evenly divide the batter among the prepared pans. Bake for 23 to 28 minutes, until a toothpick inserted into the center of each cake comes out clean. Let the cakes cool on a wire rack for 10 to 15 minutes before removing from the pans. Allow the cakes to cool completely, right-side up, on the wire rack. Level the tops of the cakes with a long serrated knife as needed.

MAKE THE MOLASSES BUTTERCREAM

Place a fine-mesh sieve over the bowl of a stand mixer.

Put the egg yolks, egg, sugar, and ⅓ cup (60 ml) water in a heat-safe mixing bowl. Whisk to combine. In a medium saucepan, bring an inch or two (2.5 to 5 cm) of water to a simmer over medium-low heat. Place the mixing bowl on top of the saucepan to create a double boiler (be sure the bottom of the bowl does not touch the water). Heat the egg mixture, stirring constantly with a heat-safe rubber spatula, until it reaches 160°F (70°C) on a candy thermometer.

Carefully pour the egg mixture through the sieve and into the mixer bowl. Carefully affix the mixer bowl to the stand mixer (it may be hot), remove the sieve, and fit the mixer with the whisk attachment. Beat the egg mixture on high speed for 4 to 6 minutes, until the mixture is foamy and pale in color and the outside of the bowl has cooled to room temperature.

Turn the mixer down to low and begin adding in the butter in thin slices, mixing until each is incorporated before adding the next. Stop the mixer and swap out the whisk for the paddle attachment.

With the mixer on low, slowly add the molasses, vanilla, and cinnamon. Turn the mixer to medium-high and beat until the buttercream is silky smooth, 1 to 3 minutes.

ASSEMBLE THE CAKE

Place one cake layer on a cake board or serving plate. Spread on ¾ to 1 cup (180 to 240 ml) of the buttercream with an offset spatula. Top with a second cake layer and repeat; place the final cake layer on top.

Crumb coat the cake with the buttercream and chill in the refrigerator for 15 minutes.

DECORATE THE CAKE

Smoothly frost the cake with the buttercream. To decorate the cake with the weave piping technique, fill a piping bag fitted with a petal tip (Wilton #104) with the remaining buttercream. Pipe borders around the top and bottom edge of the cake (see page 275).

Loosely cover the cake with plastic wrap or store in a cake box in the refrigerator until 30 minutes before serving. Let the cake sit at room temperature for 30 minutes before serving. Store leftovers loosely covered with plastic wrap or in a cake box in the refrigerator for 3 to 4 days.

NOTES: French meringue buttercream is more delicate and much softer than Swiss, so be sure to add the molasses slowly. Follow that same troubleshooting notes for Swiss meringue buttercream (page 262) if the buttercream appears curdled or soupy.

French buttercream is extremely rich, not-too-sweet, and slightly custard-like. True French buttercream is made with boiling sugar syrup, but this method ensures that the eggs are safe to consume for all. Feel free to substitute French for Swiss meringue buttercream on your favorite cakes by swapping out the molasses and cinnamon for 2 teaspoons of vanilla bean paste. This recipe yields about 4½ cups (1 l) of buttercream.

French buttercream–frosted cakes should be stored in the refrigerator. Bring to room temperature before serving.

Yule Log Cake

FEATURED DECORATING TECHNIQUE:
VERTICAL LAYER CAKE

FOR THE MERINGUE MUSHROOMS:

2 large egg whites

½ cup (100 g) granulated sugar

Pinch of cream of tartar

½ teaspoon pure vanilla extract

Unsweetened cocoa powder, for dusting

Melted chocolate, for gluing

FOR THE WHIPPED CINNAMON CHOCOLATE MOUSSE:

10 ounces (280 g) milk chocolate, finely chopped

2 cups (480 ml) heavy cream

1 cinnamon stick, crushed

Pinch of salt

FOR THE CHOCOLATE SPONGE CAKE:

¾ cup (180 ml) milk

¼ cup (60 ml) canola or grapeseed oil

¼ cup (½ stick/55 g) unsalted butter, melted and cooled

1½ teaspoons pure vanilla extract

8 large eggs

1½ cups (300 g) granulated sugar

1⅓ cups (165 g) all-purpose flour

⅔ cup (65 g) unsweetened cocoa powder

2 teaspoons instant espresso powder

2 teaspoons baking powder

1 teaspoon salt

½ teaspoon ground cinnamon

Confectioners' sugar, for dusting

FOR THE CHOCOLATE BARK:

6 ounces (170 g) dark chocolate coating wafers

FOR THE FUDGE FROSTING:

¾ cup (1½ sticks/170 g) unsalted butter, at room temperature

2½ to 3 cups (310 to 375 g) confectioners' sugar, sifted if needed

¼ cup plus 1 tablespoon (35 g) unsweetened cocoa powder

1 teaspoon pure vanilla extract

Pinch of salt

2 to 3 tablespoons whole milk

4 ounces (115 g) dark chocolate, melted and cooled

TO DECORATE:

Fresh cranberries

Red or pink edible glitter

Unsweetened cocoa powder, for dusting

Fresh rosemary sprigs

Chopped pistachios, for sprinkling

Grated white chocolate, for sprinkling

I grew up deep in the suburbs. We lived in a small neighborhood of only fourteen homes, half of which had children my age. Come Christmas, most of the neighbors would participate in a progressive dinner, where each family would serve a different course, from drinks to dessert, with a few bonus stops in between to make sure everyone had a chance to host. It would take hours! Some of my best holiday memories came from those nights with my close neighborhood friends, causing mischief and putting on amateur Christmas plays. The night always ended with a gift exchange and an epic dessert, like this Yule Log Cake.

Unlike a traditional bûche de noël, *this yule log "stump" presents itself as a vertical layer cake. Tipped on its side, each slice looks like an optical illusion. This is the type of celebration cake that calls for all the bells and whistles. Pick and choose any of the edible garnishes you'd like and have fun! Try not to stress if the cake cracks as it is being rolled; you can piece it back together as you go.* MAKES ONE 8-INCH (20-CM) CAKE; SERVES 10 TO 14

MAKE THE MERINGUE MUSHROOMS

Preheat the oven to 225°F (110°C). Line two baking sheets with parchment paper.

In the bowl of a stand mixer fitted with the whisk attachment, begin beating the egg whites on low speed until the egg whites begin to foam, form small, tight bubbles, and turn opaque. Over the course of 2 to 3 minutes, gradually increase the speed to medium while slowly adding the sugar and cream of tartar. Mix on high speed until the egg whites hold glossy, stiff peaks. Add the vanilla and mix until incorporated.

Fill a piping bag fitted with a large round tip with the meringue. Pipe meringue mushrooms onto the prepared baking sheets, using half of the meringue to pipe mushroom stems and the other half to pipe mushroom tops. For the stems, hold the piping bag perpendicular to the baking sheet and pull up on the bag as you pipe. For the tops, hold the piping bag perpendicular to the baking sheet, hovering the tip over the sheet, and apply even pressure until a small mound of meringue forms, then release the pressure before pulling up on the bag. Bake for 1 hour to 1 hour 15 minutes, until the meringues are crisp on the outside and easy to peel off the parchment. If not using immediately, the baked meringues can be stored in an airtight container at room temperature for up to 5 days.

When ready to assemble the cake, use the tip of a paring knife to gently carve out a small hole in the bottom of each mushroom cap. Using a fine-mesh sieve, dust the tops of the caps with cocoa powder. Taking care not to smear the cocoa, use melted chocolate to glue the mushroom stems into the holes in the caps.

MAKE THE WHIPPED CINNAMON CHOCOLATE MOUSSE

Put the chocolate in a heatproof bowl and set a fine-mesh sieve over the top.

In a small saucepan, combine the cream and cinnamon stick and bring to a simmer. Remove from the heat, cover, and let steep for 5 minutes. Pour the cream through the sieve into the bowl with the chocolate and let stand for 30 seconds. Discard the cinnamon stick. Add the salt and whisk until smooth. Let the ganache cool for about 2 hours, or until it is the consistency of very thick pudding.

MAKE THE CHOCOLATE SPONGE CAKE

Preheat the oven to 350°F (175°C). Grease two 9 by 13-inch (23 by 33-cm) pans and line the bottoms with parchment paper (see Notes).

In a medium bowl, combine the milk, oil, melted butter, and vanilla.

In the bowl of a stand mixer fitted with the whisk attachment, beat the eggs and granulated sugar on medium-high speed until the mixture triples in volume, about 8 minutes. Stop the mixer and sift in the flour, cocoa powder, espresso powder, baking powder, salt, and cinnamon. Using the mixer's whisk, stir the mixture, by hand, until combined. Fold in the milk mixture in two batches until thoroughly combined.

Evenly divide the batter between the prepared pans and bake for 12 to 15 minutes, until the surface springs back when gently touched. Do not overbake, or the cakes may crack.

Dust the warm cakes with a generous amount of confectioners' sugar. Place a clean tea towel on top of each cake. Carefully flip the pans upside down to release the cakes onto the towels. Peel off the parchment paper and dust the bottoms of the cakes with confectioners' sugar. While the cakes are still warm, roll them up in the towels, starting at the short ends. Set the cakes seam-side down and let cool completely in the towels, 30 to 45 minutes. Once cooled, carefully unroll the cakes, remove the towels, and discard the parchment paper. (Like muscle memory, the cake will "remember" to retain its curved shape once cooled.)

MAKE THE CHOCOLATE BARK

Place a large piece of parchment paper on your work surface.

In a microwave-safe bowl, microwave the chocolate coating at 50% power in 30-second intervals, stirring after each, until completely melted and smooth.

Working quickly, spread the melted chocolate over the parchment with an offset spatula. Roll up the parchment paper, with the chocolate inside, and let cool completely.

Once cool, unroll the parchment and break up the "bark" as needed. It should crack naturally into rugged strips.

MAKE THE FUDGE FROSTING

In the bowl of a stand mixer fitted with the paddle attachment (or in a large bowl using a handheld mixer), beat the butter until smooth and creamy. With the mixer running on low speed, gradually add 2½ cups (310 g) of the confectioners' sugar, the cocoa powder, vanilla, and salt. Pour in 2 tablespoons of the milk and mix until incorporated. Turn the mixer up to medium-high and mix until the frosting is smooth and creamy. Stop the mixer and scrape down the bowl. Add the melted chocolate and mix until smooth. Add the remaining ½ cup (65 g) confectioners' sugar ¼ cup (30 g) at a time and/or the remaining 1 tablespoon milk until the desired consistency is achieved; the fudge frosting should be soft and spreadable, not too stiff.

The melted chocolate in the frosting may start to harden as it sits. If the frosting becomes too thick/stiff and difficult to spread at any point, gently rewarm it in the top portion of a double boiler (or in a heatproof bowl set over a saucepan of simmering water; see page 14).

ASSEMBLE THE CAKE

In the bowl of a stand mixer fitted with the whisk attachment or in a bowl using a handheld mixer, whip the cooled ganache on high speed for 60 to 90 seconds. Do not overwhip, or it will turn grainy. Stop the mixer and whisk by hand until the mousse is fluffy and light in both texture and color.

Cut the cooled cakes in half crosswise to create 4 long strips of cake. Spread the whipped chocolate mousse on top of each strip of cake with a small offset spatula, using ½ to ¾ cup (120 to 180 ml) of the mousse per strip of cake. Gently roll one strip to make a spiral. Turn the rolled strip on its side and begin wrapping the remaining cakes around the center spiral, setting the start of each strip at the end of the last one to create a large spiral of cake and filling. Place the cake on a cake board or serving plate and frost it with the fudge frosting.

DECORATE THE CAKE

Put the cranberries in a small bowl and sprinkle with the edible glitter. Swirl the bowl around until the cranberries are covered.

Using a fine-mesh sieve, dust the top of the cake with cocoa powder. Press pieces of the chocolate bark into the fudge frosting to secure around the sides of the cake. Decorate the top of the cake and the cake board with the meringue mushrooms, glittered cranberries, rosemary sprigs, pistachios, and white chocolate.

If eating the cake the same day as assembled, store it at room temperature until ready to serve. If assembled in advance, store in a cake box in the refrigerator overnight. Bring to room temperature for 30 minutes before serving. Store leftovers loosely covered with plastic wrap in the refrigerator for up to 3 days.

NOTE: If working with two cakes at the same time seems intimidating, feel free to cut the cake recipe in half and bake them one at a time.

Candy Cane Marshmallows

FEATURED DECORATING TECHNIQUE: WHITE CHOCOLATE DIP

I spent the better part of my childhood memorizing Tchaikovsky's The Nutcracker, *dancing with my local youth ballet as well as the professional company in town. Many of the parts I was given were in the Divertissements—the quick routines that make up the second act that pay homage to the world's most decadent treats of the nineteenth century. From Spanish chocolate and Chinese tea to dancing candy canes and, of course, the Sugar Plum Fairy, this wondrous act easily fulfills all our sugar-related fantasies. These Candy Cane Marshmallows are my ode to my best Christmas memories of* The Nutcracker. *Sweet, fluffy, and full of peppermint, these whimsical treats capture the joy of the holidays in the form of pink, pillowy squares.* MAKES 24 TO 36 MARSHMALLOWS

About ½ cup (65 g) confectioners' sugar, for dusting

About ½ cup (65 g) cornstarch, for dusting

3 (7-g) envelopes unflavored powdered gelatin (2½ teaspoons)

1½ cups (300 g) granulated sugar

1 cup (240 ml) light corn syrup

¼ teaspoon salt

½ teaspoon vanilla bean paste

½ teaspoon pure peppermint extract

Gel food coloring (optional)

10 ounces (280 g) white chocolate, melted and cooled

¾ cup finely crushed candy canes

In a bowl, whisk together equal parts confectioners' sugar and cornstarch.

Grease a 9 by 13-inch (23 by 33-cm) baking pan and generously dust it with some of the sugar-cornstarch mixture.

Put the gelatin and ½ cup (120 ml) water in the bowl of a stand mixer and set aside for about 5 minutes to bloom.

In a saucepan, combine the granulated sugar, corn syrup, salt, and ½ cup (120 ml) water and heat over high heat until the mixture reaches 238°F (114°C) on a candy thermometer. Remove from the heat.

Affix the mixer bowl with the gelatin to the stand mixer and fit the mixer with the whisk attachment. With the mixer running on medium speed, carefully pour the sugar mixture into the gelatin. Turn the speed to high and mix until the outside of the bowl has cooled to room temperature, 10 to 12 minutes. Add the vanilla and peppermint extracts and a few drops of food coloring, if using, and mix until combined.

Coat a spatula with nonstick cooking spray and scoop the marshmallow mixture into the prepared pan. Working quickly, smooth out the top. Dust the top with some of the sugar-cornstarch mixture. Place a piece of parchment paper on top and gently press down to make sure the top is even. Set aside at room temperature until the marshmallow has set, at least 3 hours.

Coat the blade of a chef's knife with nonstick cooking spray and run it around the inside edge of the baking pan. Place a cutting board on top of the baking pan and gently invert the pan and cutting board together to unmold the marshmallow onto the cutting board. Cut the marshmallows into squares and toss each square in the bowl with the sugar-cornstarch mixture to prevent sticking.

Place a piece of parchment paper on your work surface. Put the melted white chocolate in a bowl and the crushed candy canes in a shallow dish.

To decorate the marshmallows with the white chocolate dip technique, dip the corners of the marshmallows in the white chocolate and scrape off the excess from the bottom. Roll the dipped marshmallows in the crushed candy canes, place on the parchment paper, and allow to set.

Store in an airtight container at room temperature for up to 1 week.

Gingerbread Village Cake

Christmas cookie decorating is a tradition that will always be close to my heart. And while the image has changed over the years, the act of icing cookies and decorating them with generous amounts of sprinkles continues. As a child, we celebrated by decorating my grandmother's cut-out sugar cookies. When Brett and I were first married, we started a new cookie decorating tradition with our nieces and nephews. Flash-forward a few years, we now share this tradition with our own son. Watching Everett climb up on the step stool, so eager to help, makes cleaning sprinkles out of the carpet and icing off the furniture totally worth it.

Instead of trying to construct a single gingerbread house, this Gingerbread Village Cake is decorated with tiny gingerbread structures to make a whole city out of cookies, icing, gumdrops, and peppermints. Plus, speculoos buttercream—yum! Bake your own gingerbread cookies or take the rectangular and square pieces of a gingerbread house kit and decorate them to look like individual buildings. MAKES ONE TWO-TIERED CAKE; SERVES 22 TO 28

FOR THE GINGERBREAD COOKIES:

4 cups (460 g) all-purpose flour

1 tablespoon ground cinnamon

1 tablespoon ground ginger

1 teaspoon ground cloves

¾ teaspoon baking soda

¼ teaspoon salt

½ cup (120 ml) fancy molasses

½ cup (120 ml) corn syrup

¾ cup (165 g) packed brown sugar

¾ cup (1½ sticks/170 g) unsalted butter

FOR THE 6-INCH (15-CM) GINGERBREAD CAKE:

1½ cups (190 g) all-purpose flour

1¼ teaspoons baking powder

Heaping ¼ teaspoon baking soda

¼ teaspoon salt

2 teaspoons ground ginger

¾ teaspoon ground cinnamon

¼ teaspoon ground cloves

½ cup (120 ml) fancy molasses

½ cup (1 stick/115 g) unsalted butter

3 tablespoons water

¾ cup plus 2 tablespoons (195 g) packed light brown sugar

2 large eggs

⅓ cup (30 ml) whole milk

3 tablespoons sour cream

1 teaspoon pure vanilla extract

FOR THE 8-INCH (20-CM) GINGERBREAD CAKE:

3 cups (375 g) all-purpose flour

2½ teaspoons baking powder

¾ teaspoon baking soda

½ teaspoon salt

4 teaspoons ground ginger

1½ teaspoons ground cinnamon

½ teaspoon ground cloves

1 cup (240 ml) fancy molasses

1 cup (2 sticks/225 g) unsalted butter

⅓ cup (80 ml) water

1⅔ cups (365 g) packed light brown sugar

4 large eggs

⅔ cup (160 ml) whole milk

⅓ cup (80 ml) sour cream

2 teaspoons pure vanilla extract

FOR THE SPECULOOS BUTTERCREAM:

1 small recipe Whipped Vanilla Buttercream (page 261)

¾ cup (180 ml) speculoos spread or cookie butter

FOR THE ROYAL ICING:

2 cups (250 g) confectioners' sugar, plus more if needed

4½ teaspoons meringue powder

½ teaspoon fresh lemon juice

TO ASSEMBLE AND DECORATE:

Green gel food coloring

Assorted sprinkles and candies

1 large recipe Whipped Vanilla Buttercream (page 261)

4 wooden dowels or thick plastic straws

Shredded coconut

MAKE THE GINGERBREAD COOKIES

Sift together the flour, cinnamon, ginger, cloves, baking soda, and salt into a large bowl.

In a medium saucepan, stir together the molasses, corn syrup, brown sugar, and butter. Heat over medium-high heat until the butter has melted and the sugar has dissolved. Remove from the heat and stir in half of the flour mixture until the mixture becomes thick and difficult to mix by hand.

Transfer the mixture to the bowl of a stand mixer fitted with the paddle attachment. Add the remaining flour mixture and mix on low speed for a few minutes to let some of the heat escape. Transfer the bowl to the refrigerator to chill for about 10 minutes. At this point, the dough should be smooth and pliable.

In the meantime, cut out parchment paper templates for the buildings, if desired.

Preheat oven to 350°F (175°C).

Divide the dough into 2 or 3 portions. Gather one portion into a ball with your hands, then pat it down into a flat disc. Roll out the dough between two pieces of parchment paper the size of your baking sheet to about ¼ inch (6 mm) thick. Depending on the size of your baking sheet, the dough should nearly cover the parchment paper. Peel off the top piece of parchment.

If using templates, very lightly dust the surface of the rolled dough with a touch of flour and arrange the templates on top, leaving about 1 inch (2.5 cm) between each. Using a sharp paring knife, neatly trim the dough around the templates; otherwise, cut the shapes of the buildings freehand (like I did). Cut out windows with a small square cutter. Remove the templates and peel away any excess dough between the cut-out pieces. Brush off any excess flour.

Carefully transfer the cookies, still on the parchment paper, to a baking sheet and bake for about 15 minutes, until fragrant and slightly browned. Let cool for at least 5 minutes on the baking sheet before transferring the cookies to a wire rack to cool completely.

Repeat with the remaining dough.

MAKE THE 6-INCH (15-CM) GINGERBREAD CAKE

Preheat the oven to 350°F (175°C). Grease and flour three 6-inch (15-cm) cake pans.

Sift together the flour, baking powder, baking soda, salt, ginger, cinnamon, and cloves into a large bowl.

In a large saucepan, stir together the molasses, butter, brown sugar, and water over medium heat until the butter has melted. Stir in the brown sugar and heat until dissolved. Remove from the heat.

In a medium bowl, whisk together the eggs, milk, sour cream, and vanilla. Add the egg mixture to the molasses mixture and stir until combined. Stir in the flour mixture until combined.

Evenly divide the batter among the prepared pans. Bake for 19 to 22 minutes, until a toothpick inserted into the center of each cake comes out clean. Let the cakes cool on a wire rack for 10 to 15 minutes before removing from the pans. Allow the cakes to cool completely, right-side up, on the wire rack. Level the tops of the cakes with a long serrated knife as needed.

MAKE THE 8-INCH (20-CM) GINGERBREAD CAKE

Grease and flour three 8-inch (20-cm) cake pans.

Make the batter using the same method as above. Evenly divide the batter among the prepared pans. Bake for 20 to 24 minutes, until a toothpick inserted into the center of each cake comes out clean. Let the cakes cool on a wire rack for 10 to 15 minutes before removing from the pans. Allow the cakes to cool completely, right-side up, on the wire rack before removing the parchment. Level the tops of the cakes with a long serrated knife as needed.

MAKE THE SPECULOOS BUTTERCREAM

In the bowl of a stand mixer fitted with the paddle attachment, whip the buttercream until smooth and fluffy. Add the speculoos spread and mix until combined.

MAKE THE ROYAL ICING

In a large bowl or the bowl of a stand mixer, whisk together the confectioners' sugar and meringue powder until combined. Add the lemon juice and ¼ cup (60 ml) water. Using a handheld mixer or the stand mixer fitted with the whisk attachment, beat on high until glossy, stiff peaks form. Add more confectioners' sugar or water 1 tablespoon at a time until the correct consistency is achieved; the icing should be thick but pipeable. Transfer to a clean bowl and use immediately or cover well with plastic wrap until ready to use.

DECORATE THE COOKIES

Fill a piping bag fitted with a small round tip (Wilton #102 or #103) with half of the royal icing (reserve the remainder for decorating the cake). Outline the edges of the cookie buildings and windows and allow to dry. Once dry, add details by piping on doors and icicles (see page 275). Decorate with sprinkles and candies as desired. Tint a portion of the remaining royal icing green and pipe trees and window trimmings. The cookies can be decorated in advance and stored carefully in an airtight container at room temperature for up to 2 weeks.

TO ASSEMBLE AND STACK THE CAKE

Place one 8-inch (20-cm) cake layer on a cake board or serving plate. Spread on 1 cup (240 ml) of the speculoos buttercream with an offset spatula. Top with a second cake layer and repeat; place the final 8-inch (20-cm) cake layer on top.

Crumb coat the 8-inch (20-cm) cake with the vanilla buttercream and chill in the refrigerator for 15 minutes.

Place one 6-inch (15-cm) cake layer on a 6-inch (15-cm) cake board. Spread on ¾ cup (180 ml) of the speculoos buttercream with an offset spatula. Top with a second cake layer and repeat; place the final 6-inch (15-cm) cake layer on top.

Crumb coat the 6-inch (15-cm) cake with the whipped vanilla buttercream and chill in the refrigerator for 15 minutes.

Remove the larger cake from the refrigerator and smoothly frost with the whipped vanilla buttercream. Repeat with the smaller cake.

To support the top tier, cut and insert the dowels or straws in the 8-inch (20-cm) cake as described on page 279. Using a large offset spatula, carefully lift and place the 6-inch (15-cm) cake in the center of the bottom tier.

DECORATE THE CAKE

Fill a piping bag fitted with a small round tip (Wilton #3) with the reserved royal icing. Pipe icing on the backs of the decorated cookies and gently press them to the sides of the frosted cake. Pipe icing to fill in the gaps to the top edges of the cookies. Pipe icing snowdrifts near the bottoms of the cakes and sprinkle them with shredded coconut. Add more sprinkles and candies as desired.

If eating the cake the same day as assembled, store it at room temperature until ready to serve. If making in advance, wait to add the decorated cookies and store the cake in a cake box in the refrigerator overnight. Bring to room temperature for 30 minutes before serving. Store leftovers loosely covered with plastic wrap in the refrigerator for 3 to 4 days.

Back-Pocket Essentials

BASE RECIPES, TECHNIQUES, AND TIPS TO LEARN, LOVE, AND USE FOR LIFE!

Buttercreams

Whipped Vanilla Buttercream and Swiss Meringue Buttercream may be used interchangeably in most recipes, but understand that they may not behave or taste the same as the buttercream called for in the recipes as written.

WHIPPED VANILLA BUTTERCREAM

SMALL RECIPE

MAKES 3½ CUPS (840 ML), ENOUGH TO FILL AND FROST ONE THREE-LAYER 6-INCH (15-CM) CAKE

1 cup (2 sticks/225 g) unsalted butter, at room temperature

3½ to 4 cups (425 to 500 g) confectioners' sugar, sifted if needed

2 tablespoons whole milk

1½ teaspoons pure vanilla extract

MEDIUM RECIPE

MAKES 5¼ CUPS (1.2 L), ENOUGH TO FILL, FROST, AND DECORATE ONE THREE-LAYER 6-INCH (15-CM) CAKE

1½ cups (3 sticks/340 g) unsalted butter, at room temperature

5 to 6 cups (625 to 750 g) confectioners' sugar, sifted if needed

3 tablespoons whole milk

2 teaspoons pure vanilla extract

LARGE RECIPE

MAKES 7 CUPS (1.7 L), ENOUGH TO FILL, FROST, AND DECORATE ONE THREE-LAYER 8-INCH (20-CM) CAKE

2 cups (4 sticks/450 g) unsalted butter, at room temperature

7 to 8 cups (875 g to 1 kg) confectioners' sugar, sifted if needed

4 tablespoons (60 ml) whole milk

1 tablespoon pure vanilla extract

1   In the bowl of a stand mixer fitted with the paddle attachment (or in a large bowl using a handheld mixer), beat the butter on medium speed until smooth and creamy.

2   With the mixer running on low, slowly add all but 1 cup (125 g) of the confectioners' sugar, the milk, and vanilla. Once incorporated, turn the mixer up to medium-high and mix for 3 to 5 minutes, until the buttercream is white, fluffy, and smooth. Add the remaining 1 cup (125 g) confectioners' sugar as needed ¼ cup (30 g) at a time, until the desired consistency is reached; the buttercream should be soft and spreadable, but not runny.

Whipped vanilla buttercream can be made in advance and stored in a lidded container or wrapped tightly in plastic at room temperature up to overnight, in the refrigerator for 1 to 2 weeks, or in the freezer for up to 3 months. Bring the buttercream to room temperature and mix until smooth before using.

PROS: Quick and easy! Great in high-heat situations. Takes on color easily.

CONS: Much sweeter and heavier than Swiss Meringue Buttercream. Not as smooth and silky.

SWISS MERINGUE BUTTERCREAM

SMALL RECIPE

MAKES ABOUT 3¼ CUPS (780 ML), ENOUGH TO FILL
AND FROST ONE THREE-LAYER 6-INCH (15-CM) CAKE

3 large egg whites

1 cup (200 g) granulated
sugar

2 teaspoons pure vanilla
extract

1½ cups (3 sticks/340 g)
unsalted butter, at room
temperature

MEDIUM RECIPE

MAKES ABOUT 4½ CUPS (1 L), ENOUGH TO FILL,
FROST, AND DECORATE ONE THREE-LAYER 6-INCH
(15-CM) CAKE

4 large egg whites

1⅓ cups (265 g)
granulated sugar

2 teaspoons pure vanilla
extract

2 cups (4 sticks/450 g)
unsalted butter, at room
temperature

LARGE RECIPE

MAKES ABOUT 6¾ CUPS (1.6 L), ENOUGH TO FILL,
FROST, AND DECORATE ONE THREE-LAYER 8-INCH
(20-CM) CAKE

6 large egg whites

2 cups (400 g) granulated
sugar

4 teaspoons pure
vanilla extract

3 cups (6 sticks/675 g)
unsalted butter, at room
temperature

PROS: Silky smooth. Perfect for piping
and frosting a smooth cake. Not too sweet.
Easy to add flavor.

CONS: More labor-intensive than Whipped
Vanilla Buttercream. More room for error.

/ Put the egg whites and sugar in the bowl of
a stand mixer. Gently whisk them by hand to
combine. In a medium saucepan, bring an inch
or two (2.5 to 5 cm) of water to a simmer over
medium-low heat. Place the mixer bowl on top
of the saucepan to create a double boiler (be
sure the bottom of the bowl does not touch
the water). Heat the egg mixture, whisking
intermittently, until it reaches 160°F (70°C) on a
candy thermometer.

2 Carefully affix the mixer bowl to the stand mixer
(it may be hot) and fit the mixer with the whisk
attachment. Beat the egg white mixture on high
speed for 8 to 10 minutes, until the mixture
holds medium-stiff peaks and the outside of the
bowl has cooled to room temperature.

3 Turn the mixer down to low and add the vanilla.
Add the butter a couple of tablespoons at a
time, mixing until each is incorporated before
adding the next. Stop the mixer and swap out
the whisk for the paddle attachment.

4 Turn the mixer to medium-high and beat until
the buttercream is silky smooth, 3 to 5 minutes.

*Swiss meringue buttercream can be made in
advance and stored in a lidded container or
wrapped tightly in plastic at room temperature
up to overnight, in the refrigerator for 1 to 2
weeks, or in the freezer for up to 3 months. Bring
the buttercream to room temperature and mix
until smooth before using.*

TROUBLESHOOTING

If the buttercream appears soupy, the butter was
probably added before the meringue was completely
cool or the butter was too soft. Refrigerate the
buttercream for about 15 minutes and rewhip
until smooth.

If the buttercream appears split or curdled, the
butter was probably too cold. Whip until smooth.
This may take up to 5 minutes. If it is still too cold
and clumpy, remove ½ to 1 cup (120 to 240 ml) of
the buttercream and warm it in the microwave until
slightly melted. Return the warmed buttercream to
the mixer bowl and mix until smooth.

Whipped Cream

MAKES ABOUT 3½ CUPS (840 ML)

2 cups (480 ml) cold heavy cream

3 tablespoons granulated sugar

1 teaspoon pure vanilla extract

1. In the bowl of stand mixer fitted with the whisk attachment, whisk the cream on medium speed until it starts to thicken.

2. Add the sugar and vanilla. Whisk on high until medium peaks form.

Whipped cream is best made just before assembling/serving. If you need to make it in advance, store in a lidded container in the refrigerator for up to 8 hours. Gently re-whisk by hand before serving.

Chocolate Drizzle

MAKES ENOUGH TO COVER THE TOP AND DRIP DOWN THE SIDES OF ONE 8-INCH (20-CM) CAKE

Cut the recipe in half if only adding the drips, like for the Chocolate Millionaire's Cake (page 66).

4 ounces (115 g) dark chocolate, chopped

½ cup (120 ml) heavy cream

¼ cup (60 ml) corn syrup

1 teaspoon pure vanilla extract

1. Put the chocolate, cream, and corn syrup in a small saucepan. Heat over medium-low heat until the cream begins to steam and the chocolate starts to melt.

2. Remove from the heat and stir in the vanilla until combined. Let the mixture cool to room temperature, until it is thick yet still fluid, about 10 minutes.

Chocolate drizzle may be made in advance and stored in the lidded container in the refrigerator for up to 2 weeks. Gently reheat until the correct consistency according to the recipe.

Caramel Sauce

MAKES ABOUT 1 CUP (240 ML)

¾ cup (150 g) granulated sugar

2 tablespoons corn syrup

½ cup (120 ml) heavy cream, at room temperature

2 tablespoons unsalted butter, diced

1 teaspoon pure vanilla extract

½ teaspoon salt, or to taste

1. In a small heavy-bottomed saucepan, stir together the sugar, corn syrup, and 2 tablespoons water. Heat over high heat, without stirring, until the mixture turns a light-medium amber color, 8 to 10 minutes. It will begin to rapidly boil before slowing down and darkening in color; the darker the color, the richer the caramel will taste. Remove from the heat once the correct color is reached and the bubbles start to subside.

2. Slowly and carefully whisk in the cream. The mixture may foam up and sputter, so stand clear and keep whisking.

3. Add the butter and stir until melted. Add the vanilla and salt and stir to combine. Pour the caramel into a heatproof container and let cool until it reaches the desired consistency (it will thicken as it cools), or refrigerate until ready to use.

The caramel sauce can be made in advance and stored, covered, in the refrigerator for up to 10 days.

Vanilla Pastry Cream

SMALL RECIPE

MAKES ABOUT 2 CUPS (480 ML), ENOUGH TO FILL ONE THREE-LAYER 6-INCH (15-CM) CAKE

1½ tablespoons unsalted butter, diced

1½ cups (360 ml) whole milk

6 tablespoons (65 g) granulated sugar

½ vanilla bean, split lengthwise and seeds scraped out (optional)

3 large egg yolks

2 tablespoons plus ¾ teaspoon cornstarch

1½ tablespoons all-purpose flour

1 teaspoon pure vanilla extract

LARGE RECIPE

MAKES ABOUT 2½ CUPS (600 ML), ENOUGH TO FILL ONE 9-INCH (13-CM) TART OR ONE THREE-LAYER 8-INCH (20-CM) CAKE

2 tablespoons unsalted butter, diced

2 cups (480 ml) whole milk

½ cup (100 g) granulated sugar

1 vanilla bean, split lengthwise and seeds scraped out (optional)

4 large egg yolks

3 tablespoons cornstarch

2 tablespoons all-purpose flour

1 teaspoon pure vanilla extract

1 Put the butter in heatproof bowl. Set a fine-mesh sieve over the bowl.

2 In a medium saucepan, combine the milk, 2 tablespoons of the sugar, and the vanilla bean seeds and pod (if using). Slowly bring just to a simmer over medium-low heat. Remove from the heat. Carefully fish out and discard the vanilla bean pod.

3 In a medium bowl, whisk together the remaining sugar with the egg yolks. Whisk in the cornstarch and flour until smooth.

4 While whisking, stream about half of the hot milk mixture into the egg mixture to temper the egg yolks (this slowly raises the temperature of the eggs so they don't curdle). Pour the tempered egg mixture into the saucepan with the remaining hot milk mixture and heat over medium-low heat, stirring continuously, until the pastry cream thickens and slow, large bubbles start to pop on the surface. Whisk for 1 minute more, then remove from the heat.

5 Pour the pastry cream through the sieve into the bowl with the butter. Add the vanilla extract. Stir until smooth and cover with a piece of plastic wrap, pressing it directly to the surface of the pastry cream to prevent a skin from forming. Refrigerate until cool and thick, at least 2 hours or up to 3 to 5 days. If making in advance, be sure to add the number of days the pastry cream spent in the refrigerator to the shelf life of the cake or pastry. Do not exceed 5 days total.

Decoding Vanilla Cakes

Many of the vanilla cakes in this book look similar to one another, but each carries its own unique set of characteristics. Wondering how their taste and texture are different? Here is a quick breakdown of the vanilla cake recipes used in this book:

YELLOW BUTTER CAKE

MADE WITH:
creamed butter,
mostly egg yolks,
cake flour,
and whole milk

EXAMPLES:
Vanilla Passion Fruit
Caramel Cake
(PAGE 81),

Sparkling Raspberry
Cake
(PAGE 220)

CHARACTERISTICS:
tender,
rich,
buttery,
golden in color

DOUBLE-VANILLA CAKE

MADE WITH:
oil,
melted butter,
all-purpose flour,
and whole milk

EXAMPLES:
Double-Vanilla Cake
(PAGE 140)

CHARACTERISTICS:
easy,
moist,
spongy,
similar to
boxed cake mix

WHITE CAKE

MADE WITH:
creamed butter,
egg whites,
cake flour,
all-purpose flour,
sour cream,
and whole milk

EXAMPLES:
Blueberry Galaxy Cake
(PAGE 130),

Sprinkle Surprise
Cupcakes
(PAGE 108)

CHARACTERISTICS:
light,
tender,
mild in flavor and color

REVERSE METHOD VANILLA CAKE

MADE WITH:
butter,
cake flour,
sour cream,
and whole milk

EXAMPLES:
Lavender Blackberry
Cake
(PAGE 60),

Tuxedo Checkerboard
Cake
(PAGE 172)

Milk & Cookies Cake
(PAGE 123)

CHARACTERISTICS:
fluffy,
springy,
soft, yet
tight crumb

BUTTERMILK CAKE

MADE WITH:
creamed butter,
whole eggs,
all-purpose flour,
and buttermilk

EXAMPLES:
Victoria Sponge Cake
(PAGE 206),

Cotton Candy
Cloud Cake
(PAGE 136)

CHARACTERISTICS:
versatile, tight crumb,
velvety,
slight tang from
the buttermilk

GENOISE CAKE

MADE WITH:
melted butter,
whipped whole eggs,
all-purpose flour,
no leavener

EXAMPLES:
Swedish Princess Cake
(PAGE 52),

Matcha White
Chocolate Cake
(PAGE 39)

CHARACTERISTICS:
soft,
spongy,
very mild in flavor,
sturdier than chiffon
cake

Fill and Frost a Cake

1

2

1 Level the tops of the cooled cakes as needed: Use a long serrated knife to carefully score an even line around the cake where the sides meet the top. Place the hand that is not holding the knife on the top of the cake to keep it steady, instead of on the side of the cake, just in case the knife slips through to the other side. Slice across the top of the cake, using the scored line as a guide, to remove any domed portion from the top until it is even and flat.

If called for in the recipe, cut the cakes into layers: Set one cake on a rotating cake stand. Score an even line around the center of the sides of the cake with the serrated knife. Use the cake stand to spin the cake and the scored line as a guide as you make small cuts all the way around the cake, until you reach the center and the cake splits evenly into two layers.

2 Place one of the bottom layers of cake on the rotating cake stand, a cake board, or a serving plate. For even layers of filling, fill a piping bag fitted with a large round tip with buttercream or the frosting of your choice. Pipe a ring around the outer top edge of the cake. The ring should be about half the height of the cake layer.

3 Use a rubber spatula to dollop buttercream (or the frosting of your choice) in the center of the ring.

4 Smooth out the buttercream with an offset spatula until it is flush with the outer ring.

5 Top with a second cake layer and repeat. As you continue to stack the cake, make sure that each layer is straight and level. Make adjustments as necessary.

3

4

5a

5b

267

6 a

6 b

6   Place the third cake layer on top and repeat.

7   Invert the remaining bottom cake layer cut-side down on top of the last layer of buttercream. Gently press down until it is secure. Make sure the stacked cake is flat on top and that all the layers are even. Make adjustments as necessary.

8   Crumb coat the cake: Set the stacked cake on the rotating cake stand. Place a large dollop of buttercream on top of the cake. While turning the cake stand, use an offset spatula to smooth the buttercream. A small lip of buttercream may be pushed out over the top edge of the cake.

Spread the lip of buttercream onto the sides of the cake. Add more buttercream to the sides of the cake to completely cover in a thin layer of buttercream. As you crumb coat the cake, place any excess buttercream that contains cake crumbs in a separate bowl. Smooth out the crumb coat with the offset spatula; the cake does not need to be perfect at this point. Chill the cake in the refrigerator for 15 minutes. Do not leave the cake in the refrigerator too long, or it will be difficult to apply the final coat of buttercream.

9   Remove the chilled crumb-coated cake from the refrigerator and set it on the rotating cake stand. Using crumb-free buttercream, place a large dollop of buttercream on top of the cake. Holding the offset spatula as flat as possible to the top of the cake, begin spinning the cake stand. Allow the spatula to help distribute and flatten the buttercream on top of the cake. A small lip of buttercream should be pushed out over the top edge of the cake.

10   Spread the lip of buttercream onto the sides of the cake. Working with only a small portion of buttercream at a time, apply buttercream to the top half of the sides of the cake. (Using a small portion of buttercream gives you more control.)

11

12

11 Working with only a small portion of buttercream, apply buttercream to the bottom half of the sides of the cake. The key is to create an even layer of buttercream all the way around the sides of the cake; it does not need to be smooth at this time.

Once the entire cake has been coated in an even layer of buttercream, begin smoothing it out with the offset spatula. Hold the spatula parallel to the side of the cake and spin the cake stand a couple of times to remove any excess buttercream.

12 Swap the offset spatula for an icing smoother. Place the edge of the icing smoother parallel to the side of the cake. Rest the bottom of the icing smoother on the cake stand so that it is perfectly perpendicular to the stand. This will help ensure that the sides of the cake are straight.

13 Keep the icing smoother still and begin rotating the cake stand. As the cake spins, the icing smoother will pick up excess buttercream and fill in any gaps as you go. Spin the cake only two or three rotations at a time. In between, clean off the icing smoother and assess the cake. Add more buttercream as needed. Continue until the sides of the cake are perfectly smooth.

14 As you smooth the sides, excess buttercream will be pushed up toward the top of the cake. To clean off the top, use the edge of a small offset spatula to carefully pull the extra buttercream toward the center of the top of the cake. Use a light hand and try not to disrupt the smoothed buttercream on the sides of the cake. I find it most comfortable to start with the edge of cake that is the farthest away from me and pull the buttercream in toward my body. Rotate the cake stand and repeat, cleaning off the spatula between each swipe.

15 To finish the cake, gently place the edge of the icing smoother on the very top. Spin the cake stand a couple of times while the icing smoother flattens the top of the cake.

16 If this step disrupts the sides of the cake, repeat steps 13 and 14 until the buttercream is smooth on all sides.

For an extra-smooth frosting finish, be sure that the buttercream is the correct consistency before getting started. It should be soft yet spreadable. If small bumps remain, run the icing smoother under hot water to heat up the metal, dry, and then smooth out the cake.

RUSTIC FROSTING

SIMPLE SWIRL

CLOUD FROSTING

FRILLY TWO-TONE SWIRL

CUPCAKE STYLING

TIPS AND TECHNIQUES

As my Garden Cupcakes illustrate (page 30), cupcakes can be just as elegant as any decorative cake or fanciful pastry. However, sometimes we prefer an easier approach. From simple swirls to rustic, "homemade" finishes, there are several ways to frost a cupcake:

Rustic Frosting: as seen on Sprinkle Surprise Cupcakes (page 108)

Make sure the buttercream or frosting of choice is soft yet spreadable. Place a dollop of frosting, about ¼ cup (60 ml) on top of the cupcake. Rotate the cupcake while gently pushing the frosting to the edges of the cupcake with the tip of a small spatula. Once evenly covered in frosting, place the tip of the spatula in the center of the cupcake. Apply slight pressure to the tip of the spatula and spin the cupcake to create a swirl. Continue to rotate the tip of the spatula as you pull it away from the cupcake for the perfect swoop.

Cloud Frosting: as seen on Angel Food Cupcakes (page 211)

Fill a piping bag fitted with a large round tip with buttercream or frosting of choice. Hold the piping bag straight down and hover the tip slightly above the cupcake. Apply continuous pressure to the piping bag until the frosting creates a large mound of icing on top of the cupcake. Release the pressure on the bag before pulling away.

Simple Swirl: as seen on Fancy-Pants Peanut Butter Chocolate Cupcakes (page 74)

Fill a piping bag fitted with a medium-large round tip with buttercream or the frosting of your choice. Hold the piping bag straight down and begin to apply pressure to the piping bag. Starting on the outside edge of the cupcake, pipe a ring around the edge, then begin to swirl in toward the center. Continue to pipe, about 2 to 3 rotations, allowing the frosting to build on itself to make a cone shape. Stop pressure on the piping bag when done before pulling the piping bag away.

Frilly Two-tone Swirl: as seen on Lemonade Cupcakes (page 115)

Fit a piping bag with a star tip. Use a spatula to fill the piping bag with two different shades of buttercream, one color on each side. Alternatively, fill two separate piping bags with the two different colors (one color per bag), snip the tips of the filled piping bags, and place both bags into the piping bag fitted with the star tip. Follow the same steps for creating the Simple Swirl.

Round Tip

Petal Tip

Star Tip

Playful Piping

With just a few piping bags and an assortment of piping tips, the possibilities for adding sweet decorations are endless. Pipe buttercream designs on cakes or whipped cream borders on tarts and pies. From frilly details to full-coverage cake designs, let's take a closer look at a few of my favorite piping tips and the many patterns and designs they are capable of.

ROUND TIP

I recommend Wilton #3 and #5 tips for writing and borders. For large dots, kisses, and frosting dams, use a large round tip.

Lines, stripes, and writing: Hold the piping bag at a 45-degree angle to the cake or pastry. Keeping the tip hovered just over the surface, pipe with continuous pressure on the bag until your desired design or line is complete. When done, release the pressure before pulling the piping bag away.

Dots: Hold the piping bag perpendicular to the cake or pastry surface. Apply even pressure on the piping bag until the frosting builds and forms a small mound. Release the pressure before pulling the piping bag away. If a small peak forms on top, use a clean, damp brush or fingertip to gently flatten it.

Kisses: Use the same method as making dots, but do not flatten the tops when done.

PETAL TIP

I recommend a Wilton #104 petal tip.

Ruffles: Hold the piping bag at a 45-degree angle to the cake or pastry surface. Always make sure the narrowed side of the tip is facing the direction indicated by the recipe (the narrowed side will produce the frills of the ruffle). While applying even pressure on the bag, pipe swags and ruffles by moving the tip around or across the cake or pastry. Release the pressure on the piping bag before pulling the bag away.

Weave: Hold the piping bag so the opening of the tip is at a 45-degree angle to the cake or pastry surface. Make sure the narrowed side is facing away from the direction that you will be piping. Applying even pressure, pipe interlocking "V"s, releasing the pressure before pulling the tip away as you complete each side of each "V."

Waves: Hold the piping bag so the opening of the tip is perpendicular to the cake or pastry surface. Make sure the narrowed side is facing away from the cake. Pipe with continuous pressure while moving the tip in a soft, subtle wave motion. Follow the directions for the Pistachio Truffle Cake (page 84) to create a wave pattern on the sides of a cake.

STAR TIP

I recommend Wilton #18 and #21 tips for borders and small details. For large rosettes, use a Wilton #1M tip. Use an Ateco #824 tip for fluffy borders and spirals.

Rosettes: Hold the piping bag perpendicular to the cake or pastry surface. Applying continuous, even pressure, starting from the center and working out, pipe the frosting in a tight spiral. As you complete the spiral, release the pressure to create a tail that tapers against the side of the spiral before pulling the piping bag away. Use the same technique for both mini- and large rosettes.

Stars: Use the same technique as for dots (see left).

Shell border: Hold the piping bag at a 45-degree angle to the cake or pastry surface. Apply pressure to the piping bag to create a small bulb of frosting, then decrease the pressure while dragging the tip away from the start to form a tail. Fully release the pressure. Begin the next shell slightly overlapping the tail of the previous shell. Use the same technique for small and large shell borders.

Zigzag: Hold the piping bag perpendicular to the cake or pastry surface. Applying continuous pressure, move the tip back and forth, or up and down, to create zigzags.

How to Fill a Piping Bag

1. Snip the end off a disposable piping bag or ensure that the opening of a reusable canvas piping bag is large enough.

2. Fit the piping tip into the opening of the piping bag. If using small tips, first place a plastic coupler inside the bag. Slide the tip over the coupler on the outside of the bag and secure it with the coupler's plastic ring.

3. Grasp the center of the bag with one hand and unfold the top to open it. Roll down the sides so the top portion of the bag is draped over your hand.

4. Use a spoon or spatula to scoop frosting into the bag. Use the crook of your hand that is holding the bag (between your thumb and index finger) to scrape the frosting off the spoon or spatula and into the opened bag.

5. Once the bag is partially full, stop and unroll the top of the bag. Squeeze the contents of the bag toward the tip to remove any trapped air. Twist the top of the bag and begin piping.

    If you are having trouble, stand the empty piping bag, fitted with a piping tip, in a tall drinking glass. Roll the top of the bag over the rim of the glass and fill the piping bag with a spoon or spatula.

BUTTERCREAM FLOWERS

Using similar techniques as those used to make the flowers that adorn the Garden Cupcakes (page 30), these individual flowers are perfect for adding to the top of a cake or pastry, like the Lavender Blackberry Cake (page 60). For easier placement, I pipe each flower onto its own square of parchment paper. I highly recommend using an inexpensive flower nail; secure the square of parchment paper with a dab of frosting to the top of the flower nail before getting started. Chill the flowers in the refrigerator on their parchment paper squares until firm. When ready to assemble your cake, carefully peel away the parchment paper and use a small offset spatula to place the flowers on the cake.

Buttercream Mum

1. Using a large round tip, pipe a small bulb of frosting about 1 inch (2.5 cm) wide.

2. Using a Wilton #81 tip, pipe the center of the mum: Hold the piping bag perpendicular to the bulb of frosting, apply pressure, and pull straight up. Use the curve of the tip to interlock the inner petals.

3. Continue piping petals in concentric circles around the center of the mum until the bulb of frosting is covered.

4. Angle the piping bag so that the outer petals gently flare away from the center.

Buttercream Rose

1. Using a large round tip, pipe a small cone of frosting less than 1 inch (2.5 cm) wide.

2. Using a Wilton #104 petal tip, with the narrowed side pointing up, pipe a strip of frosting that wraps itself around the tip of the cone.

3. For the inner row of petals, pipe three petals, equally spaced and slightly overlapping, around the center bud: Keeping the piping bag at a 45-degree angle leaning in toward the bud, with the narrow side of the tip facing up, pipe arcs starting at the base and then up and partially over the center bud.

4. For the outer row of petals, pipe five petals equally spaced around the flower: Keeping the piping bag slightly leaning away from the center of the flower, with the narrow side of the tip facing up, pipe arcs starting at the base and then around the inner petals.

Buttercream Blossom

1. Hold the piping bag at a 45-degree angle away from your body. Using a petal tip (Wilton #103 or #104) with the narrowed side facing away from the center, pipe one petal: Starting in the center, apply pressure to the piping bag as you move the tip out and then back to the center, creating a small, frilled edge.

2. and 3. Continue piping petals, making five total, until the blossom is complete. Release the pressure on the piping bag before pulling the tip away.

4. Finish the center with a sprinkle of sugar pearls.

Converting Recipe Sizes

The layer cakes in this book have been baked in 6-inch (15-cm) and 8-inch (20-cm) rounds. Quantities for fillings and frostings have been listed specifically for the cake size(s) indicated in the recipe. If you would like to bake a cake to serve more or fewer people than the given yield, there are some ways to alter the recipes to suit your serving needs.

Unfortunately, there is no exact, universal formula for sizing cakes up and down. But with smaller cakes like these (that is, not giant wedding cakes), no adjustments need to be made if you want to double the recipes. Just make sure not to fill your cake pans more than two-thirds full; bake any remaining batter as cupcakes. Use the following formulas to help convert the layer cake recipes in this book:

To bake a three-layer 6-inch (15-cm) round cake as a three-layer 8-inch (20-cm) round cake, multiply each ingredient quantity by 1.5 or 1.75.

To bake a two- or three-layer 8-inch (20-cm) round cake as a three-layer 6-inch (15-cm) round cake, multiply each ingredient quantity by 0.75 or 0.66.

Recipes created for 8-inch (20-cm) cake pans can also be baked in 9-inch (23-cm) pans by multiplying the ingredient quantities by 1.25. Alternatively, you can use the quantities listed, but begin checking for doneness a few minutes sooner than the given bake time; the cake layers will be slightly shorter.

These formulas may be a bit tricky when working with eggs or other ingredients that are difficult to divide. If you end up needing a fraction of an egg, whisk the whole egg, weigh it, and measure out the amount you need.

If changing the size of a cake, the filling and frosting quantities will need to be adjusted accordingly. Refer to the yields for Whipped Vanilla Buttercream (page 261) and Swiss Meringue Buttercream (page 262) as guides.

Most of the cake recipes have not been tested as cupcakes, but they should cross over without much adjustment (with the exception of genoise sponge cakes). Line a cupcake pan with paper liners and fill no more than three-quarters full with batter. Begin checking for doneness (using the toothpick test) at 20 minutes.

Storage

Most CAKE LAYERS can be baked in advance. Once cooled, wrap the cake layers in plastic wrap and store at room temperature up to overnight, in the refrigerator for up to 3 days, or in the freezer for up to 2 months. Thaw frozen cakes in the refrigerator overnight. A chilled cake will be easier to cut and assemble, but they should be served at room temperature unless otherwise stated in the recipe. Frosting will help keep the moisture inside a cake; an unfrosted or "naked" cake will dry out faster. Cakes frosted with buttercream should be served at room temperature. Follow the serving suggestions given for each recipe.

CUPCAKES and MINI-CAKES begin to dry out rather quickly and are best served within 2 days of baking (although they will still be safe to eat for a few days after that). Store cupcakes in a cake pan loosely tented with plastic wrap at room temperature overnight or in the refrigerator for up to 2 days. If frosted with cream cheese frosting or whipped cream, then store in the refrigerator. If you need to bake cupcakes or mini-cakes further in advance of serving, do not frost them; wrap the unfrosted cupcakes individually or in groups of four with plastic wrap and store in the refrigerator for 3 to 4 days or in the freezer for up to 2 months.

SIMPLE SYRUPS, SOAKS, CHOCOLATE GLAZE, and CARAMEL SAUCE can be stored in a glass jar in the refrigerator for 1 to 2 weeks.

For ASSEMBLED CAKES and BAKED PASTRIES, follow the storage suggestions given in the recipes.

Transportation and Slicing

Moving Cakes to a Cake Stand

1. If you are not using a cake board and would like to transfer the finished cake to a (stationary) cake stand, first chill the frosted cake in the refrigerator for 15 to 20 minutes. (The buttercream will firm up, making the cake easier to move.)

2. Remove the cake from the refrigerator and run the tip of a small offset spatula or thin paring knife around the bottom edge of the cake to release the buttercream from the rotating cake stand.

3. Carefully slip a large offset spatula under the cake, spinning the cake stand until the spatula is completely under the cake.

4. Carefully lift the cake up and onto a cake stand or serving plate.

5. Gently place the cake down and carefully slide the spatula out.

6. Since the buttercream should be firm at this point, use your opposite hand (the hand not holding the spatula) to gently balance the cake as you set it in place.

TRANSPORTATION

Most cakes will transport well in a standard cardboard cake box. Be sure that the cake sits on a cake board that is the same diameter as the width of the box so that it does not shift around within the box.

Cakes and other pastries involving buttercream should be chilled before transportation so they can be moved and manipulated with ease. To display the cake at your destination, follow the tips for Moving Cakes to a Cake Stand. If possible, pack a small kit for touching up minor bumps and cracks that includes extra buttercream, an offset spatula, and any piping tips/bags you used when decorating the cake.

If transporting a tiered cake, place each tier in its own box. Add dowels to support the bottom tier before you leave home. Remember to pack your cake kit to help stack the cakes at your destination and fill in the gaps between the tiers.

Pies and tarts can be transported in the pans in which they were baked. Once cool, wrap in plastic wrap or foil.

Macarons can be carefully placed in a cardboard box or lidded container. Use caution when transporting, as their delicate shells may crack.

SLICING

FOR CAKES: Use a large chef's knife to cut cakes. Clean the knife between slices or as needed.

FOR PIES: Use a serrated knife to saw through double-crust fruit pies. A serrated knife is also best for cutting fruit tarts and single-crust pies, like the Chocolate Banana Pie (page 175).

FOR CHEESECAKES: Warm the blade of a large chef's knife under hot water and wipe dry before slicing. Clean and re-warm the knife between slices or as needed.

Sources

From my favorite flea market finds to specialty ingredients, sometimes it's the little details that take a recipe or decorative dessert to the next level. I've been collecting and sourcing props, serving pieces, and baking equipment for years. I've also had a chance to test various brands and ingredients in my recipes. Here is where you might find some of my favorite products and tools.

AMERICOLOR
Soft gel paste food coloring
Americolorcorp.com

ANTHROPOLOGIE
Cake stands, linens, and specialty baking equipment
Anthropologie.com

ATECO
Rotating cake stand, baking tools, icing smoothers, and piping tips
Atecousa.com

BOB'S RED MILL
Wide variety of specialty flour, including super-fine almond meal (perfect for macarons); also available in many fine grocery stores *bobsredmill.com*

THE CROSS DÉCOR AND DESIGN
Cake stands, dessert plates, linens, and paper decorations
thecrossdesign.com

FANCY SPRINKLES
Decorating sugars, assorted sprinkles, sugar shapes, metallic decorations, and sprinkle mixes.
fancysprinkles.com

FAT DADDIOS
Cake pans, baking tools, and specialty food items
Fatdaddios.com

GLOBAL SUGAR ART
Cake decorating tools, cake pans, gel food colors, luster dusts, and more *Globalsugarart.com*

THE GOURMET WAREHOUSE
Vancouver-based restaurant supply and specialty foods store
gourmetwarehouse.com

HEDLEY AND BENNETT
Handcrafted aprons and chef gear
Hedleyandbennett.com

KITCHENAID
Stand mixers and other quality baking equipment *Kitchenaid.com*

MICHAELS
Wide array of cake pans, baking tools, paper decorations, and more *michaels.com*

NIELSEN-MASSEY
Vanilla bean paste and other high-quality extracts
Nielsenmassey.com

OH HAPPY DAY PARTY SHOP
Paper decorations, party supplies, tabletop décor, and more
shop.ohhappyday.com

VALRHONA
Gourmet chocolate *Valrhona.com*

WEST ELM
Baking tools, dinnerware, flatware, linens, and more *Westelm.com*

WILLIAMS-SONOMA
Baking tools, cake pans, and specialty food items
Williams-sonoma.com

WILTON
Cake decorating supplies and piping tips, cake pans, cupcake liners, and more *Wilton.com*

Acknowledgments

To my agent, Melissa Sarver White: Thank you for helping me navigate through unfamiliar publishing territory and supporting me from start to finish, and beyond.

To my editor, Laura Dozier: Thank you for giving me creative freedom on this project while polishing my words and reigning in my ideas in order to produce the best version of this book possible. Thank you for the support and encouragement throughout while still pushing me beyond my limits in order to create something spectacular together.

To Deb Wood and the Abrams Team: You guys make dreams come true! Thank you for your meticulous attention to detail and fabulous book design. You make truly beautiful books, and seeing my thoughts, recipes, and photographs turned into a tangible object is surreal.

To Amy Ho: Thank you for your help with food and expert flower styling abilities.

To Crystal and Colin Giles: Thank you for lending your photography skills, friendship, and fun during shoots.

To my incredible recipe testers, Erin, Joanna, Melissa, Alana, Kate, and my mom: Thank you for your careful testing and detailed notes.

To my husband, Brett: Thank you for keeping the ship afloat during late night edits and weekend photo shoots. Thank you for being my support system, designing the ultimate dishwashing routine, tackling toddler bedtime activities, and making sure I drink at least a few glasses of water throughout the day. I love you!

To my parents: Thank you for teaching me to work hard and persevere through it all but with grace and compassion. Thank you for your lifetime of support and unconditional love, no matter what my sugar-filled dreams are.

To my brother, Ryan: Thank you for your photography expertise and helping me completely change my lighting game. I would have never been able to photograph pretty cakes during Vancouver's rainy seasons without you.

To my son, Everett: Thank you for your enthusiasm in the kitchen and sheer joy for life. Thank you for reminding me to slow down and enjoy the little things with you. You've definitely inherited my sweet tooth, and watching you grow has been the greatest gift of all.

To Baby Amara: Your little kicks that I feel in my belly as I write these last few words remind me to keep working hard toward my dreams, even when I am tired and out of energy. We love you so much already, and I can't wait for you to join me in the kitchen one day soon.

INDEX

Editor: Laura Dozier
Designer: Deb Wood
Production Manager: Rebecca Westall

Library of Congress Control Number: 2018936229

ISBN: 978-1-4197-3463-2
eISBN: 978-1-68335-506-9

Abrams books are available at special discounts when purchased in quantity for premiums and promotions as well as fundraising or educational use. Special editions can also be created to specification. For details, contact specialsales@abramsbooks.com or the address below.

Abrams® is a registered trademark of Harry N. Abrams, Inc.

ABRAMS
The Art of Books

195 Broadway
New York, NY 10007
abramsbooks.com